Preparing Universities
for an Era of Change

Published by Economica, Ltd,
49, rue Héricart
75015 Paris
France

© Economica Ltd, 2014

First published 2014

Printed in France

Luc E. Weber and James J. Duderstadt (eds)
Preparing Universities
for an Era of Change
ISBN 978-2-7178-6586-8

Preparing Universities for an Era of Change

Edited by

Luc E. Weber

James J. Duderstadt

ECONOMICA

Glion Colloquium Series N°8
London • Paris • Genève

Titles in the Series

Governance in Higher Education, The University in a State of Flux,
Werner Z. Hirsch and Luc E. Weber, eds, (2001)

As the Walls of Academia are Tumbling Down,
Werner Z. Hirsch and Luc E. Weber, eds, (2002)

Reinventing the Research University,
Luc E. Weber and James J. Duderstadt, eds, (2004)

Universities and Business: Partnering for the Knowledge Economy,
Luc E. Weber and James J. Duderstadt, eds, (2006)

The Globalization of Higher Education,
Luc E. Weber and James J. Duderstadt, eds, (2008)

University Research for Innovation,
Luc E. Weber and James J. Duderstadt, eds, (2010)

Global Sustainability and the Responsibilities of Universities,
Luc E. Weber and James J. Duderstadt, eds, (2012)

Preparing Universities for an Era of Change
Luc E. Weber and James J. Duderstadt, eds, (2014)

Other publications of the Glion colloquium

The First Glion Declaration: The University at the Millennium,
The Glion Colloquium (1998)

The Second Glion Declaration: Universities and the Innovation Spirit,
The Glion Colloquium (2009)

Challenges Facing Higher Education at the Millennium,
Werner Z. Hirsch and Luc E. Weber, eds, American Council on Education/
Oryx Press, Phoenix and IAU Press/Pergamon, Paris and Oxford, (1999)

CONTENTS

PREFACE ix

CONTRIBUTORS xv

Part I   **Changing Purpose, Role and Relationships**
         of Research Universities 1

CHAPTER 1   Research Universities and the Future of America:
                A Study by the National Academies
                of the United States 3
                James J. Duderstadt

CHAPTER 2   The Strategic Repositioning of Research Universities
                to Fulfil their Global Promise 15
                Heather Munroe-Blum and Carlos Rueda

CHAPTER 3   How to Answer the Utilitarian Assault on Higher
                Education? 29
                Hunter Rawlings

CHAPTER 4   The changing nature and character of research
                universities: New Paradigms 39
                Chorh-Chuan Tan

Part II   **Changing Nature of Discovery,**
                Learning and Innovation 49

CHAPTER 5   Research Funding: trends and challenges 51
                Leszek Borysiewicz

CHAPTER 6   The Role of Universities in Regional Development 63
                Arnold van Zyl

CHAPTER 7   The Impact of Technology on Discovery and Learning
                in Research Universities 73
                James J. Duderstadt

CHAPTER 8   Can the IT revolution lead to a rebirth of world-class
                European universities? 87
                Patrick Aebischer and Gérard Escher

Part III   **Cost, Price and Value** 99

CHAPTER 9   Who is responsible for providing and paying
                for higher education? 101
                Luc E. Weber

CHAPTER 10   How and where are dominant funding models
                steering HE & Research? 113
                Howard Newby

CHAPTER 11   Fault Lines in the Compact: Higher Education
                and the Public Interest in the United States 127
                Ronald J. Daniels, Phillip M. Spector and Rebecca Goetz

CHAPTER 12   The Challenge of Transition in Public Higher
                Education 141
                Linda P.B. Katehi

Part IV   **Changing Nature and Character**
                of Research Universities: developed countries 151

CHAPTER 13   Can the French System support competitive
                Research Universities? 153
                Alain Beretz

CHAPTER 14   Contemporary challenges for the Swiss – and
                the continental European – university system 165
                Antonio Loprieno

CHAPTER 15   A Research University for both Academic Excellence
and Responsibility for a sustainable future —
does the Swedish model work?................................ 173
Eva Åkesson

CHAPTER 16   Human capital, the oft forgotten key challenge
for universities.. 187
Sijbolt Noorda

**Part V   Changing Nature and Character
of Research Universities: fast-developing countries**..... 199

CHAPTER 17   The Search for Quality at Chinese Universities............. 201
Jie Zhang and Kai Yu

CHAPTER 18   Higher Education Model for Large Developing
Economies.. 211
Raghunath K. Shevgaonkar

CHAPTER 19   Challenges and Opportunities for Public Research
Universities in Brazil... 223
Carlos Henrique de Brito Cruz

CHAPTER 20   Challenges in Establishing a Top Research
University.. 233
Nam P. Suh

CHAPTER 21   The Asian Tiger University Effect................................ 249
John Niland

Part VI   Summary and Conclusion................................... 269

CHAPTER 22   Summary and Conclusion.................................. 271
James J. Duderstadt and Luc E. Weber

PREFACE

The Glion Colloquium has established itself as an influential resource in addressing both the challenges and responsibilities of the world's research universities. Every two years, the Glion Colloquium provides a forum for research university leaders to consider together the role that the world's leading universities should play in addressing the great challenges and opportunities of our times and to explore together how universities, in partnership with governments, industry and society, can contribute both to solutions of global challenges and especially as partners and leaders in change. These activities, consisting of papers prepared by participants prior to three days of intense discussions in Glion-above-Montreux, Switzerland, are captured in subsequent books given wide circulation throughout the world.

Over the past 15 years, over 200 leaders of higher education, business and government agencies have participated in the Glion activities to consider issues such as the challenges of the new millennium, the governance of universities, the increasingly interdisciplinary nature of teaching and research, the globalization of higher education, the relationship between universities and industry, the role of university research in driving innovation and ways to address the challenges of global sustainability. The publications resulting from the Glion activities are now regarded as an important resource for better aligning higher education with the needs of a rapidly changing world.

The topic of the IX Glion Colloquium in June 2013 concerned the ability of the world's research universities to respond to an era of challenge and change. Interestingly enough, this topic arose during discussions at the 2011

ix

Glion Colloquium concerning the role of the world's research universities in addressing the challenges of global sustainability. In the closing session of this earlier conference, the question was raised as to whether the current paradigm of the research university itself was facing serious challenges of sustainability as the world was changing, hence both stimulating and defining the focus of IX Glion.

Today, our world has entered a period of rapid and profound economic, social and political transformation based upon an emerging new system for creating wealth that depends upon the creation and application of new knowledge and hence upon educated people and their ideas. Paradoxically, the accelerating pace of events is driving our societies towards unknown futures in which the role of learning and new knowledge has become ever more important. It has become increasingly apparent that the strength, prosperity and welfare of a nation in a global knowledge economy will demand a highly educated citizenry enabled by development of a strong system of tertiary education. It will also require institutions with the ability to discover new knowledge, develop innovative applications of these discoveries and transfer them into the marketplace through entrepreneurial activities while enabling social organizations, such as governments and corporations, to develop new skills of policy development and decision-making.

Today, the institutions most responsible for advanced education and basic research are the world's research universities. Yet these are being challenged by the powerful forces characterizing the global economy: demographic change, environmental risks, increasing ethnic and cultural diversity, hyper-competitive markets, failing governments and disruptive technologies such as information, biological and nanotechnologies. More specifically, markets characterized by the instantaneous flows of knowledge, capital and work, and unleashed by lowering trade barriers are creating global enterprises based upon business paradigms such as out-sourcing economic activity and off-shoring jobs, a shift from public to private equity investment, and declining identification with or loyalty to national or regional interests.

The populations of most developed nations in North America, Europe and Asia are aging rapidly, while developing nations in Asia, Africa and Latin America are characterized by young and growing populations. Today, we see a serious imbalance between educational need and educational capacity. In a sense, many of our universities are in the wrong place, where populations are aging and perhaps even declining rather than young and growing, driving major population migration and all too frequently the clash of cultures and ethnicity.

New technologies are evolving at an exponential pace, obliterating both historical constraints such as distance and political boundaries, and enabling new paradigms for learning, such as open educational resources, virtual organizations, social networking and technology-enabled learning systems (e.g., massive open online courses and intelligent tutor automated learning systems) that threaten traditional approaches to learning, innovation and economic growth.

On a broader scale, the education investments demanded by the global knowledge economy are straining the economies of both developed and developing regions. In the developed economies of Europe, America and Asia, the tax revenues that once supported university education for only a small elite are now being stretched thin as they are extended to fund higher education for a significant fraction of the population (i.e., massification) at ever rising levels of quality and standards. Developing nations are overwhelmed by the higher education needs of expanding young populations at a time when even secondary education is only available to a small fraction of their populations.

The changing purpose, role and relationships of research universities became the focus of the opening session of the colloquium. This began with a panel discussion (Duderstadt, Munroe-Blum, Newby) of a recent study by the National Academies of Science, Engineering and Medicine of the United States concerning the future of the American research university. This study, requested by the U.S. Congress, found that, despite the increasing importance of graduate education and research for prosperity and security in a knowledge-driven global economy, the partnership among research universities, government, industry and philanthropic organizations had deteriorated significantly, putting both the quality and capacity of U.S. institutions at considerable risk. While the study recommended several bold actions to address these concerns, the National Academies were concerned that today's weakened economy and political divisiveness in the United States would likely require a decade-long, sustained effort to make progress.

This discussion was broadened (Munroe-Blum) using the experience of Canadian universities as they attempted to address global challenges and expand international research programs in the face of instabilities in government funding and eroding public trust and confidence. As costs have risen and priorities for tax revenues have shifted to other public policy goals, governments have asked more and more stridently, what are universities for? The imperatives of a knowledge-driven global economy have provided a highly utilitarian answer: to provide the educated workforce and innovation necessary for economic competitiveness (Rawlings), despite the importance of their more fundamental primary responsibilities of education, scholarship and the conservation and promotion of cultural heritage. The session concluded with discussion of the remarkable contrasts provided by higher education in Asian nations such as Singapore (Tan), characterized both by strong government commitments of funding and a willingness to explore exciting new paradigms

xii   Preface

for the research universities involving innovative international partnerships, uses of technology and novel efforts to better integrate the fundamental missions of teaching and research.

The second session concerned the changing nature of discovery, learning and innovation, driven by the changing needs of society, government policy and technology. The discussions began with the changing nature of research sponsorship in the United Kingdom, as government funding transitioned from the support of research grants to individual investigators to grand challenges requiring the creation of multidisciplinary theme centres in universities (Borysiewicz). Campus research activities have been further influenced by the impact of the European Research Area, stressing key themes, large-scale research facilities and innovation and technology transfer that challenge the highly disciplinary structure of universities and faculty training. The discussion then shifted to the third mission of universities as they moved beyond their classical roles of teaching and research to actively engage with the socio-economic and political environment (Van Zyl). The discussion revealed sharp contrasts between such engagement in developed economies, where efforts were heavily focused on the technology transfer to industry, and developing economies in regions such as Africa, where both poverty and resource limitations required quite different roles for universities. The last two presentations (Duderstadt and Aebischer) addressed the impact of rapidly evolving technologies on teaching and research with the emergence of new paradigms such as MOOCs (massively open online courses) and learning analytics for the universities' educational mission, with clouds, big data and disciplinary convergence driving a shift in research paradigms from hypothesis-driven to data-correlation-driven discovery. While the powerful impact of technology-driven activities such as MOOCs to efficiently access gigantic student markets opens up enormous opportunities for both access and quality, there is still very limited evidence on the effectiveness of these approaches.

The third session focused on the complex issues of the cost, price and value of higher education, or more specifically, who benefits and who pays for research universities. The presentations began with a very thorough analysis (Weber) of these issues from the perspectives of both economic and social policy, including the sharp differences in the approaches taken by Europe and North America, where the current model for financing higher education in nations heavily dependent upon public tax support is simply incapable of sustaining massification while achieving world-class quality, and Asia where rapidly developing economies have given high priority to higher education. It was noted (Newby) that even as governments in Europe and America are providing our universities with less resources, they are attempting to exert greater influence through increasing regulation and a more forensic focus on impact and value for money, imposing more accountability for both the educational and research activities of universities. The extreme example of this has been the devastating cuts in state appropriations (over 60%) experienced by the University of California (Katehi), perhaps the most prominent research university system in the world. While there was considerable discussion of the many factors driving these challenges, there was also an effort to develop an agenda involving both universities and governments to address them (Daniels) that would encompass issues such as the growing inequality in access to higher education.

The fourth session concerned the particular nature of the changing nature of research universities in developed countries, such as the emergence of research universities in France (Beretz), where world-class quality has become a major priority for the universities (in addition to the traditional "grandes écoles" system). Similarly, Swiss universities are evolving (Loprieno), under some pressure from the Bologna process, to embrace the Bildung/Ausbildung paradigm of broader education at the college level and focused disciplinary training in graduate schools, essentially transitioning from "universitas" to "university". While both funding and quality are still strong in Swedish universities, the high tuition and visa requirements recently placed upon international students could cripple their ability to sustain globally competitive and relevant research programs (Akesson). The final discussion focused on the challenges of providing a smooth transition in university faculties from one generation to the next, both addressing the attractiveness of the academic profession for junior faculty and the appropriate role and mobility of senior faculty (Noorda).

The fifth session shifted to a discussion of the experiences of building world-class research universities in developing economies. China's achievement in building sufficient university capacity to increase participation of 18- to 22-year-olds from 1% in 1982, to 26% today with a goal of 40% in 2020 was particularly impressive (Zhang), as was the commitment to attract faculty of international quality. There was also discussion of India's experience (Shevgaonkar) in providing the capacity to serve a very large student population, while achieving world-class quality through both creative use of online learning and focusing research support on elite institutions such as the IIT and IIM systems. Of particular interest was the recent effort in Korea to elevate the Korean Advanced Institute of Science and Technology to MIT quality through a combination of investment, discipline and cultural changes (Suh). The discussion was broadened to examine the experience of the other "Asian tigers" (Singapore, Hong Kong, Taiwan) in building world-class research universities (Niland).

The final session consisted of a broad discussion of both the format and funding of the Glion Colloquium. There was a strong sense of the great value of attracting a truly global representation of university leadership with a flexible agenda that provided considerable opportunity for open discussions informed by short papers prepared in advance by each participant. Following the IX Glion Colloquium, these papers have been refined by the authors and are included as chapters in this book, although with a summary chapter containing several of the key points made in the discussions in each session.

The IX Glion Colloquium was arranged under the auspices of the University of Geneva and the Graduate Institute of International Studies and Development in Geneva, and made possible by the generous support of the National Science Foundation of the United States (NSF), the Swiss State Secretariat for Education, Research and Innovation (SERI), the Board of the Swiss Federal Institutes of Technology (ETH Board), the Swiss Federal Institute of Technology Zurich (ETH Zurich), the University of California, Davis (UCDavis), and Jubilant DraxImage, India. We are also particularly grateful for the efforts of those who contributed to the colloquium and to the production of this book, in particular Natacha Durand, Roxana Voconavu-Bota and Manuela Wullschleger of the University of Geneva for their kind and efficient help, as well as Edmund Doogue in Geneva, who provided rigorous editorial assistance.

Luc Weber   James Duderstadt
University of Geneva   *University of Michigan*

CONTRIBUTORS

AEBISCHER, Patrick

Patrick Aebischer trained as an MD (1980) and Neuroscientist (1983) at the Universities of Geneva and Fribourg in Switzerland. From 1984 to 1992, he worked at Brown University (U.S.) as an Assistant and then Associate Professor. In 1992, he returned to Switzerland as a Full Professor at the Centre Hospitalier Universitaire Vaudois (CHUV) in Lausanne. Since 2000, Patrick Aebischer has been President of the Ecole Polytechnique Fédérale de Lausanne (EPFL) and continues to pursue his research in the field of neurodegenerative diseases.

ÅKESSON, Eva

Eva Åkesson is Professor of chemical physics and Vice-Chancellor of Uppsala University, Sweden. From 2009 to 2011, she was Deputy Vice-Chancellor of Lund University, with special responsibility for basic and advanced level studies issues, quality work and related internationalization matters. From 2003 to 2008, she was Vice-Rector of Lund University with special responsibility for undergraduate education and the Bologna Process. Eva Åkesson has served on numerous boards, including CSN (Central Board for Student Aid), SI (Swedish Institute) and the National Committee for Chemistry.

BERETZ, Alain

Alain Beretz is a pharmacologist. He was Vice-President in charge of technology transfer, and then President of the Louis Pasteur University in Strasbourg.

He then became the first president of the University of Strasbourg, resulting from the innovative merger of the three universities. He was re-elected in 2012 for a second term and is a member of the Board of Directors of the League of European Research Universities (LERU).

BORYSIEWICZ, Leszek

Sir Leszek Borysiewicz has been Vice-Chancellor of the University of Cambridge since October 2010, and was earlier Deputy Rector of Imperial College London. From 2007 to 2010, he was Chief Executive of the U.K.'s Medical Research Council, the national agency responsible for the allocation of £750 million (€890 million) in research funding.

BRITO CRUZ, Carlos Henrique de

Carlos Henrique de Brito Cruz was born in Rio de Janeiro, Brazil. He graduated in Electronics Engineering and has an MSc and a DSc in Physics. He is a professor at the Physics Institute at Unicamp. He worked at the University of Rome and at AT&T Bell Laboratories. Brito Cruz has been the President of the São Paulo Research Foundation, FAPESP, and the Rector of Unicamp. Since 2005 he has been Scientific Director of FAPESP. He is a member of the Brazilian Academy of Sciences.

DANIELS, Ronald J.

Ronald J. Daniels became the 14th president of The Johns Hopkins University in March 2009. Previously, he was provost and professor of law at the University of Pennsylvania (2005-2009) and dean and James M. Tory Professor of Law at the University of Toronto (1995-2005). Since arriving at Johns Hopkins, President Daniels has focused his leadership on three overarching themes: enhanced interdisciplinary collaboration, increased student accessibility and community engagement. As Chair of the Executive Committee for Johns Hopkins Medicine, he works closely with the trustees of Johns Hopkins Medicine, serving as a bridge between the university and health system.

DUDERSTADT, James J.

James J. Duderstadt is President Emeritus and University Professor of Science and Engineering at the University of Michigan. His teaching, research and service activities include nuclear science and engineering, applied physics, computer simulation, science policy and higher education. He has served on or chaired numerous boards and study commissions, including the National Science Board, the Executive Board of the National Academies, the Policy and Global Affairs Division of the National Research Council, the Nuclear Energy Advisory Committee of the U.S. Department of Energy, the National Commission on the Future of Higher Education and the National Academies

Committee on Research Universities. At the University of Michigan he currently co-chairs the program in Science, Technology and Public Policy, and directs the Millennium Project, a research centre exploring the impact of over-the-horizon technologies on society.

ESCHER, Gérard

Gérard Escher obtained his diploma in Biology at the University of Geneva, and his PhD (Neuroscience, 1987) at the University of Lausanne, where he led a research group working on synapse formation, after a postdoctoral fellowship at Stanford University. He worked for 10 years as scientific advisor and assistant director at the Swiss State Secretariat for Education and Research. Since 2008, he has been senior advisor to President Patrick Aebischer (EPFL).

GOETZ, Rebecca

Rebecca Goetz is a business analyst at Fannie Mae who previously worked as a researcher in the Office of the President of The Johns Hopkins University. She graduated in 2012 from Johns Hopkins with a degree in International Studies and Economics.

KATEHI, Linda P. B.

After a distinguished career at the University of Illinois at Urbana-Champaign, Purdue University and the University of Michigan, Linda Katehi was named UC Davis chancellor in August 2009. The university is widely recognized as one of the top public research universities in the world. Chancellor Katehi earned her bachelor's degree in electrical engineering from the National Technical University of Athens in her native Greece and went on to earn her master's and doctoral degrees in electrical engineering from UCLA. Her work in electronic circuit design has led to numerous national and international awards and she has 19 U.S. patents and five U.S. patent applications.

LOPRIENO, Antonio

Trained in Egyptology, Linguistics and Semitic Languages and Literatures at the University of Turin (Italy), Antonio Loprieno was appointed Associate Professor of Afro-asiatic Languages at the University of Perugia (Italy) in 1987, and then as Professor of Egyptology at UCLA in 1989, where he was also Chairman of the Department of Near Eastern Languages and Cultures until 2000. In 2000, he returned to Switzerland as Professor of Egyptology at the University of Basel and was appointed Rector in 2006. He also heads the Conference of Swiss University Rectors (CRUS). Professor Loprieno is a member of the Academy of Sciences in Göttingen, of the German Institute of Archaeology and various other national and international Boards of Regents.

MUNROE-BLUM, Heather

Heather Munroe-Blum is Principal and Vice-Chancellor (President), McGill University. She holds a B.A., B.S.W. (McMaster University); M.S.W. (Wilfrid Laurier University); Ph.D. in epidemiology (University of North Carolina-Chapel Hill). She is a member of the boards of the Association of American Universities; Association of Universities and Colleges of Canada (AUCC); AUCC Committee on University Research (Chair); Canada Pension Plan Investment Board; Royal Bank of Canada. She is also a member of Canada's Science, Technology and Innovation Council; Canada Foundation for Innovation; Trilateral Commission; President's Council of the New York Academy of Science. She is an Officer of the Order of Canada and of the National Order of Quebec, as well as a Specially Elected Fellow of the Royal Society of Canada.

NEWBY, Howard

Sir Howard Newby, KB, CBE, BA, PhD, AcSS, is Vice-Chancellor of the University of Liverpool. He was previously Vice-Chancellor of the University of the West of England (UWE) in Bristol, having earlier spent five years as the Chief Executive of the Higher Education Funding Council for England (HEFCE). He was Vice-Chancellor of the University of Southampton from 1994 to 2001 and was previously Chairman and Chief Executive of the Economic and Social Research Council (ESRC). From 1999 to 2001, Sir Howard was President of Universities U.K., the U.K. body which represents the university sector. He was also President of the British Association for the Advancement of Science for 2001-2002. He was made a CBE in 1995 for services to social science and granted a knighthood in 2000 for services to higher education. Sir Howard was formerly a Professor of Sociology in both the U.K. and U.S., and has published numerous books and articles on social change in rural England.

NILAND, John

John Niland was President of the University of New South Wales (UNSW), Australia, from 1992 to 2012. He is the standing Chairman (2012 to 2015) of the International Academic Review Panel of Singapore Management University (SMU), and is an Independent Director of Macquarie Bank-Group, where he chairs its governance and compliance committee. He was a foundation member of the SMU Board of Trustees (2000 to 2012) with particular responsibility for governance, finance and remuneration strategies. He served on the University Grants Committee of Hong Kong (2003 to 2011) and led several reviews, involving HKUST and university mergers. His *Fit for Purpose* report on management and governance reforms for Hong Kong University led to fundamental changes there and at other Hong Kong Universities. He has been a Faculty member at Cornell, ANU and UNSW.

NOORDA, Sijbolt

Sijbolt Noorda is the former president of the University of Amsterdam and the Dutch research universities association VSNU. He is an advisor to many European universities (in Austria, Germany, The Netherlands, Romania and Turkey) and writes and lectures on a wide array of issues in Higher Education and Research policies. He is president of ACA (Academic Cooperation Association) and council member of MCO (Magna Charta Observatory).

RAWLINGS, Hunter

Hunter Rawlings is President of the Association of American Universities, a group of 62 leading research universities in the United States and Canada. Previously, Rawlings served as President of Cornell University for nine years, and, before that, as President of the University of Iowa for seven years. Hunter Rawlings is a Professor of Classics and History, and the author of several books and a number of articles on Greek Historiography. He is a member of the American Academy of Arts and Sciences, and of the Board of Trustees of the American School of Classical Studies at Athens.

RUEDA, Carlos

Carlos Rueda is a PhD candidate at the Desautels Faculty of Management at McGill University. He is currently working on management and leadership development under the advisory of Henry Mintzberg and Paola Perez-Aleman. He graduated with a B.A. in Economics from Universidad del Pacifico (Lima, Peru) and completed the Global Competitiveness Leadership Program at Georgetown University. In 2012, he was elected as a Vanier Scholar at McGill University.

SHEVGAONKAR, Raghunath. K.

Raghunath K. Shevgaonkar is Director of the Indian Institute of Technology Delhi, the top-ranked institution in India. He has been a leading educationist and researcher for more than 30 years. He is Fellow of IEEE, Indian National Academy of Engineering, National Academy of Science, Institution of Electronics and Telecommunication Engineers, Optical Society of India, and recipient of IEEE UG Teaching Award 2011 and Academic Leadership Award of Times Now.

SPECTOR, Phillip M.

Phillip Spector is the Vice President for Strategic Initiatives at The Johns Hopkins University. Previously, he served as Senior Advisor to the Legal Adviser at the U.S. Department of State and Senior Counsel to then-Senator Hillary Rodham Clinton. He is a graduate of Yale Law School and Swarthmore College.

SUH, Nam Pyo

Nam Pyo Suh is the Cross Professor Emeritus at M.I.T. and former President of KAIST. He was awarded the ASME Medal, the General Pierre Nicolau Award of CIRP and many others. He advanced axiomatic design theory, wear theories and microcellular plastics. He invented a large number of products and processes, including the OLEV, MH and MuCell. He has received nine honorary degrees from four continents.

TAN, Chorh Chuan

Tan Chorh Chuan is President of the National University of Singapore (NUS), Chairman of National University Health System, Deputy Chairman of Singapore's Agency for Science, Technology and Research, and Member, Board of Directors, Monetary Authority of Singapore. A renal physician, he obtained his MBBS, Master of Medicine (Internal Medicine) and PhD from NUS, MRCP (U.K.) from the Royal College of Physicians, and research training at the Institute of Molecular Medicine, Oxford. He served as Dean of Medicine from 1997-2000, and Director of Medical Service, Ministry of Health, from 2000-2004, where he lead the public health response to the 2003 SARS epidemic. Prof. Tan has been a member of the World Economic Global University Leaders Forum since 2008 and sits on the WEF's Science Advisory Committee.

WEBER, Luc

Luc Weber was professor of Public Economics at the University of Geneva and an adviser to Swiss governments. Since 1982, he has been strongly involved in university management and Higher Education policy in the capacity of vice-rector, then of rector, of the University of Geneva, as well as Chairman of the Swiss Rectors' Conference. More recently, he served on the Steering Committee for Higher Education and Research of the Council of Europe, the International Association of Universities and the European University Association.

YU, Kai

Dr Yu is Associate Professor and Assistant Dean of the Graduate School of Education, Shanghai Jiao Tong University. His research focuses on higher education in China, graduate education and higher education management. Dr Yu obtained his PhD from University of Oxford in the field of educational studies. He studied Computer Science at Queen's University of Belfast where he received a Bachelor's degree in Engineering with First-Class Honours.

ZHANG, Jie

Professor Zhang became the 39th President of Shanghai Jiao Tong University in 2006. He is a prominent physicist recognized for his pioneering research in laser-plasma research and a strong advocate and outstanding practitioner of higher education. Professor Zhang is a member of the Chinese Academy of Sciences (CAS), German Academy of Sciences Leopoldina, Fellow of Third World Academy of Sciences (TWAS), International Fellow of the Royal Academy of Engineering (FREng) and Foreign Associate of the U.S. National Academy of Sciences (NAS).

ZYL, Arnold van

Trained in Chemical Engineering at the University of Cape Town (South Africa), Arnold van Zyl was a post-doctoral Fellow at the Max Planck Institute for Solid State Research in Stuttgart, before occupying various leading positions in the R&D sector of Daimler in Stuttgart, Ulm and Brussels. From 2008 to 2012, he was Vice-Rector for Research and Innovation at the University of Stellenbosch (South Africa). He is currently Rector of Chemnitz University of Technology in Germany.

PART I

•••••••••••••

Changing Purpose, Role and Relationships of Research Universities

CHAPTER 1

Research Universities
and the Future of America:
A Study by the National
Academies of the United States

James J. Duderstadt

In June 2012, the National Academies of the United States released the results of an important study concerning the future of the American research university requested by the United States Congress (Holliday, 2012). The crucial importance of the research university as a key asset in achieving economic prosperity and security is widely understood, as evidenced by the efforts that nations around the globe are making to create and sustain institutions of world-class quality. Yet, while America's research universities remain the strongest in the world, they are threatened by many forces: the economic challenges faced by the nation and the states, the emergence of global competitors, changing student demographics and rapidly evolving technologies. Even as other nations have emulated the United States in building research universities to drive economic growth, America's commitment to sustaining the research partnership that built a great industrial nation seems to have waned, hence stimulating the growing concern of our government.

Today, our nation again faces a period of rapid and profound economic, social and political transformation driven by the growth in knowledge and innovation. Educated people, the knowledge they produce and the innovation and entrepreneurial skills they possess have become the keys to economic prosperity, public health and national security. As President Obama stated the challenge in his 2011 State of the Union Address (Obama, 2011):

*"The world has changed. In a single generation, revolutions in technology have trans-
formed the way we live, work and do business. The competition for jobs is real. But
this shouldn't discourage us. The future is ours to win. But to get there, we can't just
stand still. We need to out-innovate, out-educate and out-build the rest of the world."*

Investing in innovation creates the jobs of the future. Investing in education prepares our citizens to fill these jobs. Building the infrastructure for a
knowledge-based economy will ensure prosperity and security for our nation.
Economists estimate that 40% to 60% of economic growth each year in the
United States is due to research and development activity. Another 20% of
the increased resources each year is based upon the rising skill levels of our
population. (Augustine, 2007) When asked to identify the one federal policy
that could most increase the long-term economic growth rate, economists put
further investment in education and research at the top of the list.

Key to the achievement of all three of these goals is the American research
university, which, through its research, creates the new knowledge required
for innovation; through its advanced graduate and professional programs produces scientists, engineers, physicians and others capable of applying innovation to create economic value; and through its development and deployment
of advanced infrastructure, such as information and communications technology, provides the foundation for the knowledge economy. (Cole, 2009)

But America is not adequately investing in its research universities, nor has
it developed a national strategy to support them. For many years, public universities have seen steep reductions in state appropriations per student. Federal support for university research has also been declining in real terms, at the
same time that other countries have increased funding for research and development. Meanwhile, American business and industry have not fully partnered
with research universities to create the industrial leadership that was found in
the past in large corporate research labs, such as the former Bell Laboratories.

The unfortunate consequence of the low priority given to support the
unique missions of the American research university by the states, the federal
government, industry and the public puts not only the quality of higher education at risk, but also threatens the economic prosperity and security of the
nation.

A REQUEST FROM THE UNITED STATES CONGRESS

To address these concerns, in 2010, leaders of Congress made the following
request to the National Academies of Science and Engineering and the Institute of Medicine (Holliday, 2012):

*"America's research universities are admired throughout the world, and they have
contributed immeasurably to our social and economic well-being. Our universities, to*

an extent unparalleled in other countries, are our nation's primary source of long-term scientific, engineering and medical research. We are concerned that they are at risk.

"We ask the National Academy of Sciences, the National Academy of Engineering and the Institute of Medicine to assemble a distinguished group of individuals to assess the competitive position of American research universities, both public and private, and to respond to the following question:

"What are the top 10 actions that Congress, state governments, research universities and others can take to maintain the excellence in research and doctoral education needed to help the United States compete, prosper and achieve national goals for health, energy, the environment and security in the global community of the 21st Century?"

In response, the National Academy leadership recruited a group of top national leaders, roughly balanced among those from American research universities, industry, government and science, to serve on a committee to respond to the request made by Congress. Over the past two years, this committee, chaired by Chad Holliday, former CEO of DuPont, met frequently to receive testimony and written input from an array of stakeholders from both the public and private sectors. Supported by a strong team of National Academy staff, the committee also conducted a number of studies of both key issues and possible actions. Those exercises influenced the committee's decision to frame its recommendations within the theme of the research partnership — among universities, the states, the federal government and business and industry — that has been key to the evolution and leadership of the American research university.

Because of the importance of this study, the National Academies also developed a rigorous review process for the report, involving 23 reviewers from an unusually broad array of backgrounds and constituencies. The committee responded to hundreds of suggestions from those reviewers to arrive at its final report. In my roles as both a member of this committee and the chair of the Policy and Global Affairs Division of the National Research Council of the National Academies to whom it reported, my paper will concern both the findings and the recommendations of this important study.

KEY FINDINGS

During past eras of challenge and change, our national leaders have acted decisively to enable universities to enhance American prosperity and security (Cole, 2009). While America was engaged in the Civil War, Congress passed the Morrill Land-Grant Act of 1862 to forge a partnership between the federal government, the states, higher education and industry aimed at creating universities that could extend educational opportunities to the working class, while conducting the applied research that would enable Americans to become world leaders in agriculture and industry. Eighty years later, emerging from the Great Depression and World War II, Congress acted once again to strengthen that partnership by investing heavily in basic research and graduate education to build the world's finest research universities, capable of providing the steady stream of well-educated graduates and scientific and technological innovations central to our robust economy, vibrant culture, vital health, enterprise and national security in a complex, competitive and challenging world.

Yet, today, each member of the national research partnership appears to be backing away from the earlier commitments that created and sustained the American research university. The policies and practices of our federal government no longer place a priority on university research and graduate education (Berdahl, 2010). In the face of economic challenges and the priorities of aging populations, our states no longer are either capable or willing to support their public research universities at world-class levels. American business and industry have largely abandoned the basic and applied research that drove American industrial leadership in the 20th century (e.g., Bell Laboratories), largely ceding this responsibility to research universities, but with only minimal corporate support. Finally, our research universities themselves have failed to achieve the cost efficiency and productivity enhancement in teaching and research required of an increasingly competitive world.

While, in the wake of the 2008 meltdown of the equity markets and subsequent recession, all American research universities were facing challenges, there was general agreement that perhaps the more serious challenges were faced by the nation's public research universities as the states withdrew support (McPherson et al., 2009). The endowments of private universities will recover rapidly, but state support is unlikely to recover for at least a generation.

KEY RECOMMENDATIONS

Today, our nation faces new challenges, a time of rapid and profound economic, social and political transformation driven by the growth in knowledge and innovation. A decade into the 21st century, a resurgent America must stimulate its economy, address new threats, and position itself in a competitive world transformed by technology, global competitiveness and geopolitical change. Educated people, the knowledge they produce, and the innovation and entrepreneurial skills they possess, particularly in the fields of science and engineering, have become key to America's future. Hence, the National Academies study stressed as its key theme the importance of both reaffirming and revitalizing the unique partnership that has long existed among the nation's research universities, the federal government, the states and business and industry.

The approach taken in our recommendations was framed by several key principles. We sought a balanced set of commitments by each of the partners — federal government, state governments, research universities and business and industry — to provide leadership for the nation in a knowledge-intensive world and to develop and implement enlightened policies, efficient operating practices and necessary investments. To this end, we attempted to create linkages and interdependencies among these commitments that provide strong incentives for participation at comparable levels by each partner. We sought sufficient flexibility in our recommendations to accommodate the differences among research universities and the diversity of their various stakeholders. While merit, impact and need should continue to be the primary criteria for awarding research grants and contracts by federal agencies, we believed that investment in infrastructure should consider additional criteria, such as regional and/or cross-institutional partnerships, program focus and opportunities for building significant research capacity. Furthermore, we stressed the importance of supporting the comprehensive and interdependent nature of the research university, spanning the full spectrum of academic and professional disciplines, including the arts and humanities. Finally, we believed success would require a decade-long effort when both challenges and opportunities are likely to change, evolving from an early emphasis on more efficient policies and practices to later increases in investment as the economy improves.

In particular, we framed our recommendations of actions involving each member of the research partnership to accomplish these three broad goals. The first four actions were aimed at strengthening the partnership among universities, federal and state governments, philanthropy and the business community in order to revitalize university research and speed its translation into innovative products and services. The next three actions sought to streamline and improve the productivity of research operations within universities. The final three actions were intended to ensure that America's pipeline of future talent in science, engineering and other research areas remains creative and vital, leveraging the abilities of all of its citizens and attracting the best students and scholars from around the world.

Revitalizing the Partnership

*Recommendation 1: Within the broader framework of United States innovation and research and development (R&D) strategies, the **federal government** should adopt stable and effective policies, practices and funding for university-performed R&D and graduate education.*

Over the next decade as the economy improves, Congress and the administration should invest in basic research and graduate education at a level sufficient to produce the new knowledge and educated citizens necessary to achieve national goals. As a core component of a national plan to raise total national R&D funded by all sources (government, industry and philanthropy) to 3% of GDP, Congress and the administration should provide full funding of the amount authorized by the America COMPETES Act. (America COMPETES, 2010) That would double the level of basic research conducted by the National Science Foundation, the National Institute of Standards and Technology, and the Department of Energy Office of Science, as well as sustain our nation's investment in other key areas of basic research, including biomedical research funded by the National Institutes of Health. Note that this recommendation is not calling for new programs, but rather asking the Congress to achieve funding goals authorized earlier for various federal research agencies.

Recommendation 2: The states should strive to restore appropriations for higher education to levels that allow public research universities to operate at world-class levels, while providing them with greater autonomy to enable them to compete strategically and respond with agility to new opportunities.

Over the past two decades, in the face of shifting public priorities and weak economies, states have decimated the support of their public research universities, cutting appropriations per enrolled student by an average of 35%, totaling more than $15 billion each year nationally (McPherson *et al.*, 2009). Yet, even as the states have been withdrawing the support necessary to keep these institutions at world-class levels, they have also been imposing upon them increasingly intrusive regulations. As the leader of one prominent private university put it, "The states are methodically dismantling their public universities where the majority of the nation's campus research is conducted and two-thirds of its scientists, engineers, physicians, teachers and other knowledge professionals are produced." (Holliday, 2012).

Hence, we challenge the states to recognize that the devastating cuts and meddlesome regulations imposed on their public research universities are not only harming their own future, but also putting at great risk the nation's prosperity, health and security. While strongly encouraging the states to begin to restore adequate support of these institutions as the economy improves, we also urged them to move rapidly to provide their public research universities with sufficient autonomy and agility to navigate an extended period with limited state support.

Recommendation 3: The role of business in the research partnership should be strengthened, facilitating the transfer of knowledge, ideas and technology to society and accelerating "time to innovation" in order to achieve our national goals.

We recommend strongly that the relationship between business and higher education should shift from that of a customer-supplier — of graduates and intellectual property — to a peer-to-peer nature, stressing collaboration in areas of joint interest and requiring joint commitment of resources. Strong support of a permanent federal tax for research and development, and more efficient management of intellectual property by businesses and universities to improve technology transfer are also needed. Such a tax credit would stimulate new research partnerships, new knowledge and ideas, new products and industries in America, and new jobs. Better management of intellectual property would result in more effective dissemination of research results, thus also generating economic growth and jobs.

Recommendation 4: *Universities must increase cost-effectiveness and productivity in order to provide a greater return on investment for taxpayers, philanthropists, corporations, foundations and other research sponsors.*

It is essential that the nation's research universities strive to address the concerns of the American public that their costs are out of control. To this end, universities should set and achieve bold goals in cost-containment, efficiency and productivity. They should strive to constrain the cost escalation of all continuing activities — academic and auxiliary — to the national inflation rate or less through improved efficiency and productivity. This will require the development of more powerful, strategic tools for financial management and cost accounting, tools that better enable universities to determine the most effective methods for containing costs and increasing productivity and efficiency. It is essential that universities, working together with key constituencies, intensify efforts to educate people about the distinct character of American research universities and cease promoting activities that create a public sense of unbridled excess on campuses.

Strengthening Research Universities

Recommendation 5: *Create a Strategic Investment Program that funds initiatives at research universities that are vital to advancing education and research in areas of key national priority.*

We recommend that the program begin with two 10-year initiatives. The first would be an endowed faculty chairs program to facilitate the careers of young investigators. During a time of economic difficulty and limited faculty retirements, it would help ensure that America is developing the research faculty we need for the future. We also call for a research infrastructure program that is initially focused on advancement of campus cyber-infrastructure, but perhaps evolves later to address, as well, emerging needs for the physical research infrastructure as they arise. (Atkins, 2003) Matching grant requirements would generate additional funds from private or state support.

Recommendation 6: *Strive to cover the full costs of research projects and other activities they procure from research universities in a consistent and transparent manner.*

Today, many research universities are forced to subsidize underfunded sponsored research grants from resources designated for other important university missions, such as undergraduate tuition and patient fees for clinical care. This is no longer acceptable and must cease. If the federal government and other research sponsors would cover the full costs of the research they procure from the nation's research universities, they, in turn, could hold steady or reduce the amount of funding from other sources they have had to provide to subsidize this federal research. Universities should be able to allocate their various resources more strategically for their intended purpose. Both sponsored research policies and cost recovery negotiations should be applied in a consistent fashion across all academic institutions (COGR *et al.*, 2011).

Recommendation 7: *Reduce or eliminate regulations that increase administrative costs, impede research productivity, and deflect creative energy without substantially improving the research environment.*

Federal and state policy-makers and regulators should review the costs and benefits of federal and state regulations, eliminating those that are redundant, ineffective, inappropriately applied to the higher education sector, or impose costs that outweigh the benefits to society. (COGR *et al.*, 2011) Furthermore, the federal government should also harmonize regulations and reporting requirements across all federal agencies. Reducing and eliminating regulations could trim administrative costs, improve productivity and increase the nimbleness of American universities. With greater freedom, they will be better positioned to respond to the needs of their constituents and the larger society.

Building Talent

Recommendation 8: *Improve the capacity of graduate programs to attract talented students by addressing issues such as attrition rates, time to degree, funding and alignment with both student career opportunities and national interests.*

Research universities should restructure doctoral education to enhance pathways for talented undergraduates, improve completion rates, shorten time-to-degree, and strengthen the preparation of graduates for careers both in and beyond the academy. (Wendler *et al.*, 2010) To this end, the federal government should achieve a better balance of fellowships, traineeships, and research assistantships. Both universities and research sponsors should address the many concerns characterizing postdoctoral research appointments including the excessive length and low compensation of such service and the misalignment of these experiences with career opportunities. Such efforts would increase cost-effectiveness and ensure that we can draw from the "best and brightest" for our nation's future doctorates.

Recommendation 9: *Secure for the United States the full benefits of education for all Americans, including women and underrepresented minorities, in science, mathematics, engineering, and technology.*

Research universities should intensify their efforts to improve science education throughout the education ecosystem, including K-12 and undergraduate education. Furthermore, all research partners should take action to increase the participation and success of women and under-represented minorities across all academic and professional disciplines and especially in science, mathematics and engineering. As careers in STEM fields continue to expand, recruiting more under-represented minorities and women into those fields is essential in order to meet the workforce needs of our nation and to secure economic prosperity and social well-being.

Recommendation 10: Ensure that the United States will continue to benefit strongly from the participation of international students and scholars in our research enterprise.

Federal agencies should make visa processing for international students and scholars who wish to study or conduct research in America as efficient and effective as possible, consistent also with homeland-security considerations. This should include the possibility of granting residency to each foreign citizen who earns a doctorate in an area of national need from an accredited research university ("attaching a green card to each diploma").

CONCLUDING REMARKS

These recommendations reflect the consensus of extensive testimony before the National Academies committee, both oral and written, from many constituencies including federal agencies, business leaders, state governments, and, of course, leaders of American higher education. While sometimes bold and ambitious, the committee believes that these recommendations and actions are necessary to preserve one of the nation's most important assets: its world-class research universities. While achieving these goals will be challenging, particularly in a rapidly changing economic environment, we believe that it is important to state what we think is needed and then to develop implementation strategies in collaboration with the various constituencies that are key to achieving these goals.

It is important to keep the recommendations and the report sufficiently flexible to adapt to unforeseen challenges and opportunities as they arise. For example, the staging of implementation steps will depend significantly upon economic circumstances. During the current economic recession, most of the focus should probably be on those federal and state policies and university practices designed to improve cost-containment and productivity. As the current economic crisis recedes and the economy improves later in the decade, attention should turn to restoring or increasing investments in research and graduate education.

Since the release of the National Academies report last summer, members of the committee have been working closely with leaders of business and government to build traction on several of the key recommendations. Although, during the current economic crisis, further investment will be difficult to achieve, other recommendations — such as the relaxation of burdensome regulation, the achievement of greater autonomy for public research universities, and a major transformation of immigration policies — seem possible in the near term.

The actions recommended by the National Academies will require significant policy changes, productivity enhancement, and investments on the part of each member of the research partnership: the federal government, the states, stakeholders such as business and philanthropy, and most of all, the nation's research universities. However, we believe these recommendations comprise a fair and balanced program that will generate significant returns to the nation. Such commitments are necessary for the future prosperity, health and security of America.

REFERENCES

America COMPETES Act (2010). *America Creating Opportunities to Meaningfully Promote Excellence in Technology, Education, and Science Act*, Public Law No. 110-69 (reauthorized 2010).

Atkins, Daniel E. (chair) (2003). *Revolutionizing Science and Engineering Through Cyberinfrastructure*. Report of the National Science Foundation Blue-Ribbon Advisory Panel on Cyberinfrastructure. Washington, DC: National Science Foundation.

Augustine, Norman (chair) (2007). National Academies Committee on Prospering in the Global Economy of the 21st Century, *Rising Above the Gathering Storm: Energizing and Employing America for a Brighter Economic Future*. Washington, D.C.: National Academies Press.

Berdahl, Robert (2010). *"Maintaining America's Competitive Edge: Revitalizing the Nation's Research University"*. Testimony to the National Academies Committee on Research Universities. Washington, DC: Association of American Universities.

Cole, Jonathan R. (2009). *The Great American University*. New York, NY: Public Affairs.

COGR, AAU & APLU (2011). *"Regulatory and Financial Reform of Federal Research Policy"*. Recommendations to the National Research Council Committee on Research Universities. Council on Government Relations, Association of American Universities, Association of Public and Land-Grant Universities, 21 January 2011.

Holliday, Chad (chair) (2012). National Academies Committee on Research Universities. *Research Universities and the Future of America: Ten Breakthrough Actions Vital to Our Nation's Prosperity and Security*. Washington, D.C.: National Academy Press. (The complete report, summary, and videos of the press conference can be found on the National Academies website: http://sites.nationalacademies.org/PGA/bhew/researchuniversities/index.htm)

McPherson, P., Shulenburger, D., Gobstein, H. & Keller, C. (2009). *Competitiveness of Public Research Universities and Consequences for the Country: Recommendations for Change*. Washington, D.C.: Association of Public and Land-Grant Universities.

Obama, President Barack (2011). State of the Union Address before the United States Congress, 25 January 2011.

Wendler, C., Bridgeman, B., Cline, F., Millett, C., Rock, J., Bell, N. & McAllister, P. (2010). *The Path Forward: The Future of Graduate Education in the United States*. Princeton, NJ: Educational Testing Service.

CHAPTER 2

The Strategic Repositioning of Research Universities to Fulfil their Global Promise

Heather Munroe-Blum and Carlos Rueda*

INTRODUCTION

The relevance of universities has become a theme of public debate, reflecting the anxiety and excitement surrounding changing forces in the larger context of globalization, as well as widespread concern with regard to basic economic and societal well-being.

Despite a whirlwind of change and transformation, universities have been stable, resilient and durable social institutions. A study done for the U.S. Carnegie Commission on Higher Education identifies 66 institutions in Europe that have prevailed since the 16th century. Remarkably, apart from two churches and two parliaments, the other 62 institutions are universities (Neilson & Gaffield, 1986, p. xiii). Given this staying power, we can ask: is this ability of universities to adapt to changing forces and circumstances sufficient to ensure their central place, contribution and viability, going forward? How is higher education responding to the transformation of information and communication technologies with the rise of the internet, and the global impacts of major economic and social events? And, are universities optimally organized and managed to address the fundamental global challenges that exist, and to do so at the pace of change required be effective?

It is evident that the world's research universities must be active and flexible in the face of global powerful forces: demographic change, environmental unpredictability, increasing population mobility, a rapidly changing landscape of ethnic and cultural diversity, hypercompetitive markets, unstable govern-

15

ments, the internet, disruptive technologies, and a decline of deference for leadership and institutions, across sectors — from governments to industry, NGOs and universities. In the context of these fundamental shifts, we identify five themes or forces that have strong relevance for the world's research universities and, perhaps most critically so, for the great public research-intensive universities.

At large, these five main forces include:

- Urgency of global challenges and shifting mandate of universities; Instability of government funding for universities, and public trust/confidence in universities;
- Rapid expansion of massive online information and education; Increased tensions with respect to differentiation of mission in post-secondary systems; Expansion of large-scale, international research programs.

While fundamental aspects of the mission of the research-intensive university are enduring, today's top public research-intensive universities face different concerns than their predecessors: difficult, fundamental questions with regard to purpose, role and relationships. This was well demonstrated in a 2012 study published by the National Research Council, "Research Universities and the Future of America", which highlights the threat to the future of top U.S. research universities and to the prosperity and security of society. The report finds that U.S. state funding for higher education, already eroded over the past two decades, has fallen further in the recent recession, and recommends that, especially in these tough times, governments cannot afford to defer investment in research universities. If the nation is willing to renew its commitment to keeping these institutions the best in the world, they will lead the way to the next generation of scientific and technological breakthroughs that propel prosperity, just as they have in the past.

THE URGENCY OF GLOBAL CHALLENGES AND THE SHIFTING MANDATE OF RESEARCH UNIVERSITIES

The "Global Challenges Survey", a United Nations-led effort within the context of the Millennium Development Goals program, gives an overview of some of the most urgent global challenges to humanity. These challenges, primarily man-made, are selected and prioritized based on indicators of damage and risk to life and health, economic and social development, and the natural resources on which human life depends (Global2015, 2010). Among the 24 challenges analysed, the Survey identifies the following four as top priorities: world nutrition and poverty eradication; elimination of epidemics; sustaining a livable climate; and achieving safe birth conditions.

The figures are startling. Every year these four global issues combined are responsible for the premature death of at least 11 million people (equivalent to one-third of Canada's population) and affect nearly two billion people worldwide. No country escapes problems of nutrition, poverty, epidemics, climate and negative birth conditions. These immediate threats have prime implications for our societies, our education systems and their perceived and actual societal relevance.

Against this background, what then is the role of higher education and research in creating a sustainable future for us all and generations to come? The concept of "university" goes back to the classical understanding of the learning and teaching community. As knowledge and talent have become ever-stronger driving forces for the development of healthy, civil society, the perception and expectation of universities have both shifted and broadened considerably. Universities cannot be relevant today as self-contained systems without direct links and contributions to the rest of society. Universities are well placed to make a difference, by playing a significant role in shaping and responding to the change process and contributing to the alleviation of many local and global challenges — including poverty, disease and malnutrition — but also in positioning communities and nations for international competitiveness in distinctive fields and sectors of high global importance. This is particularly so when one considers the necessity of achieving globally competitive talent, products and services to sustain local community progress in a global economy and with global demographic factors at play. Our universities can play a prime role in shaping policies and programs, developing leaders, shaping existing sectors, creating new sectors and industries, and promoting the fundamental ideas and learning that influence every one of us and that enhance civil society as a whole.

As Duderstadt and Womack (2003, p. 6) note:

The public university provides a model of how social institutions, created by public policy and supported [...at least in part...] through public tax dollars, evolve in response to changing social needs. They exist to serve the public interest. As the needs and aspirations of society have changed, so too have public universities.

These challenges are all "public" problems for today's world. They cross beyond our notion of a "public-as-national" interest or concern, and emerge into the "public-as-global" imperative. They are front and centre to discussions of the future of the public, research-intensive university.

In this context, McGill University has a long history of contributing to progress and responding to global challenges. McGill's involvement in shaping the international human rights agenda dates back to the drafting of the UN Declaration of Human Rights by Professor John Peters Humphrey in 1948, right up to current programs, such as the McGill International Community Action Network, a fellowship program in the School of Social Work that engages and educates young scholars from war-torn regions in the Middle East and encourages them to apply their learning towards the betterment of their home countries. Similarly, a creative new collaboration of the MasterCard Foundation with a small consortium of universities, in which McGill is a partner, aims to advance social and economic progress in sub-Saharan Africa, by educating talented young people drawn from the most economically disadvantaged sub-Saharan regions and preparing them to lead change in their home communities. In a conservational context, the sustainability and food safety and security programs of McGill's Faculty of Agricultural and Environmental Sciences and the School of Dietetics and Human Nutrition are geared towards meeting industrial and public sector demands for professional development in the fields of food safety, nutrition, water resources management and environmental sciences. And, lastly, to name just one example of student-driven social change: most recently, a team of five MBA students from McGill's Desautels Faculty of Management won the Boston Regional Finals of the 2013 Hult Prize competition for their novel plan to combat famine in urban slums. Their submission outlines the development of a manufacturing plant to grow edible crickets to use as a safe and affordable source of protein to fight hunger and malnutrition.

Such innovations and educational programs, as described here and found broadly in our university, are compelling, and there is more to do at home and abroad, to fulfil the mission of our research universities. The "public" nature of universities goes beyond financial or legal relationships to local jurisdictions and governments. Indeed, it rests in the broad public domain that public research-intensive universities serve, adapt and respond, providing solutions to prime societal challenges as a collective responsibility.

INSTABILITY OF GOVERNMENT FUNDING AND CHANGE IN PUBLIC TRUST

The last financial meltdown demonstrated both how vulnerable our financial markets really are, and how vulnerable our system of higher education can be in regard to the vicissitudes of government financing. Instability in public finances translates into big impacts on public universities. The year following the financial crisis of 2007-08, and again in the past year, many national and regional governments in jurisdictions including Canada, the U.K. and the State of California imposed dramatic cuts to their university systems. These cuts were a wake-up call about universities' financial over-dependence on government funding, leading to and imposing major constraints in operations for public universities around the world. With unstable and declining government finances, public universities worldwide experience unrelenting pressure to take measures to increase and diversify revenues, while at the same time working to retain their capacity to fulfil the core mission. The Canadian Association of University Teachers (CAUT) reports that between 1979 and 2009 the proportion of university operating revenue pro- vided by government sources has declined from 84% to 58%. Federal govern- ment cash transfers for post-secondary education in Canada, when measured as a proportion of GDP, have declined by 50% from 1992-1993 to 2011-2012; that is, from 0.41% to 0.21% (CAUT, 2013). Most recently, many Canadian provinces have also imposed sudden, drastic funding cuts to their universities: $250 million in Quebec, $146 million in Alberta, $121 million in Ontario, and $70 million in British Columbia. The Quebec government announced its decision to cut funding for the current fiscal year eight months into the 2012- 2013 fiscal year, leaving Quebec's universities under order to cut $120 million within four months.

University research is complex in terms of its sources of funding and its impact on the operations of the institutions. The just-released Canadian State of the Nation 2012 report shows that Canada's gross domestic expenditures on R&D (GERD) declined from a peak in 2008 and, when measured in relation to gross domestic product (GDP), since 2001 (STIC, 2013). In contrast, the GERD and GERD intensity of most other countries has been increasing. Can- ada's declining GERD intensity has pushed its rank down from 16th position in 2006 to 17th in 2008 and to 23rd in 2011 (among 41 economies). While there have been shifts in funding among sectors in Canada over time, the more recent declines in the country's total R&D funding efforts are attributable pre- dominantly, but not only, to low levels of private sector funding of R&D.

In other places such as the U.K., continental Europe, North America and Japan, government investment is also increasingly unstable and limited, espe- cially at the state/regional level. Beyond influences such as economic slow recovery, structural factors — escalations in healthcare costs, heavy and grow- ing public and private debt, and the demographic deficit reflected in the aging of populations — contribute greatly to the weakening of public finances and are correlated with a decreased investment in education. Universities, as well as countries, are responding in different ways to the financial consequences of the economic downturn and such structural factors. In the U.S., for example, 71.2% of universities with doctoral-level programs cut their academic pro- grams and activities, 59.3% increased tuition fees by 5% or more (already high by international standards), 57.8% cut administrative operations and services, and 50.8% laid off administrative staff (Green, Jaschik & Lederman, 2011).

Universities require a high degree of financial stability and predictability to ensure effective and sustainable operations, to maintain the capacity to hire and retain outstanding talent, to enhance quality and to innovate in infra- structure, pedagogy and research programs.

In return, this investment serves all sectors of society. Universities are talent magnets, employers, innovation and workforce catalysts, infrastructure and product creators, and community collaborators. University graduates are the principal leaders and workforce in creating and building the knowledge-based industries that fuel innovation (Munroe-Blum *et al.*, 1999; STIC, 2013). These essential roles shift higher education from an economic mainstay, primarily, to serving as a driver of the next generation of leaders, and of regional economies and indeed, the health of nations; 51% of Canada's adult population has a university or college education — one of the highest levels in the world; however, Canada lags others in its production of PhDs, especially in the STEM disciplines (STIC, 2013). University graduates today play an especially important role in building high value-add companies and the jobs that contribute to economic prosperity in the new global context.

Despite their central importance for society, public universities have been simultaneously facing an increasingly burdensome regulatory framework, along with declining public respect. At the federal and provincial/state levels in Canada and elsewhere, universities are staggering under a range of growing administrative and regulatory burdens as new government reporting and regulation requirements are added to existing ones. Research shows that increased university performance is favoured by less regulation and increased autonomy (Oliveira Martins *et al.*, 2009), when accompanied by strong institutional governance and institution-specific compacts with governments; that is, when the focus is on accountability via results rather than on a large burden of rules, regulations and reports. Universities work better under accountability mechanisms that foster agility such as those requiring a commitment to accessible information on high-performance, cost-effective operations, services and programs, and research and educational program impacts consistent with the institution's prime academic mission (Munroe-Blum, 2012 & 2013). Highly prescriptive regulatory environments encourage a "one-size-fits-all" culture and lead to drifts downward in attention to mission-targeted performance and results, in general.

Public institutions are experiencing a decline in the confidence of publics, universities included. A survey commissioned by the Association of University and Colleges of Canada (AUCC) shows that although universities continue to be viewed to be among the most ethical of public institutions, trust in them has declined over the last decade by nearly 30% (AUCC, 2013). The decline of trust in academia, and for science in particular, is a trend observed in many parts of the world. Perhaps one powerful explanation is the interaction of the uncertainties of global economies with the eradication of "expertise", as it has been known and respected, in lieu of accessible information; and, collaborative content-generation repository such as Wikipedia, in lieu of evidence, experience and wisdom.

The loss of trust from and in government agencies may be related to a seemingly unstoppable expansion in public health care costs without perceived increases in healthcare services and outcomes, and a related significant decline, therefore, of public investment available for education. Both factors stand to negatively affect the value placed on education by the public, and pose potential risks to the health and well-being of society.

THE RAPID EXPANSION OF MASSIVE ONLINE INFORMATION AND EDUCATION

Related to these phenomena, and as we move further into the 21st century, information and knowledge are increasingly democratized. Google and Wikipedia organize information and disseminate it quickly and more widely than could have been imagined 20 years ago or less. Paradoxically, at this very time, as the privileged sites of critical inquiry, intellectual debate and knowledge generation, research-intensive universities may be uniquely positioned authorities with respect to knowledge validation and adjudication of competing claims to truth. "Evidence-based" now takes on new meaning.

The world's top-ranked public research universities are increasingly positioning both to transform their own facilities, networks and practices to take full advantage of the modern-day, high-tech environment, and to stand as global leaders in innovative, technology-enhanced teaching and learning, for both enhanced campus-based learning and benefitting communities of students around the world.

Massive Online Open Courses (or MOOCs) present a special, yet mixed opportunity to develop new pedagogical models and educational outreach. *The New York Times* dubbed 2012 "The Year of the MOOC", and MOOCs have since become one of the most discussed topics at educational conferences and workshops (Pappano, 2012). *Time* magazine noted that free MOOCs open the door to the "Ivy League for the Masses" (Ripley, 2012). This assertion has been reinforced by several well-financed providers, associated with top universities, including:

- The edX Cosortium (edx.org), a not-for-profit organization launched by MIT and Harvard. More than 100,000 students signed up for the first prototype course offered by MIT. McGill University, among others, has recently joined the edX Consortium.
- Coursera (coursera.com), a for-profit start-up founded by Stanford professors. It has almost 3.5 million users and offers more than 300 courses.
- Udacity (undacity.com), another for-profit, founded by a Google VP. It currently offers 25 courses, five of which can serve as credit courses at San Jose State University.

While MOOC providers address a variety of interests, they are unlikely to deliver in the absence of active assessment and R&D to develop and position these online courses effectively, as any new teaching and learning model would demand. According to a survey of MOOCs' professors, on average 33,000 students enrol in a MOOC; however less than 8% of them successfully complete the course with a passing grade (*The Chronicle*, 2013). These figures point clearly to a broad surface interest and, as well, to the significant work ahead in developing optimal online and campus enhanced e-learning experiences. The edX Consortium, for one, is taking on the challenge of researching and developing online learning, using technology to enhance campus-based learning for the "born digital" student. This could allow technology to assist in providing a research experience as a hallmark of the undergraduate learning experience.

No one institution on its own will likely be able to gather the quantity of data necessary to understand what features of these new and emerging tools are best deployed, what aspects will engage students best to enhance their learning experience, the role of interactive learning, and how preferences interact. Research collaborations with peer institutions, such as those in the edX Consortium, are positioned to contribute new pedagogical methods in an evidence-based context and stand to advance the effectiveness of the research-intensive university in a world where technology is prevalent and more and more of the world's population are born digital.

A GREATER EXPRESSION OF MISSION, SPECIFICALLY IN POST-SECONDARY SYSTEMS

Widespread cuts to government-supported student aid and tertiary education threaten the quality of higher education. A concomitant rise in the world's youth population and global fiscal challenges combined are expected to produce an unprecedented need for education. These and other factors will require greater diversification of revenues for teaching (and research). While new sources of funding should not replace public funding, diversification of income sources is increasingly essential if financial risks are to be shared and quality preserved.

The California three-tier system has long served as the gold standard for differentiation of resources in higher education systems, notwithstanding the financial constraints discussed earlier. With 10 campuses of the University of California, 23 campuses of the California State University, and 112 California Community Colleges, the state has three clearly differentiated institutional models, by law, and differential resources and funding models assigned to each group of universities through public funding, tuition fees and other revenue sources, including state and federal research programs. The three-tier system has been credited with helping to shape and nurture the strengths of California's economy. Today, five out of the 10 universities in the University of California system rank among the top 50 universities in the world (*Times Higher Education*, 2013).

Many countries have introduced policies to vigorously support world-class, research-intensive universities. Countries such as the U.K., the U.S. and Australia have traditionally focused their research funding on their most competitive universities; the U.K.'s Russell Group, an association of 24 public research universities, receives approximately two-thirds of all university research grant and contract income (from among a total of 115 public universities); according to a study by the National Science Foundation, in FY 2011, the top 30 academic institutions in the U.S. accounted for approximately 40% of total federal R&D support (of all 896 schools that received federal money for R&D) (NSF, 2012); and Australia's "Group of Eight" leading research institutions receives approximately 70% of national competitive research grants (from among a total of 39 accredited Australian universities).

Germany and France have also developed targeted programs: in 2006, the German Excellence Initiative created a national program in which top universities received additional support in order to promote cutting-edge research and raise their international visibility (in 2012, out of the 140 universities in Germany, 11 universities were chosen as "elite universities"); while in 2010, France's Initiatives d'excellence promoted university clusters with international visibility to compete with the best universities in the world, selecting projects led by eight research-intensive universities and providing financial support of €7.7 billion over a period of at least four years. In recent years, many Asian economies, including China, India, Japan, South Korea, Singapore, Hong Kong, Chinese Taipei and Malaysia, have developed ambitious plans to strategically build world-class universities in support of their economic and societal development. In 2011, China allocated CAD $11.4 billion of its education budget towards achieving world-class status for 100 of its more than 3,000 universities; while India has selected nine universities — with six more to come — under its University with Potential for Excellence scheme, to provide "substantial support" to these universities with the amount to be decided on the merit of the proposal (STIC, 2013).

Funding research-intensive universities on an equal footing with liberal arts, state and community colleges is an unproductive trend increasingly referred to as the disposition of governments to "vocationalize" universities and their research. This approach stands at odds with the core principles and mission of the research university, but also with the evidence. Performance-driven, mission-differentiated funding models enable institutions to take advantage of their unique pasts, strengths, assets and missions, and to craft appropriate results-oriented niches, including appropriate programs and modalities of teaching and learning, of research and scholarship.

Canadian provincial governments (which hold prime jurisdiction over education), unlike most of the governments mentioned earlier, have long favoured a more homogenous approach to university funding; allocating the majority of operating grants according to headcounts vs. funding formulas that advance performance according to mission; the former approach being process- rather than results-oriented. Consequently, Canada's most productive and highest-performing research universities are often the least well-funded to perform their mission, relative to their peers elsewhere, or to regional and undergraduate liberal-arts-focused universities. To address this, the Higher Education Quality Council of Ontario prepared the policy report "The Benefits of Greater Differentiation of Ontario's University Sector" (HEQCO, 2010), presenting four key benefits to greater differentiation in institutional mission and funding. The report notes that "greater differentiation" is one of the most powerful levers available to government, especially in resource-constrained times, to achieve goals of greater quality, competitiveness, accountability and sustainability; it provides clarity to students as to the postsecondary institutions that may best serve their career goals, talents and personal aspirations; it helps institutions and society to be cost-effective and outcomes-oriented by preventing mandate dilution and mission creep; it allows institutions to allocate their resources most effectively by providing clarity as to mandate, performance goals and public expectation; and finally, it allows for a results-focused accountability framework for universities, and also provides a framework for best determining the differential costs of education and research by mission and results, and levels of required funding.

Canada has strong science, technology, education and innovation foundations on which to build, but stands to do better in investing at internationally competitive levels in programs that reward research, excellence, top talent and institutional performance. All participants in the educational ecosystem have a role to play in driving enhanced performance and lifting Canada into the top ranks of the world's leading innovative economies. It is not only about investing more, but about investing more strategically and coherently, focusing resources and efforts, learning from the experience of leading nations and improving agility to create and seize emerging opportunities. Differentiation in mission and funding, building upon institutional assets, strengths and performance, will foster institutions and nations that "run with the best."

EXPANSION OF LARGE-SCALE, INTERNATIONAL RESEARCH PROJECTS

NASA's Apollo program was a great scientific collaboration involving government, academia and industry. Landing humans on the moon by the end of 1969 required an intense burst of technological creativity, and the largest commitment of resources ($24 billion) ever made by any nation in peacetime. At its peak, the Apollo program employed 400,000 people and involved over 20,000 industrial firms and universities. The Apollo project provides some useful reflection about large-scale R&D initiatives. Can humanity harness collaborative knowledge beyond industrial or military applications, for the public good?

Knowledge — and even more importantly, the production of knowledge — is highly relevant for the economy of today. Collaboration channels between universities and industry stand to be enhanced. On the one hand, new ventures and established companies are increasingly seeing universities as sources of scientific discoveries that can be transformed into innovations for the market, as well as places to recruit innovation-minded workers trained in rich research environments. On the other hand, universities are increasingly seeing companies as effective agents to transform research results into concrete solutions for society and new support for financing basic research. This situation creates a natural, powerful partnership between research-intensive universities and innovative companies.

The modern research-intensive university is characterized by the increasing internationalization of its activities and a related rise in collaboration, including open innovation, among different players and across national borders. Universities can anchor clusters of innovative activity in their local communities and act as bridges between businesses, governments and other countries. They also play a critical role in developing and advancing knowledge and its application. Much of the knowledge underlying today's innovation resulted from research conducted in the higher education sector. Through their research activities, universities play a critical role in linking local economies to the global pool of knowledge, technology and talent. Through research collaboration with foreign counterparts and through attraction of world-class researchers and scholars to their institutions, universities advance regional knowledge and talent advantages. Today, building local strength in priority areas is no longer enough. Only clusters that are competitive, connected and recognized on the world stage will achieve sustained local economic benefit (Munroe-Blum, 2011).

The Canadian government, with this aim, created the Networks of Centres of Excellence (NCE) program in 1989. The program has since invested $1.8 billion in research, commercialization and knowledge translation; leveraged $1.1 billion in contributions from industry and other partners; helped train more than 39,000 highly qualified personnel; and created 107 spin-off companies (NCE, 2013). One of these networks, BioFuelNet Canada, based at McGill University and led by Prof. Don Smith, connects 25 post-secondary institutions, nearly 100 leading researchers, 40 industrial partners, dozens of governmental and nongovernmental organizations, and 6 international partnerships. The goal is to develop the knowledge, the tools and the policies that will facilitate 25% of the fuel used in Canada to come from advanced biofuels, within 10 to 20 years.

Innovation rarely happens in isolation. Collaboration, whether between two researchers or on the large scale such as the BioFuelNet, is the key to answering big questions. For instance, the Natural Sciences and Engineering Research Council of Canada's (NSERC) CREATE program helps science and engineering graduate students add job skills to their academic achievements. CREATE recently awarded funding for six years to McGill projects in green chemistry, and medical image analysis. Launched in 2010 by UN Secretary-General Ban Ki-moon, The United Nations Academic Impact (UNAI) is a powerful initiative bringing together postsecondary institutions from around the world with the joint goal of advancing ten basic principles, including addressing issues of poverty, promoting universal access to education, and encouraging global citizenship. Currently, more than 700 institutions in over 100 countries and some 40 academic networks have joined the initiative.

It is our position that targeted large-scale, international research consortia of distinction can create networks of scientists, scholars, practitioners and public and private-sector decision-makers that, on a wide scale, can usefully advance the development of solutions to global challenges. The strategic creation and expansion of targeted international research programs to achieve innovation breakthroughs may be one of society's most powerful strategies to tackle the world's "grand challenges". They can provide exciting opportunities for public, research-intensive universities to lead in creating synergies in research and innovation, while furthering the development of tangible projects with concrete results for a sustainable future.

CONCLUDING REMARKS

Unlike the State of California, Canadian provinces and many other regions in the U.S. and Europe have taken more of a unitary approach to university funding: a one-size-fits-all criterion favouring headcounts over more sophisticated distinctions of funding based on mission, quality, and results. But increasing global demand and a domestic demographic deficit, along with greater global population mobility, shrinking public resources and emerging online learning models, among other factors, challenge the role of all public institutions of higher education — especially top-ranked public research universities. Greater recognition of the differentiation of postsecondary institutions stands to enhance the strategies and contributions of all universities while increasing the benefits of the world's top public universities to the jurisdictions and nations in which they reside. Public research universities require re-configured relationships with governments, the private sector and civil society in order to build on their strengths and reaffirm and strengthen their contributions, domestically and internationally. This will require a move away from highly regulated and bureaucratic government oversight to funding-based performance contracts, at the level of institutional-contracts that recognize mission specific goals and reward according to performance.

* The authors acknowledge, with gratitude, the supportive editorial contributions of Ms. Karin Lornsen.

REFERENCES

Association of Universities and Colleges of Canada (AUCC) (2013). "Public perceptions of university autonomy and accountability". Presentation given by David Turpin, President and Vice-Chancellor of the University of Victoria.

Canadian Association of University Teachers (CAUT) (2013). 2012-2013 CAUT Almanac of Post-Secondary Education in Canada / Almanach de l'enseignement postsecondaire au Canada de l'ACPPU. Available at: http://www.caut.ca/docs/almanac/2012-2013-caut-almanac-of-post-secondary-education-in-canada.pdf?sfvrsn=0

Duderstadt, J. & Womack, F. (2003). *The Future of the Public University in America: Beyond the Crossroads.* Baltimore and London: The Johns Hopkins University Press.

Global2015 (2010). Global Challenges Survey; Special Edition for the UN Summit on the Millennium Development Goals, High-Level Plenary Meeting of the United Nations General Assembly, 20-22 September 2010. Berlin, Global2015. Available at: http://www.global2015.net/file/global2015mdg.pdf

Green, K. C., with Jaschik, S. & Lederman, D. (2011). Presidential Perspectives: The 2011 Inside Higher Ed Survey of College and University Presidents. Inside Higher Ed.

Higher Education Quality Council of Ontario (HEQCO) (2010). The Benefits of Greater Differentiation of Ontario's University Sector: Final Report. Available at: http://www.heqco.ca/siteCollectionDocuments/DifferentiationENG.pdf

Munroe-Blum, H., Duderstadt, J. & Davies, G. (1999). Growing Ontario's Innovation System: The Strategic Role of University Research. Government of Ontario.

Munroe-Blum, H. (2011). Higher Education and Innovation: The Canada-U.S. Story. Published in *Policy Options*, March 2011. Available at: http://www.irpp.org/en/po/canada-us-conversations-and-relations/higher-education-and-innovation-the-canada-us-story/

Munroe-Blum, H. (2012). Our research universities can lead ahead. Published in The *Globe and Mail*, June 25, 2012. Available at: http://www.theglobeandmail.com/commentary/our-research-universities-can-leap-ahead/article4365206/

Munroe-Blum, H. (2013). 10 Lessons over 10 Years. Speech given to the Canadian Club of Montreal, Montreal, Canada, March, 11 2013. Available at: http://www.cerclecanadien-montreal.ca/assets/files/Events_docs/2012-2013/discours-heather-munroe-blum-eng.pdf

National Science Foundation (2012). Universities Report Highest-Ever R&D Spending of $65 Billion in FY 2011. NCSES Infobrief, November 2012.

Neilson, W. & Gaffield, C. (1986). Universities in crisis: A mediaeval institution in the twenty-first century. Montreal: The Institute for Research on Public Policy.

Networks of Centres of Excellence of Canada (2013). Quick facts about the NCE. Available at: http://www.nce-rce.gc.ca/About-APropos/QuickFacts-QuelquesFaits_eng.asp (Accessed 24 May 2013).

Oliveira Martins, J., Boarini, R, Strauss, H. & de la Maisonneuve, C. (2009). The Policy Determinants of Investment in Tertiary Education. OECD Journal: Economic Studies, Volume 2009, No. 1.

Pappano, L. (2012). The Year of the MOOC. Published in *The New York Times*, 12 November 12, 2012. Available at: http://www.nytimes.com/2012/11/04/education/edlife/massive-open-online-courses-are-multiplying-at-a-rapid-pace.html?pagewanted=all&_r=1& (Accessed 24 May 2013).

Ripley, A. (2012). College is Dead. Long Live College! *Time U.S.*, October 18, 2012. Available at: http://nation.time.com/2012/10/18/college-is-dead-long-live-college/

Science, Technology and Innovation Council (2013). State of the Nation 2012. Canada's Science, Technology and Innovation System: Aspiring to Global Leadership. Available at: http://www.stic-csti.ca/eic/site/stic-csti.nsf/vwapj/StateOfTheNation2012-may16-eng.pdf/$file/StateOfTheNation2012-may16-eng.pdf

The Chronicle of Higher Education (2013). The Minds Behind the MOOCs: Additional Results from *The Chronicle*'s Survey. Available at: http://chronicle.com/article/article-content/137905/#id=results

Times Higher Education (2013). World University Rankings 2012-2013. Available at: http://www.timeshighereducation.co.uk/world-university-rankings/2012-13/world-ranking

U.S. National Research Council (2012). Research Universities and the Future of America: Ten Breakthrough Actions Vital to Our Nation's Prosperity and Security. National Academies Press, Washington, DC.

CHAPTER 3

How to Answer the Utilitarian Assault on Higher Education?

Hunter Rawlings

American universities are facing unprecedented pressure to adopt a purely utilitarian mission, both in the education of their students and in the research they conduct.

GROWING PRESSURES
TO ADOPT UTILITARIAN MISSION

Across the country, state governors and governing boards are demanding that undergraduate education focus on the preparation of students for immediate jobs, thus promoting vocationalism above all other purposes of education, in fact, often to the exclusion of all other purposes.

- In some cases, governors suggest making state funding for public universities dependent on recent graduates' employment rates. "Are young people getting degrees in jobs that are open and needed today, not just the jobs that the universities want to give us, or degrees that people want to give us?" asks Wisconsin Governor Scott Walker. North Carolina Governor Pat McCrory is even more explicit, declaring that state funding for education should "not [be] based on butts in seats, but how many of those butts can get jobs."
- States such as Virginia have passed laws requiring universities to publish the salaries of very recent graduates, *by major*, as an "aid" to families considering their options in higher education.
- Under this highly reductive scheme, a college education becomes nothing more than short-term job preparation and students nothing more than workers-in-training.

- By prioritizing immediate employment, these governors create a hierarchy of majors, suggesting that some fields of study are more worthy than others.

Science and engineering fields often earn high praise as fueling innovation and preparing students for a knowledge economy, while the social sciences, humanities and the arts are overtly attacked. "Is it a vital interest of the state to have more anthropologists? I don't think so," says Governor Rick Scott of Florida.

From this perspective, the societal benefits of higher education warrant public investment only in vocational fields. Any field of study that does not lead directly to an industry pipeline does not merit public support. Governor McCrory, again, makes it plain: "If you want to take gender studies, that's fine, go to a private school and take it. But I don't want to subsidize that if it's not going to get someone a job."

There are now clear signs that this movement has reached the national level, where new efforts are under way to measure the salaries of recent college graduates, *by major*, as well as by college, through the creation of a new national data base. The Wyden/Rubio bill in the United States Senate will probably be more broadly based than some state legislation, in the sense that it will require several measures, rather than just an economic one, of student "success", but it is giving impetus to the trend we have noted in the states.

The argument that many college degrees are impractical, that students would be better off in vocational training programs, that liberal arts degrees are a waste of time and money is utterly absurd, even from a purely *economic, utilitarian* standpoint. A new, not-yet-published paper by John Etchemendy, Provost of Stanford, makes this point more cogently than previous research.

- Multiple studies have shown that the "college premium — the difference between the earnings of the average college graduate and the average high school (only) graduate — stands at record levels," as high as 97%. The precise bump in salary conferred by a college degree varies by the location of employment, but in the United States, there is "no combination of major and state that does not see a wage premium for a baccalaureate degree" (Etchemendy). Furthermore, the wage premium exists across nearly all occupations, including many that do not require a college degree. Why should universities compromise their dedication to knowledge in favour of vocational skills when students already earn a significant — and lifelong — economic boost from their studies?
- The economic benefits of a college education also accrue to society at large. A recent report by the Milken Institute has shown that each additional year of college for the average worker in a given region

increases the region's per capita GDP by 17.4%. The wages of the average worker also rise by 17.8%, including workers with only a high school diploma. (DeVol *et al.*, 2013)

• These are hard numbers, statistics backed by large sets of data, just the sort of information that should resonate with those utilitarian governors and governing boards. If student employment is such an important outcome of university education, should we not at least acknowledge the fact that the unemployment rate for college graduates is less than half that of high-school graduates? (Carnevale *et al.*, 2012)

• In America, at least, the obsession with vocationalism stems in part from a sense that college students are not actually learning anything. Despite the economic gains to be had from earning a college degree, there is widespread acceptance of the proposition that most college students who graduate do so without acquiring the skills they will need to serve them in the workplace.

STUDENT LEARNING GAINS AND THE RHETORIC OF CRISIS

These attitudes arise in large part from the book *Academically Adrift*, a study of student learning gains as measured in the first two years of college. The authors, Arum and Roksa (2011), famously claimed that 45% of students enrolled in a wide variety of institutions showed no significant improvement on the CLA, a standardized test used to measure critical thinking and reasoning skills.

This assertion has prompted a great deal of hand-wringing both inside and outside the academy. If nearly half of all college students are not learning anything, then surely something must be wrong!

While there is no doubt that many improvements could be made to the American system of higher education, a more nuanced appraisal of the data behind *Academically Adrift* suggests that panic is not (yet) necessary. Etchemendy has thoroughly reviewed Arum and Roksa's claims, and come to the following conclusion:

"Once we strip away Arum and Roksa's rhetoric of crisis and look at the actual data they present, it takes on an entirely different cast. Using a methodology that is biased toward understating student progress, they nonetheless see evidence of a reassuring degree of learning across a very broad base of students attending a wide variety of colleges and universities. They see this progress using a test that targets a set of abstract reasoning and communication skills widely known to be among the most difficult to teach, and they see the improvement after only three semesters of the students' college experience.

This is not evidence of a system that is academically adrift, but evidence entirely consistent with what the economic data tell us: graduates produced by American colleges and universities display a significant skill differential that employers reward with the most substantial wage premium offered in the economically developed world."

A DEFICIT IN PRACTICALITY?

Academic research has also now come under attack for a perceived deficit in practicality.

- At the national level, Congress has essentially defunded political science research and is poised to do the same to all social science research, with the justification that these fields do not produce benefits to society.
- Under the new regulations, political science research can be funded by the government only if it improves national security or contributes to economic growth. In these exceptions, our government has clearly laid out its priorities. Greater understanding of the functioning of our democracy, gained through political science research, is by this reasoning not worthwhile, but anything that produces jobs can find support.
- Even more dangerous is a new attempt in the House of Representatives to make ALL scientific research funded by the federal government pass a utilitarian test. A discussion draft of a bill called the "High Quality Research Act" would stipulate as follows: "Prior to making an award of any contract or grant funding for a scientific research project, the Director of the National Science Foundation shall publish a statement on the public website of the Foundation that certifies that the research project — (1) is in the interests of the United States to advance the national health, prosperity, or welfare, and to secure the national defense by promoting the progress of science; (2) is the finest quality, is ground breaking, and answers questions or solves problems that are of the utmost importance to society at large...."
- Thus the purpose of this draft bill is to refocus NSF's entire program on applied, targeted research that leads to economic development or national security, period.

This trend in legislation appears to be gaining momentum during a time of budget shortages and calls for stringent accountability and oversight. It clearly prioritizes short-term, economic results and targeted research. And it clearly ignores the crucial role of fundamental research in leading, over time, to often unanticipated discoveries that enhance human life and usher in whole new industries, products and jobs.

Utilitarianism thus encompasses the vocationalization of education and the instrumentalization of research, through which technical fields of knowledge achieve greater status at the expense of other fields. This shift constitutes the repurposing of the entire university enterprise. Teaching and research are, in this new paradigm, no longer valued for the pursuit of knowledge, for the stimulation of human curiosity and intellect, nor even for the public good of a well-educated citizenry. Instead, it is economic growth alone that rules the day.

A GROWING TREND

Unfortunately, this trend is not limited to the United States.

- In Britain, the adoption of the Research Excellence Framework has created a new funding model in which 25% of government funding for research depends on the "impact" of previous research. That impact must extend beyond the academy and must be readily quantifiable, a difficult assessment in many fields. After all, how do you measure the impact of a study of a poem by Ovid? Even in more technical fields, predicting the impact of a given scientific study is a fruitless endeavour. Crucial advances, in medicine, technology, communications may find applications years or even decades after their first invention. Yet British researchers must now submit an assessment of the total impact of their research or risk losing government support.
- Australia is following Britain's lead, conducting case studies with a limited number of research universities to determine the cost of requiring an "impact" assessment for future research funding.
- These various efforts represent a collective shift towards narrow utilitarianism, a shift towards evaluating universities by limited and reductive metrics — jobs for students and economic impacts of research.

As Western governments lead the way in this shift, it is instructive to observe the behaviour of universities elsewhere on the globe. Asian universities have recently begun embracing the liberal arts, in contrast to their previous focus on technical and engineering programs.

- Universities in South Korea and Japan have adopted new curricula that include the liberal arts; in Hong Kong and China, new colleges have been created explicitly for the liberal arts. Bo Ya college, at Sun Yat Sen University, even requires its students to study Latin. And Singapore is investing in a new liberal arts college on the American model, designed and implemented with Yale University.
- These new colleges and programs adhere to their own understanding of what constitutes the liberal arts, and many remain in the early stages. And they certainly do not represent a major shift away from technical fields to the liberal arts. Yet it is clear that for these Asian

countries, the utilitarian approach to higher education is no longer sufficient. As China and Singapore rise in economic stature, they see value in supporting a broader definition of a university education. We might do well to consider that stance as our governments and societies seem poised to reject or at least to devalue education as mind-expanding rather than as vocational training.

PUTTING DOLLAR SIGNS

A great problem in the West lies in the fact that we academic leaders have often aided and abetted the movement towards utilitarianism. We trumpet research parks and technology transfer, spinoff companies and the economic impact our universities produce. We quantify our achievements, put dollar signs on much of what we do and stand for, and lobby mostly on the basis of what we can do for society in the short term. We are no longer effective or even ardent advocates of the so-called softer disciplines, such as the arts, the humanities and the social sciences.

One of the consequences of our general tendency now to emphasize economic measures of success is that higher education has come to be seen as a purely private interest, rather than as a public good. We are all aware of the seemingly inexorable withdrawal of state support from public universities in the U.S. The recession has clearly contributed to this reduction in support, but a more significant and primary cause is the loss of faith in higher education as a public good.

We need to address this problem before all others. And if *we*, higher education leaders, do not, no one else will.

COMPLEXITIES OF A FUNDAMENTAL DEFINITION

While it is true that universities perform many functions, and that they serve society in a number of ways, and that in the U.S. land grant universities were founded to contribute to social and economic welfare, at its fundamental level the university exists for the truth.

- Acknowledging and promoting this fundamental definition — that the primary purpose of the university is the truth, is not always easy. While the economic benefits of a college degree and of university research remain as valid as ever, the fact is that, ultimately, universities are *not* practical. They do not exist to make a profit. They are concerned with intellectual pursuits that may have no immediate, practical impact whatsoever and yet still have value. How to measure that value becomes a difficult question — here is an outcome that is not easily quantified.

- How does one quantify intellectual satisfaction, the inspiration to pursue lifelong learning, the capacity and the desire to thoughtfully contribute to civil society? They are not utilitarian, but they are perhaps the most valuable aspects of a college education.
- How does one quantify humanities scholarship and basic scientific research? Citations help, as do a few other measures, but in the end, it is difficult, and often reductionist in the extreme, to evaluate quality effectively.
- For some time now we have been content to emphasize our utilitarian achievements and to view them as compatible with, even supportive of, our fundamental intellectual purpose. And this strategy has worked well for at least three decades. But we have reached the point, I am afraid, when our facile combination of utilitarian and intrinsic values has become dangerous to our enterprise. Partly induced by our own rhetoric, many politicians now view us largely through an instrumentalist lens. (And I am not even going to get into the political and social roles of intercollegiate athletics in the U.S., a domain in which the risks of conflict of interest make technology transfer look like child's play).

So we are going to have to make the case for the intrinsic value of the university in order to preserve that value in the face of the utilitarian assault. How to make that case effectively?

One good place to start is the Group of Eight's April, 2013, discussion paper entitled "The role and importance of research intensive universities in the contemporary world." Among many other good arguments, the paper identifies key "attributes of research intensive universities": openness and autonomy; detached engagement; and radical conservatism. These are three paradoxical formulations that nicely capture the university's identity: a remarkable combination of innovation and preservation. While innovation holds sway today in our hyper-utilitarian culture, it is essential for us to be just as forceful and adept in expressing our commitment to the preservation of the best thinking from the past. As we are reminded nearly every day in this interconnected world, political and scientific and military power are not enough to solve crises: culture turns out to matter more than anything else.

OTHER RHETORICAL STRATEGIES

Many other rhetorical strategies present themselves as means of making the case for the intrinsic purpose of higher education. By way of conclusion, I offer an entirely unconventional one. It has to do with pleasure.

Henry Cabot Lodge was a student at Harvard in the 1870s. In spite of his aristocratic roots (or perhaps because of them), he was an unmotivated, indifferent student. As he wrote later in life to a friend,

- "In all my four years, I never really studied anything, never had my mind roused to any exertion or to anything resembling active thought until in my senior year I stumbled into the course in medieval history given by Henry Adams, who had then just come to Harvard. How I came to choose that course I do not exactly know. I was fond of history, liked to read it, and had a vague curiosity as to the Middle Ages, of which I knew nothing. I think there was no more intelligent reason than this for my selection. But I builded better than I knew. I found myself caught by strong interest, I began to think about the subject, Mr. Adams roused the spirit of inquiry and controversy in me, and I was fascinated by the stormy careers of the great German emperors, by the virtues, the abilities, the dark crimes of the popes, and by the tremendous conflict between church and empire in which emperors and popes were antagonists. In just what way Mr. Adams aroused my slumbering faculties I am at a loss to say, but there can be no doubt of the fact. Mr. Adams has told me many times that he began his course in total ignorance of his own subject, and I have no doubt that the fact that he, too, was learning helped his students. But there was more than this. He had the power not only of exciting interest, *but he awakened opposition to his own views, and this is one great secret of success in teaching*. In any event, I worked hard in that course *because it gave me pleasure*. I took the highest marks, for which I cared, as I found, singularly little, because marks were not my object, and for the first time I got a glimpse of what education might be and really learned something. I have never lost my interest in the Othos, the Henrys and the Fredericks, or in the towering figure of Hildebrand. They have always remained *vital and full of meaning to me*, and a few years ago I made a pilgrimage to Salerno with Adams himself to see the burial place of the greatest of the popes, who had brought an empire to his feet and had died a beaten exile. Yet it was not what I learned but the fact that I learned something, that I discovered that *it was the keenest of pleasures to use one's mind*, a new sensation, and one which made Mr. Adams's course in the history of the Middle Ages so memorable to me." (Wills, 2005, p. 89) (my italics)
- There are many points to note in this letter, but I will mark three. First, a professor does not have to be an "expert" in his discipline to be a great teacher. Henry Adams had no PhD, and very little expertise in medieval history when he offered this course at Harvard.

- Second, a good professor in the humanities, and perhaps in most disciplines, not only excites interest in his students, but encourages opposition to his own views. Learning at university is not simply about mastering material; it is about gaining the tools and the desire and the confidence to develop one's own views.
- Third, the goal of education is to discover that to use one's mind is the keenest of all pleasures. Why did Lodge finally find the will to work hard? Because work in Adams's course gave him pleasure.

TRILLING'S ANALYSIS

This matter of pleasure was also the subject of an acute analysis by one of America's great 20th century critics and essayists, Columbia professor Lionel Trilling.

Trilling addressed the significance of pleasure and of knowledge for its own sake in his definition of what he called "contemplative experience".

- "Such, it seems, is the opinion of the great mass of people, for by *contemplative experience* I mean those pursuits in which the faculties, though engaged, are concerned with their own exercise chiefly; for the mass of people such experience takes the form of engaging in difficult sports or watching complicated games...."
- "But however concerned it may be with purposive activity, literature in its essence is concerned primarily with *how* the act is done and how its own powers deal with the act. This interest in *how* and the intense pleasure it can afford are what literature has traditionally tried to create. And if we abandon the idea of literature as an independent, contemplative experience, as a pleasure,... if we continue to make it conform to philosophies of immediate ends,... and do not keep clear its own particular nature, we shall be contributing to the loss of two things of the greatest social value. Of these one is the possibility which art offers of an experience that is justified in itself, of nearly unconditioned living. Upon such experience, or even the close approach to it, we have learned to turn hostile faces; that is one of the strategic errors of our culture, for in the long run the possibility of such experience is a social necessity. The second thing we shall lose is the awareness — it is ultimately practical — which comes only from the single-minded contemplation of works that arise from the artist's own contemplation of events and objects; this is an awareness of the qualities of things. In the realm of art we call these qualities style, in the realm of morals we call them character, in the realm of politics we have no name for them but they are finally important. To these qual-

ities, especially in times of crisis, society seems to be stolidly indifferent; actually they are, after survival, the great social concern."
- "*Contemplative experience* has dangerous connotations. We think at
  once of *active thought* and in our time we know which of the two is better, for we have in mind purposive, constructive action which, in a
  time of crisis, seems the only possible way of survival. Well, crisis
  requires its sacrifices, but it is a good rule to sacrifice one's interests, if
  one must, by suspending them rather than by distorting them." [Trill-
  ing, 1940, pp. 440-442]

Is this a time of crisis? The word is overworked. But we are certainly confronted with disruption in our enterprise, and at such a time, we need to focus
upon the *qualities of things*, in our case, the essential qualities of the university.
When education is purely vocational, and research is purely utilitarian, contemplative experience vanishes. With Trilling, I believe that, contrary to the
common view, the single-minded contemplation of intellectual and artistic
works, whether they be in science or the humanities, is ultimately practical:
paradoxically, what appears to be abstract is in fact utilitarian. Because it is
only through such contemplation that one can see the qualities of things. And
such awareness is indeed the "great social concern."

REFERENCES

DeVol, Ross C., Shen, I-Ling, Bedroussian, Armen & Zhang, Nan (2013).
    *A Matter of Degrees: The Effect of Educational Attainment on Regional Economic
    Prosperity*, Milken Institute.
    http://www.milkeninstitute.org/publications/publications.taf?func-
    tion=detail&ID=38801395&cat=resrep
Etchemendy, J. "Are our Colleges and Universities Failing us?" Yet to be published.
Group of Eight (2013). "The role and importance of research intensive universities in
    the contemporary world." ACT, Australia.
    http://www.go8.edu.au/__documents/go8-policy-analysis/2013/role-importan-
    ceofresearchunis.pdf
Carnevale, A.P., Cheah, B., & Strohl, J. (2012). "Hard Times". Georgetown Center
    on Education and the Workfoce http://cew.georgetown.edu/unemployment/
Arum, Richard & Roksa, Josipa (2011). *Academically Adrift: Limited Learning on Col-
    lege Campuses*. University of Chicago Press.
Trilling, Lionel (1940). "Literature and Power", *The Kenyon Review* II.4, pp. 433-442.
Wills, Garry (2005). *Henry Adams and the Making of America*. Houghton Mifflin, Bos-
    ton and New York.

CHAPTER 4

The changing nature and character of research universities: New Paradigms

Chorh-Chuan Tan

WHY NEW PARADIGMS ARE NEEDED FOR RESEARCH UNIVERSITIES

The research university in its current form represents a remarkable and successful model where education and research and its application are brought together in synergistic ways that produce valuable new ideas, insights, products and services, as well as thought-leadership that informs policy and action (National Research Council of the National Academies, 2012).

However, the world in which research universities have thrived is changing fundamentally and rapidly. As a result, many businesses, social enterprises and public agencies have had to respond by transforming their strategies and operations (UNDP, 2013). Research universities will not be immune to the need to adapt to these changes and to seek fresh ways to remain relevant and contribute significantly to the advancement of society.

GLOBAL DRIVERS FOR CHANGE IN HIGHER EDUCATION

Potent global drivers for change in higher education include the following:
(a) The massive ongoing explosion of information and its ready availability anytime and anywhere. This has been driven by the dramatic advances in information technology and disruptive models of information creation, dissemination and use (such as Google, Wikipedia, open innovation). The

introduction of Massive Open Online Courses (MOOCs) has been accompanied by predictions of potential disruptions to the current models of delivery and credentialing in higher education.

(b) New generations of students who are highly IT-savvy and network through social media, and who would expect the same in their education. They are already making use of on-line learning resources and materials to supplement (or in some cases, replace) what they are being taught in their respective universities.

(c) The changing nature of work due to the forces of globalization, the demands imposed by rapid obsolescence of knowledge, and the ever-growing impact of technology (Brynjolfsson & McAfee, 2011). For example, the U.S. Department of Labor reported that in the U.S., men and women with a Bachelor's degree would have on average held 11.4 jobs and 12.2 jobs respectively, between the ages of 18 and 46 years (Bureau of Labor Statistics, 2012). As these jobs could be in very different sectors, educators need to consider how to give the best grounding to university students, which would enable them to re-skill more easily to meet the demands of different types of work in the course of their careers.

(d) Increasing complexity and volatility. The major challenges the world faces are truly complex and cross-disciplinary. Our graduates will need a broader intellectual base and the intellectual and personal abilities to deal effectively with complexity. Universities will need to reshape the way they pursue research and collaborate across borders in order to address complex research questions more holistically.

(e) In the U.S., some commentators are increasingly questioning the value of the research university model, arguing that it is too costly and of declining relevance relative to the changed needs of the economy and of graduate employability (Research Universities Futures Consortium, 2012).

Many of these drivers and trends are being perceived and framed as challenges. It is crucial to recognize, however, that they will also present many exciting new opportunities for research universities to innovate to create distinctive new educational models and value, and fresh approaches to tackle the large-scale complex problems the world faces.

MAJOR IMPLICATIONS FOR RESEARCH UNIVERSITIES

In an environment where information is so readily accessible, university education will need to go beyond content mastery. It needs to help students develop the intellectual scaffolding by which they can cope effectively with information overload by being better able to categorize, place and connect new knowledge. The ability to ask relevant and appropriate questions is more critical than ever before, as is the capacity to make sense of complex data and

to think imaginatively and differently about issues. In our tightly interconnected world, interpersonal skills such as teamwork, communication and
cross-cultural effectiveness will also become increasingly important.

For research universities, there is the added dimension of creating greater
synergies between research and teaching activities that take place within the
institution, so that the former has a clearer positive impact on the education
being provided.

The increasingly global nature of education and research is greatly intensifying competitive pressures on universities. However, the key drivers of
change, while pervasive, will likely present individual research universities
with different challenges. Each research university will need to reconsider its
distinctive value proposition to its students and the community it serves, and
this would clearly vary in different regions of the world, with their different
contexts and aspirations.

In most countries, the value proposition of research universities often
extends to playing important roles in driving and supporting local economic
growth and development. In this context, the changing global environment
makes it more urgent and crucial for more effective linkages to be developed
between education and research in the university, and local and regional economic activities, sectors and industry.

WHERE NEW APPROACHES MAY BE ESPECIALLY IMPACTFUL

In responding to these fundamental external drivers, research universities may
need to consider new approaches that represent much larger qualitative or
step-wise transformations in their activities. This is particularly pertinent for
rapidly growing countries that are in the process of ramping up investments in
research and higher education, the best example of which is China. Given the
scale of investment and ambition, appropriate innovations could potentially
enable research universities in these countries to "leap-frog" forward in their
development. The same is true at the other end of the spectrum — for small
countries with no natural resources such as Singapore, continued investment
and bold educational innovation are also important for universities to remain
competitive and maintain their relevance in a dynamic global economy.

While this paper will focus on new paradigms in education and research, it
is worth noting that new approaches are also required in other important
areas.

For example, in a complex and volatile world, "new" models of university
governance that increase nimbleness and the ability to create and seize opportunities are critical. To be successful, these would need to be accompanied by
greater diversification of sources of funding for the universities. While these
concepts are not new, as exemplified by long-standing practices in the leading

universities in the United States, they are not the norm in many other parts of the world, and, certainly, in Asia.

New paradigms are also required that more effectively and efficiently bridge the gap between knowledge creation and its application and commercialization, since these represent important dimensions of the overall value-proposition of research universities.

NEW PARADIGMS IN EDUCATION AND RESEARCH FOR RESEARCH UNIVERSITIES

Some proponents of MOOCs predict that on-line learning will completely disrupt the traditional university educational model (Forbes, 2012). Meanwhile, the report "An avalanche is coming" (Barber, Donnelly & Rizvi, 2013) warns that the functions currently served by universities are at the risk of being "unbundled" with each being better and more efficiently delivered by alternative providers or forms of delivery.

While there is little doubt that educational approaches and pedagogies will have to change substantially in research universities, it seems unlikely that there will be a "one-size-fits-all" model that would apply ubiquitously.

As the strategies and responses of individual research universities will have to be appropriate and relevant to their particular contexts and the needs and aspirations of the wider community that they serve, I would discuss three such new paradigms by referencing the example of the National University of Singapore (NUS), as the institution that I understand the best.

'GLOBAL EDUCATION'

While there are many definitions of "global education", at NUS this concept encompasses three main ideas.

First, that being effective in diverse cross-cultural settings, international and Asian, would be one of the distinguishing features of our graduates, and that this quality can only be gained through experiential immersion. This is particularly relevant for Singapore, which is a key hub for many large multinational companies, a major trading nation and a global shipping and logistics centre.

Second, NUS is not just a physical campus in Singapore that offers a rigorous education, but also a portal and bridge to excellent academic programs and professors in renowned universities around the world. In other words, our students would not just have the benefit of an NUS education in Singapore, but, through NUS, will also be able to study in some of the best, and complementary, programs overseas. For example, about 30% of NUS undergraduates currently spend six months or more on overseas student exchange programs, with a further 30% having at least one overseas educational experience, which may be for 3-8 weeks.

Third, a related concept is that of "mutually beneficial academic outsourcing". In regular student-exchange-programs (SEPs), students typically choose from a menu of courses, but the sum may lack academic coherence and relevance and may miss out on areas of particular academic strength in their host university. An alternative is for two institutions with complementary academic strengths to develop programs of study that deliberately exploit these complementarities, hence providing a distinct new value proposition for the students and universities. An example of this more structured approach is the NUS-University of Toronto's joint minor programs in environmental studies that leverage on the academic strengths in environmental biology and environmental chemistry at University of Toronto, and in environmental biology and nanoscience at NUS. In a similar way, joint-, double- and concurrent Bachelors-Masters programs between universities represent structured academic offerings that create new educational synergies, while providing students with an immersive overseas experience. In line with this philosophy, NUS currently has a significant number of such programs, in a range of disciplines, with partner universities around the world.

In such structured programs, the sharing of on-line learning materials and resources, and the use of video-conferencing to conduct joint classes across countries, can be readily, coherently and usefully integrated into the overall curriculum.

The NUS Overseas Colleges (NOC) program represents a different variation of the "mutually beneficial academic outsourcing" concept. Through the NOC, NUS undergraduate students have the opportunity to intern for a year at small start-up companies in the world's most entrepreneurial hubs, while taking courses at partner universities at these sites, namely Silicon Valley (Stanford University); Philadelphia (University of Pennsylvania); Shanghai (Fudan University); Stockholm (KTH); and Beijing (Tsinghua University); and for 3 to 6 months in social enterprises and high-tech start-ups in India and Israel respectively. The goal of the NOC program is to provide an experiential entrepreneurship education for a selected number of entrepreneurially inclined students. We judge this 10-year-old program to be very successful — for example, NOC students and alumni have founded 163 start-up companies (of which 99 are in operation) and are in high demand by employers both within and outside Singapore.

In tandem with such study abroad opportunities, we feel it critical that rich opportunities to develop cross-cultural effectiveness should also be developed on the NUS campus in Singapore — a sort of "internationalization-at-home". The NUS campus comprises a very diverse community of students and faculty, and we have introduced various approaches to enhance the peer learning opportunities arising from this. The most notable example is the NUS's newly opened University Town, which includes four new undergraduate residential colleges, each with 600 students. Admission to each college is randomized to create the most diverse student body possible in terms of disciplines, backgrounds (including students who are financially needy where specific support is provided) and with the ~30% of international students coming from about 40 countries. To ensure that students interact academically, they take a number of courses together, in small groups over two years, within the college. The College-based modules are designed to encourage exploration, sharing and uncovering of perspectives and ideas from different disciplinary and cultural backgrounds.

INTERNATIONALIZATION IN SITU: CREATING NEW EDUCATIONAL MODELS THROUGH DEEP STRATEGIC UNIVERSITY PARTNERSHIPS

NUS has pursued deep strategic partnerships with a small number of universities to establish major new programs in Singapore, which represent new learning approaches or novel models of education. These include the establishment of the Duke-NUS Graduate Medical School in partnership with Duke University, and most recently, the setting up of the Yale-NUS College. I will discuss the latter as an illustrative example of this approach.

Yale-NUS College: A new model of liberal arts education for Asia

In 2008, NUS started studying the feasibility of establishing a liberal arts college within our university. This was motivated by our conviction that as the world became increasingly complex and volatile, we needed to offer very high-potential students from Singapore and beyond, an educational option which emphasized breadth of multidisciplinary learning, but which was combined with rigour and the nurturing of critical thinking. Our review concluded that these learning outcomes would be most effectively achieved through a liberal arts education. However, our aspiration from the outset was that we should not simply adopt existing practices, but instead, endeavour to develop a new approach. In particular, with the rapid growth of Asia, with its attendant serious challenges and exciting opportunities, we believed that it was critical that the graduates of such an educational program should also have a deep appreciation of the culture and perspectives of this vast and populous region of the world.

This concept resonated strongly with the visionary leader of Yale University, President Richard Levin. In April 2011, after more than two years of detailed discussions and consultations, NUS and Yale signed an agreement to set up the Yale-NUS College, as an autonomous college of NUS in Singapore.

The partnership is founded on the strongly shared vision and excitement of re-imagining liberal arts education for the 21st century, and the unique opportunity to create an entirely new educational program in Singapore from scratch. The Yale-NUS College would therefore not be a wholesale "import" of the existing liberal arts model from Yale or the U.S., outstanding as this is, but would seek to break new ground. In particular, the College would endeavour to bring the major ideas, cultures and perspectives of the Western civilization into meaningful conversation with the intellectual traditions, cultures and contexts of Asia.

Groups of NUS and Yale faculty worked intensively and closely together to outline the broad contours of such a curriculum. Since the success of these new approaches would not just depend on the design of the curriculum, but on the actual teaching and learning that takes place, the College adopted a unique selection process for the appointment of the inaugural faculty. From the more than 2,500 applicants for the initial 50 faculty positions, shortlisted candidates were invited to workshops at Yale and at NUS, where they critiqued the proposed curriculum, suggested enhancements and described how they could personally contribute to its teaching. This process has enabled the College to identify faculty who are not just highly talented in their particular fields, but who have a passion for cross-disciplinary learning and a strong commitment to teaching outside of their areas of expertise.

With the progressive recruitment of the inaugural group of Yale-NUS College faculty in 2012, the faculty embraced the task of giving detailed form to the goals, directions and shape of the curriculum and developing the specific courses with impressive passion and commitment. Apart from curricula design, the faculty are also keenly working to introduce and innovate new pedagogies, including the integration of technology-enhanced learning. Besides the use of on-line learning resources and flipped classroom formats which free up face-to-face classroom time for conversation and argumentation, students and Professors in Yale-NUS College and Yale University could also be video-linked, encouraging dialogues across continents and providing opportunities to learn across institutions and cultures.

Beyond the formal curriculum, the College is dedicated to creating strong linkages between learning within and outside the classroom. To create a vibrant community of learning, the College will be fully residential and offer a myriad of experiential learning opportunities for its students that would enable them to grow intellectually and as well-rounded individuals. In a prospective world of technology-dominated education, one of the key differentiating factors for university education would be the opportunity to develop other dimensions of young people beyond the intellectual. Social and emotional intelligence, resourcefulness and resilience of individuals are as important in society, economy and polity as knowledge, critical thinking and other intellectual capacities. Arguably, such social and emotional development is best achieved through opportunities such as residential living and learning. As this would include cross-cultural effectiveness, all students of the College will also have a significant global educational experience. The College's physical facilities, which are currently being constructed and which will be completed in 2015, have been carefully designed to support and enable the educational vision and desired learning outcomes.

The inaugural class of 157 highly talented Yale-NUS College students has just been admitted, selected from a pool of more than 11,000 applications to date. The College and both NUS and Yale are looking forward in great anticipation as the College's educational programs formally begin in August 2013.

It is perhaps a little ironic that at a time when there are debates in the U.S. about whether liberal arts colleges still have a place, there is strong interest and growing recognition in Asia of liberal arts education as a valuable and complementary model of higher education. The reasons vary, but, in part, this has been driven by an increasing acceptance that the narrow, early specialization that characterizes much of higher education in Asia would not adequately prepare graduates for a world of much greater complexity, in which individuals would need a much broader intellectual base to make an impact. Others look to the liberal arts model as an educational program that fosters critical thinking and creativity, qualities that will be of increasing importance in rapidly emerging economies in Asia.

Within this context, the Yale-NUS College represents a bold, future-oriented initiative which has the potential to serve as a model for others in Asia and around the world, who have a similar interest and desire to respond to changing global and local circumstances by diversifying their higher education models away from a purely research-university only approach.

'An international research collaboratory': Singapore National Research Foundation's Campus for Research Excellence And Technological Enterprise (CREATE)

Over the past two decades, Singapore has progressively and substantially stepped up its investments in Research and Development, particularly in Science and Technology. The scale of this investment has been intensified since the year 2000, to help support and drive Singapore's development into a knowledge- and innovation-based economy and society.

As part of this overall effort, Singapore's National Research Foundation (NRF) launched a bold and novel initiative by establishing the Campus for

Research Excellence and Technological Enterprise (CREATE) in 2006. The goal is to internationalize and increase the diversity and vibrancy of Singapore's R&D ecosystem by forming collaborative research programs between world-class institutions and Singapore universities. This would eventually involve up to 1,200 researchers working physically together in a single 67,000 m^2 complex which is located in NUS' University Town.

At present, there are 15 collaborative research programs between Singapore universities (NUS and the Nanyang Technological University) and 10 overseas partners, namely MIT, ETH Zurich, University of Cambridge, University of California Berkeley, Technical University of Munich, Shanghai Jiaotong University, Peking University, Technion University, Hebrew University of Jerusalem and Ben Gurion University.

The 15 programs are in research areas of relevance to Singapore and similar cities, in four broad areas, namely Human Systems; Energy Systems; Environmental Systems; and Urban Systems.

Under Urban Systems, for example, researchers from ETH Zurich, Shanghai Jiaotong University, MIT and the Technical University of Munich work with faculty from NUS and NTU on developing solutions for the sustainable development of buildings, cities, districts and regions; developing decentralized waste-to-energy systems and building modelling and data management tools to track and mitigate emerging environmental contaminants; using modelling to develop a new paradigm for the design and operation of urban mobility systems; and developing electric vehicle technologies for use in megacities respectively.

CREATE's stated objectives are to "raise Singapore's research quality and to attract international research talent. Such international collaborations will allow Singapore to tap into state-of-the-art research overseas, while promoting knowledge spillover through cross-fertilization of ideas and enhancing efficiency through pooling of resources".

CREATE represents an exciting new paradigm that enables top researchers from Singapore and around the world to work in a cluster of research programs that, taken together, should contribute significantly to novel insights and solutions for some of the important and complex challenges that the world and Asia face. Another important dimension is that this arrangement greatly facilitates the joint supervision of PhD students from the partner universities and NUS and NTU, who will benefit from the unique experience of working within these cross-national, multidisciplinary research programs.

CONCLUSION

Some may argue that the new paradigms described above still revolve around the traditional activities of the research university, and may not stand the test of true disruptions to higher education that may be brought about, for example, by a revolution in on-line learning.

An alternative view, to which I also subscribe, is that these approaches, which may themselves involve the integrated use of on-line learning, can substantially increase the distinctive value-proposition of the face-to-face and experiential learning components within the university. In turn, this could more effectively motivate and prepare students for work and life in an increasingly complex and uncertain world. It is true that we would need to objectively evaluate the impact and outcomes of these new approaches. While this will take time, it should not detract from the need for research universities to continue to explore and innovate new ways in which their relevance could be extended or re-defined in a complex, fast-paced and volatile world.

REFERENCES

Barber, Michael, Donnelly, Katelyn & Rizvi, Saad (2013). "An Avalanche is Coming". pp. 32-47. IPPR. Available from:
http://www.ippr.org/images/media/files/publication/2013/04/avalanche-is-coming_Mar2013_10432.pdf
Brynjolfsson, Erik & McAfee, Andrew (2011). Race Against The Machine — how the digital revolution is accelerating innovation, driving productivity, and irreversibly transforming employment and the economy. Digital Frontier Press.
Bureau of Labor Statistics (2012). U.S. Department of Labor. News release on 25 July 2012. Available from: http://www.bls.gov/news.release/pdf/nlsoy.pdf
Forbes (2012). "Massive Open Online Courses — A Threat or Opportunity to Universities?" Forbes.com. Available from:
http://www.forbes.com/sites/sap/2012/09/06/massive-open-online-course-a-threat-or-opportunity-to-universities/
National Research Council of the National Academies (2012). "Research Universities and the Future of America", The National Academies Press. Available from:
http://www.nap.edu/openbook.php?record_id=13396&page=R1
Research Universities Futures Consortium (2012). "The Current Health and Future Well-Being of the American Research University", p. 9. Available from:
http://www.researchuniversitiesfutures.org/
RIM_Report_Research%20Future's%20Consortium%20.pdf
UNDP (2013). Human Development Report 2013, p. 14, 17. Available from:
http://hdr.undp.org/en/media/HDR_2013_EN_complete.pdf

PART II

•••••••••••••

Changing Nature
of Discovery,
Learning and Innovation

CHAPTER 5

Research Funding:
trends and challenges

*Leszek Borysiewicz**

INTRODUCTION

Research — the generation or collection of knowledge — is of the greatest importance. It can affect individual lives, society at large and even the fate of our planet. Uncountable sums of money are spent, and usually well spent, on moving forward our understanding of academic disciplines. Researchers access these funds in a variety of ways and account for their use, similarly, in a variety of ways. As each individual researcher knows painfully well, obtaining funding is a competitive activity — many more grants are sought than are awarded. And yet the effectiveness and efficiency of the various methods of allocating research funding are not well understood. What one might call "research about research" is thin on the ground. There is little agreement even on the appropriate methodologies to use to track either efficiency or effectiveness, and although the great majority of funds are dispensed to scientists by scientists (the arts, humanities and social sciences requiring less equipment and fewer consumables), it is in the social sciences that the necessary methodologies are to be found. Scientific funding boards, by implication, are not the best placed to rate their own success.

The principal thesis of this paper is that, in a context of poor data, trends in research funding methods and objectives need tracking. These trends are shaped by different funders, not necessarily acting with regard to each other, and so the possibility arises that by pulling the trend line up and down different axes, gaps can open up in provision.

The humanities have typically chosen to present their case for funding according to arguments of beauty and value, including (recently) economic value. Science has argued for funding on the basis of utility: and so it is entirely

51

reasonable that funders should particularly ask scientists to account for their success in those terms, and demonstrate the impact of their research. That there is an inherently long delay between funding a research project and observing the impact of the funding is generally understood — but a funder will naturally want to know that the research proposed is meaningful. As Gordon Graham, Professor of Philosophy and the Arts at Princeton Theological Seminary, writes, knowledge is not always valuable. "There is a fact of the matter as to how many people listed in a telephone directory between, say, pages 171 and 294 have surnames beginning with the same letter as the street in which they live, and quite some time could be spent ascertaining this fact. But the knowledge we would come to possess ... would be quite worthless". (Graham, 2008, p. 88). A researcher proposing such a project for funding would have to do better than to argue "it may prove useful in some way, eventually". In this extreme example, a funder would have no difficulty concluding that any value in the research would be too small and too distant; in other cases (most, indeed) careful judgment is needed to weigh the scale, likelihood and imminence of a potential benefit.

Funders of research often have multiple options on where to place their investments: research institutes, R&D divisions of companies, or universities. Universities are a unique sort of organization and can make a strong case, based on that uniqueness, to attract research investment.

WHAT CHARACTERIZES GLOBAL UNIVERSITIES?

Leading, research-led universities are characterized by three commitments:

Excellence in both education and research. The best research-led universities are also committed to teaching, in a variety of modes from intensive supervisions to large-scale lectures, often using innovative technology, at both undergraduate and graduate level. We place heavy bets that enough of our faculty members (hired principally for their research excellence) will also have a taste and aptitude for teaching — bets which are hedged by the great variety of modes of teaching we employ, and bets which at institutional level pay off: it is unusual to find an excellent research-led university whose teaching is assessed poorly. The essence of a university in the 20th and 21st centuries has been the unity of teaching and research. Although universities have local, national and international responsibilities to admit talented students and to teach them to the highest degree of excellence, it is by our research performance that we stand or fall, and that our global reputations are made.

Disciplinary breadth. Universities are characterized by a broad span of disciplines, from the arts to the physical and often the medical sciences. The best universities actively find ways to encourage the productive cross-fertilization of ideas between disciplines, helping the creative process of determining research directions, and also providing new applications, by employing the innovations of one discipline in another. Cambridge is fortunate to have inherited from medieval times a College system which achieves this mix superbly. Other institutions have consciously evolved other strategies to obtain a similar result.

Relevance to society. Both our teaching and research efforts are relevant to the societies which we serve. If ever there was an age which contrasted ivory tower universities with "the real world", that age is over. Serving society, disinterestedly, is at the core of what we do. Many universities capture that purpose in their formal mission statements — Cambridge's mission statement for example is "to contribute to society through the pursuit of education, learning, and research at the highest international levels of excellence". Though national and local missions remain important, in the 21st century, society is construed globally.

Universities are the only providers of research in which all these benefits are unified in one institution.

LEAGUE TABLES

Measures of education, research and contribution to society are used (often indirectly) in league tables — which, although artificial and tendentious, are of course enormously influential. Their simplicity is seductive (University A immediately appears "better than" University B because A scored 82.3, whereas B only scored 82.1), and their proper interpretation requires, but doesn't often receive, some sophisticated analysis.

Positions in institutional league tables are almost absurdly sensitive: my university, currently at the top of U.K. league tables, could easily drop several places simply by sneezing — or, as frequently happens, by small adjustments in the weightings given to various factors by the creators of the league tables. Nothing substantive about the quality of our education or research would have changed, but external perception certainly would change.

What are funders to do with the information that they think league tables are giving them? Industrial funders of research often identify partner universities by their strengths specific to the industry in question, and government agencies funding research typically make funding decisions on the merits of the particular grant application before them. In each case, the institution's overall position in league tables is less relevant than excellence in more specific areas. This allows for the emergence of "pockets of excellence": high-performing research teams and centres within an otherwise average institution. Such "pockets" have three possible fates — most die away when the key researchers move or retire, but more productively a "pocket of excellence" might move wholesale to another institution — or the home institution might succeed, during a brief window of opportunity, in creating new critical mass by combining and supporting them, and thus contribute to the whole institution's movement up the quality scale. A funding system based on institutional league tables would squander that opportunity.

In the worst cases, governments can use league tables to direct short-term research funding to favoured institutions, particularly in countries where funding decisions are not robustly separated from the priorities of the government of the day — making it almost impossible for research groups in lower-ranked institutions ever to progress. Although governments have a legitimate interest in asking the research community to solve particular problems of practical public policy (for example in understanding patterns of criminal offending), the decision of which research groups receive that commission is best made by the community of researchers themselves. At that level of granularity, governments cannot, and should not, pick winners.

HOW DO FUNDERS CHANNEL RESOURCES TO RESEARCH?

Since we have ruled out governmental whim as an effective means of putting funds in the hands of individual research groups, how is that decision best made?

At its best, the relationship between funder and researcher is a continuing dialogue, tailored to individual talents, interests and objectives. Government research funders have an obligation to part with their money; philanthropic and industrial funders often do not, and the difference can shape relationships. In practice, most large funders run competitions of one sort or another, and funding models are designed often in *pointilliste* detail in the hope of obtaining an increasingly closely-defined outcome.

Impact versus Excellence

In the U.K. at least, a veneer of "impact" now colours pretty much every sort of research (e.g. from the Research Councils U.K. website, "Excellent research with impact is central to Research Council activities" [RCUK, 2013]). In considering the impact of research, the U.K.'s Research Excellence Framework also requires 2* minimum quality ("very good") in the underpinning research. The equivalent exercise in Australia makes no such requirement, the underlying logic being that quality of research need not be a pre-requisite for impact. Do research contributions that are effective in meeting practical challenges also need to be academically excellent?

Peer review

Research proposals are usually vetted by others in the field who are not compromised by being in direct competition for the same funds. This process produces a self-evaluating community of scholars and helps ensure excellence and independence. As an evaluation tool, peer review is used in over 90% of formal funding allocations — but here particularly the evidence base for effectiveness and efficiency is lacking. RAND Europe, a widely-respected research consultancy, evaluated 13 frequent criticisms made of peer review, and found sufficient evidence in studies (i.e. "research about research") to conclude that three of those criticisms were valid; one was not valid; and the remaining nine were "unclear" — in other words, that there was insufficient data. (Guthrie *et al.*, 2013)

- The three "valid" **criticisms** — those for which there was sufficient evidence — are interesting.
- **High cost.** Although research assessment is inherently bureaucratic, peer review is particularly so. The cost is principally measured in the time required, and is exacerbated by the opportunity cost: universities want their best researchers to be researching, not reviewing. The Wellcome Trust — a global U.K.-based charitable foundation which funds biomedical research in several ways including responsive-mode grants — found that fewer than 50% of those approached contribute a review (and the Trust has since introduced a peer-review college, which enjoys a higher review rate. Members join the college on the understanding that they will not be approached for more than six reviews in a year). Anecdotally, the more successful and renowned the reviewer, the less likely they are to contribute a review — though again, data is lacking.
- **Unreliability**, evidenced by wide variety of ratings given by different reviewers. There is a question as to how effective peer review is at discriminating between several research projects which are all at an international level of excellence: U.K. Research Councils routinely grade a much higher proportion of research as A* (meaning internationally excellent), than they are able to fund — so need tools to discriminate — but it is arguable that though peer review is good at defining whether a piece of research is internationally excellent, it can't readily distinguish at a more granular level than that.
- **Lack of transparency**, in the common case of reviews being provided anonymously.

The principal conclusion of the RAND review however was that the great majority of the criticisms — whether they proved to be valid or not — were anecdotal, and had little firm evidence behind them. There are few ethnographic studies, and no studies of how gender balance on a panel might affect the outcome; conversely, there is evidence that the time of day when applications are considered does have an effect. The general conclusion was that peer

review, though still the best mechanism for assessing academic merit, is itself
a rather unscientific process: it is carried out by fallible human beings.

Typology

It is possible to sketch a rough typology of funding models and reasons for their
variety, and the paragraphs below attempt this.

Investigator-led, responsive-mode grants

In this mode, an individual investigator (or, in a few cases, several such investigators acting as a consortium, perhaps across more than one institution) sub-
mits a project funding proposal in response to an open competition. The idea
for the topic and scope of the proposed research comes from the mind of the
researcher, and is most likely of all the possible modes to warrant the description of "blue-skies" research: inherently risky experiments which may or may
not work. (Society at large may or may not be supportive of this risk, where it
derives from taxpayer investments.) The proposal is peer-reviewed, and
awards made on the basis of the review. This is a well-understood method,
whose benefits include providing a gathered field of competing bids.

Funders are encountering problems with this model which they find difficult to address, and other models, considered below, are gaining ground. In the
U.K., the three-year project grant, for which a tenured researcher makes a case
through a grant application, was once the norm, but is now much more
restricted. Reasons for its decline include:

- Demand far exceeds supply. The U.K.'s six Research Councils are
  charged with the allocation of public funds to research across the arts,
  humanities, sciences and social sciences. The median success rate
  they reported in 2010-11 for responsive-mode standard research
  grants was 22.2%. The highest success rate was 33% (at the Engineering and Physical Sciences Research Council); the lowest 15% (at the
  Medical Research Council).
- Bias against younger researchers. The average time in years between
  appointment as a Principal Investigator and the award of a first
  research grant is increasing. Early-career researchers do not have as
  high as success rate as established investigators. Further, the National
  Institutes of Health in the U.S. reported that most investigators were
  now in their 40s before they succeeded in obtaining their first award
  (37 in 1980, compared to 42 in 2008). (National Institutes of Health,
  2008, p. 53).
- Administrative costs to the funding body. It is much more cost-effective for funding bodies to administer one £30m grant than 30 £1m
  grants.

Grand Challenge model

In response to weaknesses in the responsive mode, and in order to marshal the resources of the research community, several large funders now favour what is called the "Grand Challenge" model. This is a spectrum: the challenge can be more or less closely defined. The U.S. Defense Advanced Research Projects Agency, DARPA, uses the (bureaucracy-light) "prize" model; its "Grand Challenges" are open competitions, with teams constructing driverless vehicles (and more recently humanoid robots) which compete against each other. This approach has a distinguished history: in the 18th century the British Parliament established a generous financial prize, administered by the Board of Longitude, to stimulate innovation to solve a specific problem: the measurement of longitude at sea, vital for the increased maritime trade of the period (Cambridge Digital Library, 2013). In this format, there may be prizes for the "top" few places, but it is entirely possible for a competitor to incur significant expense with no reward.

The Bill and Melinda Gates Foundation led the way in popularizing a different sort of "grand challenge" model which identifies an ambitious target — the eradication of malaria, for example — and funds large teams to contribute to meeting that challenge. Multi-disciplinarity is well catered for in this model — as is multi-institutional research, since the concept is that the very best researchers from around the world bring their minds to bear on a single problem, but from different angles. This version seeks to combine the virtues of top-down and bottom-up methods.

Depending on the point along the spectrum of broad to narrow, downsides to this model include:

- **Risk of homogeneity.** Universities and institutes all want a slice of these very large pies, and so configure themselves to meet the best-known challenges: meaning that they all end up focusing on the same problems.
- **Risk to the pipeline.** This model tends to produce thematic "centres" in universities (Energy Centres, Institutes for Food Security, etc.) which attract talented researchers (and, particularly, researchers who talk a good talk) — potentially depriving the discipline-based faculties and departments of funds and people to develop and retain core skills upon which successful research relies. The depth of understanding created in the latter sorts of department is critical to the pipeline that will enable the thematic centres to solve the grand challenges.
- **False impression of the tractability of the problem.** Awarders can be ill-informed about the "researchability" of a topic. Some challenges are not particularly sensitive to the number of dollars thrown at them, and can be susceptible to fashions. An example is the U.K.'s fixation

with superconductivity in the late 1990s. The central assumption was that superconductive materials would allow highly efficient overhead cables in the electricity grid, at potentially transformative cost savings. "Proof of concept" existed, and funding was narrowly directed at research teams who were challenged to create the ideal material. Expensive centres sprang up in U.K. universities, and it was considered only a matter of time before the key breakthrough was made; it never was, and the funding eventually ceased.

If the challenge is sufficiently broad — as in the Gates Foundation's mission to eradicate malaria — then to the individual investigator, bidding for funds, it will be almost indistinguishable from "blue-skies" research. Crucially, the key idea for which funds are sought is the researcher's. To a researcher, "explain how your idea contributes to this public good" is much more attractive than "solve this specific [and potentially insoluble] problem".

Awards to support individuals, rather than projects

Especially in the sciences, investigators building a serious program of research will have several research projects in their lab. Since many more grant proposals are made than are funded, investigators are constantly writing (often fruitless) grant applications. To break out of this pattern, the research community has petitioned funding bodies to make large, bold investments in stellar individuals, so that this generation of Einsteins does not spend their time and energy on writing grant proposals. (As noted above, the peer review process is not good at supporting true paradigm-changing research, so it is entirely possible that today's Einsteins will have their grants rejected.)

It is also recognized that in responsive-mode grants, investigators tend not to perform the experiments which they originally set out (and applied for funds) to perform. The funders know that, even if their funding scheme intends to support ideas, what they are actually doing is investing in people, whom they can trust even if they divert from their original and intended path.

The Howard Hughes Medical Institute in the U.S. has had great success with the "people not ideas" approach. The 330 current HHMI Investigators include 164 members of the National Academy of Sciences and 15 Nobel Laureates (Howard Hughes Medical Institute, 2013).

Despite obvious successes, this approach like the others has its downsides:

- **Pressures other than excellence.** Even if the lion's share of award-worthy individuals are in one department or one institution or one country, the unhelpful signals sent by allocating resources accordingly are often too unpalatable for the funding body, which may impose — probably without articulating it — a quota.

- **The gap in the middle.** Several significant funding schemes target young researchers (including for example the E.U.'s Marie Curie Fellowships). Several others reward senior, established professors. Fellowships for those in mid-career are rare in comparison, especially in the sciences: many post-doctoral scientists find themselves too senior (and expensive) to be employed on another contract, but too junior to be appointed to an established position.

- **The vicious spiral.** Investing in individuals rather than responsive-mode grants takes out of circulation a large sum that would have gone into thematic research — introducing the possibility of a vicious spiral whereby researchers can't show the track record of competitive project funding necessary to qualify for fellowship awards, precisely because the funding bodies are focusing resources on such awards and not on project funding. Data to support this theoretical possibility is not available, but Wellcome Trust evidence does show that while the total amount spent by the Trust is the same, the number of grants awarded is decreasing, while the size and length of grants are increasing. Competition, therefore, is higher.

- **Two-tier research.** The approach also picks "winners" at an early age, risks creating a demoralizing two-tier system — those with individual funding and those without — and potentially leaves very able researchers without the means to set up their research group.

European structures

The development of the European Research Area (ERA) and the increasing importance of European funding to research-intensive universities have significantly challenged our thinking. The overall budget for Horizon 2020, the E.U.'s eighth framework program for science and innovation, is 70.2 billion euro (US$92 billion), built on three pillars:

- Excellent science, delivered primarily through the European Research Council
- Industrial leadership
- Societal challenges

There are many positives in this approach, but it is the case that many of the themes have been decided "top-down", with limited input from the community of European research-led universities. I believe that there are echoes of this trend in other parts of the world.

GENERAL TRENDS

The trends identified in the above typology are away from shorter grants towards longer; away from individual applicants towards collaborative work; away from single-discipline focus towards multi-disciplinary breadth; and away from blue-skies, investigator-led speculative approaches towards centrally-defined themes to which investigators are expected to respond. The effect of any one of these trends would be small — but the net effect of the combination may be to damage the generation of genuinely new knowledge.

Tackling global grand challenges is laudable and is indeed among our core duties, but doing so relies on what Donald Stokes, sometime Dean of the Woodrow Wilson School at Princeton, has called "basic research with considerations of use": the sort of work Pasteur did, which Stokes contrasts both with the pure curiosity of Niels Bohr, and — critically — with the applied focus of Thomas Edison. The combined trends in research funding appear greatly to favour our Edisons at the expense of our Pasteurs. As with all else, moderation is key: it is valuable for some of our researchers to be looking at this year's grand challenge, as long as they are not all doing so (Stokes, 1997).

This package of trends brings with it a shortening of time horizons. Every proposal now needs to demonstrate a measurable short-term impact. "Strategic themes" are identified, sometimes under political (fiscal) influence, as those responding to a perceived *current* challenge. The risk to the pipeline of research is obvious; and the risk to institutional and individual autonomy is obvious too. There is an associated risk to universities: it is much easier for politicians to control the inputs and outputs of short-term research if it is performed in government-funded research institutes.

SOME RECOMMENDATIONS,
SOME CONCLUSIONS AND SOME QUESTIONS

The assertion at the beginning of this paper — that the large sums spent on research are usually well spent — does not rely on a mass of trustworthy and verifiable data, but on anecdote and experience. Nevertheless, it is an assertion which the research community overwhelmingly believes to be true. The inefficiencies in the system, particularly around peer review, result chiefly from the need to design out the worst flaws of caprice and bias. The need to track trends, and to make corrections where gaps in provision emerge, is nonetheless clear.

It is imperative that universities retain their depth and continue to supply fundamental research of the first quality. As a system, research funding bodies must always keep funds available for individuals (not just large collaborations) and for basic research (not just applied). It is difficult though to know how much is enough. Responsive-mode grant-giving (or at least, enough of it) should be genuinely un-earmarked, and open to speculative bright ideas. Responsive-mode programs renounce a good measure of their usefulness if they are hijacked by fashion, and by the temptation to pick winners.

The diversity of funding models is valuable, and the trends identified in section 4 above eventually risk damaging diversity, by tending towards homogeneity. Agencies should maintain separation of roles. National public-funded bodies (e.g. in the U.S., the National Science Foundation, the National Endowment for the Humanities; in the U.K., the six Research Councils) lend themselves to responsive-mode, investigator-led basic research: supporting *ideas*. In Europe, the European Research Council can play the complementary role of supporting excellent *individuals*.

The systems-oriented changes outlined above will have a tremendous impact on research-intensive universities. It leaves them with challenges, which include:

- Ensuring that a university structure which is still largely based in discipline-based units can deliver multi-disciplinary solutions
- Combining grand-challenge approaches with investigator-led research, preserving the distinct benefits of both
- Avoiding the institutional instability that can result from increasing support for star individuals, coupled with increased mobility of researchers and increasing requirements for costly infrastructure
- Promoting strategic research partnerships, with academia and with the private sector, domestically and across national borders, in the changing research environment illustrated above.

These new shifts and tensions in research funding carry enormous implications, with risks and opportunities in equal measure, both for funders and performers of research — but also for the wider world. We have a responsibility to get it right.

* The author gratefully acknowledges the assistance of Matthew Moss of the University of Cambridge in helping to write this contribution; and of Dr Steven Wooding and colleagues, at RAND Europe, and Dr Liz Allen of the Wellcome Trust.

REFERENCES

Cambridge Digital Library (2013). Board of Longitude. http://cudl.lib.cam.ac.uk/collections/longitude.
Graham, Gordon (2008). *Universities: The Recovery of an Idea*, (Societas). 2nd Edition. Imprint Academic.
Guthrie, S., Guerin, B., Wu, H., Ismail. S. & Wooding, S. (2013). "Alternatives to Peer Review in Research Project Funding: 2013 Update." Santa Monica, CA: RAND Corporation, 2013. http://www.rand.org/pubs/research_reports/RR139.

Howard Hughes Medical Institute (2013). Investigator Program. http://www.hhmi.org/programs/biomedical-research/investigator-program.

National Institutes of Health (NIH) (2008). 2007-2008 Peer Review Self-Study: Final Draft. Washington, D.C. National Institutes of Health (NIH), 29 February. http://enhancing-peer-review.nih.gov/meetings/NIHPeerReviewReportFI-NALDRAFT.pdf

RCUK (2013). "Why do RCUK consider demonstrating and maximising the impact of research to be significant?" http://www.rcuk.ac.uk/kei/impacts/Pages/maximisingimpact.aspx.

Stokes, D. E. (1997). Pasteur's Quadrant: Basic Science and Technological Innovation. Brookings Institution Press.

CHAPTER

The Role of Universities in Regional Development

Arnold van Zyl

INTRODUCTION

In addition to the classic functions of research and teaching, universities worldwide are fulfilling additional functions within their communities. This activity is generally described as the so-called "third mission" of the university and reflects the transfer of knowledge through various forms of community engagement with a wide range of stakeholders.

The perspectives gained from working in the university and industry environment in Europe, the USA and Africa have sensitized me to the different approaches universities take in the global North and global South towards fulfilling their third mission. Amongst others, these approaches differ with respect to the stakeholders involved, as well as the respective impact on the curriculum and the research agenda.

This paper reflects on the differences in approach with respect to the third mission of universities in the global South and global North, and describes the advantages, benefits and risks for the universities and the associated stakeholders.

The terms often used so loosely — the Global South and by implication also the Global North — do not exclusively refer to location. They also relate to the broader context and history in which the particular academic institution is embedded.

In the Global South — characterized by a high birth rate — the demographic structure results in an enormous demand for higher education. Many students are disadvantaged by the structural legacy of the historically inequitable education system and hence face academic as well as financial barriers to higher education. The unfavourable staff-to-student ratio, the uncertain academic career prospects and the general resourcing situation are, in general, not conducive to a vibrant, sustainable research environment. On average, for example, around 40% of South African university academics have a PhD qualification (Dell, 2010, p. 1). Student and staff mobility is in general restricted to incoming mobility. Despite this situation, there is an omnipresent consensus on the value and transformative power of education. University research in the global South is quite heterogeneous, as it needs to respond to the needs of a far broader set of stakeholders who do not have access to a sophisticated, differentiated research infrastructure.

The Global North, on the other hand, is characterized by an inverse demographic structure resulting from declining birth rates. In certain areas of Europe for instance, it is postulated that the student population will decline by 20% within the next 10 years (Sächsisches Staatsministerium für Wissenschaft und Kunst, personal communication, 9 April 2013). The education system of the Global North provides broad access to university education with student and staff mobility (at least theoretically) encouraged by the Bologna system and by targeted funding. In the Global North, university research tends to be focussed on basic, fundamental issues, with applied research being conducted in state research institutions and the industry.

Thus the Global South and the Global North differ fundamentally in their state of development, their demographic structure and the resulting demand for by higher education, the level of preparedness of the students, the mobility of students and staff, the resourcing of the institutions and the respective research foci — basic versus applied.

The Global South, in most cases, has an additional historic legacy of colonialism with consequences that still persist. The disempowerment and social dislocation resulting from colonialism, as well as the inability to respond to rapid, unexpected and unexplained change, are still very relevant in our contemporary world!

THE EVOLVING MISSION OF UNIVERSITIES

In addition to the classic functions of research and teaching, universities worldwide are increasingly fulfilling additional functions within their communities. This enhancing of the classical functions is described as the so-called third mission of the university (Laredo, 2007, p. 1 of 11).

In the broadest generic sense, the third mission encompasses the interrelationship between a university and its non-academic partners. Ideally, it should encompass more than the transfer of knowledge towards economic actors through patents, licences and spin-off companies. The complexity of the stakeholder involvement reflects the richness of the inter-linkage of the university with a society at large.

Universities are called upon to provide the knowledge and the appropriate responses for communities that are successively exposed to rapid, unexpected changes. Our communities are faced with globalization, climate change, economic uncertainty and rapid, disruptive technological advancement. In these circumstances, universities can empower communities to respond to these challenges.

In the light of these rapid societal changes, universities — especially those in the Global South — have an enhanced responsibility to their local communities. Universities need to put the issue of individual human rights and concerns for the environment at the centre of their enquiries. Universities need to provide the necessary facts and arguments for the articulation of a critical, public academic voice through, for example, active participation in policy formulation. In those societies still plagued by inequity, the academics should be those who never cease to question and criticize and speak out against past and present systems of structural exclusion in society.

In order to effectively exercise the third mission, universities need to actively engage and enter into alliances with a number of stakeholders: These stakeholders include — but are not limited to — schools, community organizations, local and national authorities, non-government organizations, industry and commerce, the media and, of course, other institutions of tertiary learning. Such alliances should (1) aim at establishing mechanisms to articulate the knowledge generated at universities into action and societal change and (2) serve as a sounding board for establishing the relevance of the research and teaching activities of the institution.

Most importantly, though, the effective implementation of the third mission requires a fundamental change of the mind-set by members of the university community. It requires a broad academic commitment towards a better future, an attitude that seeks, through knowledge, to realize the horizon of new possibilities. In the words of the German theologian Eberhard Jüngel — "we should aim at imagining and prioritizing the possible over the contemporary reality." (Jüngel, 2000). This can only be realized if the sceptical, logical truth-seeking mind of the researcher enters into an uncomfortable but essential alliance with the (utopian) vision of "a better life — a better society" as articulated by Ernst Bloch in his book *Das Prinzip Hoffnung* (Bloch, 1985). The basis and prerequisite are a firm grounding in excellent, basic scientific disciplines, as well as a creative imagination that seeks practical solutions beyond the classical disciplinary boundaries.

Third mission of universities in the Global North

In the global industrialized North, the third mission of the universities is in general focused mainly on knowledge transfer to industry partners. This is enabled by the embodiment of knowledge graduates and PhD students, through codified knowledge produced by the University in the form of intellectual property such as patents, licences or copyright or through coproduction of knowledge via contract research with industry. These aspects of the third mission most often result in mutual benefit —industry benefits in the form of innovation and universities benefit from additional funding sources.

Further aspects of the third mission focus on entrepreneurship with the university and regional authorities providing the required incubator function for spin-off companies. Expertise from universities is also required in the process of the shaping and/or implementation of policy.

Involvement in social and cultural life is restricted to the urban domain in which the university is located and mostly focuses on involvement with museums, orchestras, sports facilities, libraries and schools. An important aspect of this activity is the dissemination of knowledge with the general public through contribution to the public understanding of science through lectures, laboratory demonstrations or open days.

In many cases universities still operate in isolation from their socioeconomic and political environment. Articulating the third mission in a meaningful way with the classical functions of teaching and research is a continual challenge and source of tension within the university. Here the particular challenge is to balance the involvement with industry (as a well-paying partner) and the community at large.

In a recent article in the *New Yorker*, this risk was illustrated by posing the provocative question: is Stanford still a university? The article explores what it calls the unhealthy synergy between Stanford University and Silicon Valley start-up companies and concludes that: "…it seems like all the myriad identities are being subsumed in process of cooperation. Students can still study Chaucer, and there are still lovely palm trees. But the centre of gravity at the university appears to have shifted. The school now looks like a giant tech incubator with a football team." (Thompson, 2013, p. 1)

The challenge remains to find a meaningful engagement that enriches the community and simultaneously rejuvenates the key functions of teaching and research of the institution.

Third mission of universities in the Global South

In the Global (postcolonial) South, university communities are in general in a position of privilege and are often still associated with historical systems of structural exclusion. Thus their isolation from their socioeconomic and political environment is exacerbated. This situation places an added dimension of pressure on the institutions to meaningfully engage with and change their communities.

One useful framework for structuring this engagement is the Millennium Development Goals of the United Nations.

In September 2000, the General Assembly of the United Nations adopted a document — 55/2 United Nations Millennium Declaration (2000) — that described eight global development goals to be reached by 2015. These goals have become known as the so-called Millennium Development Goals (MDGs) and can be summarized as follows:

- Eradicate extreme poverty and hunger
- Achieve universal primary education
- Promote gender equality and empower women
- Reduce child mortality rates
- Improve maternal health
- Combat HIV/AIDS, malaria, and other diseases
- Ensure environmental sustainability
- Develop a global partnership for development

The MDGs represent a significant, global anti-poverty push. Governments, international organizations and civil society groups around the world have helped to cut in half the world's extreme poverty rate. More girls have been enrolled in school. Fewer children are dying of preventable diseases. The world continues to fight killer diseases, such as malaria, tuberculosis and AIDS.

The visibility of universities or global university alliances actively engaging with issues such as hunger, access to education, improved sanitation, maternal health and gender equality as part of their third mission activity has been disappointing. Nevertheless, some individual universities in the Global South — Notably the University of Cape Town and the University of Stellenbosch in South Africa — have taken up the challenge of addressing the Millennium Development Goals as part of their third mission and as an integrated part of their research and teaching activities. These universities have positioned themselves to harness their expertise to assist in those aspects of the Millennium Development Goals where a contribution could be made.

Examples of third mission university initiatives in the Global South

Ukwanda Rural Clinical School of the University of Stellenbosch

The Ukwanda Rural Clinical School of the University of Stellenbosch (Stellenbosch, 2012) — illustrates how community engagement and stakeholder involvement were structured to achieve the optimal impact of the university activity in the community.

The activity supports the achievement of the following Millennium Development Goals: reducing child mortality rates, improving maternal health and combating infectious and other diseases.

Ukwanda is a Xhosa word that can be translated as "to grow" and "develop" within the community; to make a positive difference. In keeping with its name, the Ukwanda Centre for Rural Health, established in 2001, has, central to its vision, a commitment to train healthcare professionals with applicable knowledge and hands-on experience of the health issues facing rural and underserved communities in South Africa (Stellenbosch, 2012, online). The philosophy of the Centre is based on the following principles:

- "Teach where the patients are" to ensure relevant exposure to the burden of disease and practical experience
- Enable immersion within the community for better service orientation and the specific social, legal and economic contextualization of health problems
- Establish partnerships at a local level with the community via NGOs, the local Municipality and the provincial Department of Health
- Catalyse research in the context of the complex rural social structures
- Support multi-professional learning (physicians, nurses, teachers, lawyers, agriculturalists) to foster interdisciplinary solutions
- Make use of IT solutions and MOOCs to overcome geographic distances
- Promote a community orientated approach/community engagement/ sense of social responsibility for a defined population

Ukwanda pursues an "immersion model" where students are exposed to the realities of working/caring in a resource-limited environment. Students work within the existing health care system and not alongside it, to provide assistance and support to health care personnel, while gaining valuable "real-life" experience at the same time. Currently 970 undergraduate students rotate to rural towns for periods of 2-6 weeks per year. Students are currently from the disciplines of Human Nutrition, Physiotherapy, Occupational therapy, Speech, hearing and language therapy, as well as medicine (MB ChB). An extension of the program to involve students from the disciplines of Education, Law and Agriculture is being planned.

Students are exposed to the full spectrum of health care services provided at these sites including primary health care platforms such as: community health centres, primary care clinics, mobile clinics and home visits, NGO encounters, as well as private sector exposure. The extended plans include a one-year clinical rotation for final-year medical students and trainee specialists. On a postgraduate level, the school will allow for additional registrars (medical specialists) to be trained in the rural environment, as well as provide opportunities for research for Masters and doctoral students. The selection criteria for students will be expanded to include those of rural origin. Selected medical students will complete their final year in one of the five participating district hospitals. This integrated training at district and regional level is a new approach for undergraduate students.

The Centre is a good example of how structured community engagement has had an impact on the curriculum and research agenda of the entire Health Sciences Faculty, and the impact is also noticeable in the activities of other faculties. In this case, the third mission has not only provided community benefits but has also had a positive influence on the development of the key focus areas of the university, namely that of teaching and research.

African Climate & Development Initiative of the University of Cape Town

With the institutional strategic initiative — African Climate and Development Initiative (ACDI) — the University of Cape Town (UCT) is focussing on the MDG of ensuring environmental sustainability.

The African Climate and Development Initiative (ACDI) has been established to facilitate, stimulate and coordinate partnerships and knowledge across disciplines on climate and development issues. With a strong African and Global South perspective, the ACDI's work is focused on research, teaching at post-graduate level, public awareness and close interaction with policy-makers, business and civil society. Its interdisciplinary focus provides a multi-layered perspective on climate change and development, bringing interdisciplinary breadth and specialist depth to problems and solutions through research partnerships, graduate and professional training and community engagement (University of Cape Town, 2013, online).

In addition to cross-university activities, the ACDI supports innovative research in partnership with government, business and civil society. For example, the Climate Change Think Tank is a partnership between ACDI, the African Centre for Cities and the City of Cape Town, where researchers work with the city to develop better understanding of key mitigation and adaptation issues facing the City of Cape Town, and to incorporate research insights into city policy. The Wild Coast Living Laboratory is an alliance between UCT, several other universities, Eastern Cape Parks and a local community that undertakes research and community education to address the issues of climate, development and conservation in community-owned nature reserves.

ACDI convenes a one-year coursework Masters in Climate Change and Development, which provides students with interdisciplinary training in climate change and sustainable development, with a specific focus on the issues of relevance to African development. The Masters course includes core modules in Climate Science, Energy, Development Economics and Adaptation, and optional courses across a spectrum of disciplines, including Business Sustainability, Biodiversity, Climate Prediction and Environmental Law. Many of these modules can also be taken as professional short courses, and a number of summer and winter courses for practitioners are also offered. ACDI supports Masters and PhD research through the ACDI Graduate Network, a forum for students from different departments to interact across disciplinary boundaries to explore innovative approaches to their research.

The Initiative engages with civil society and NGOs to enhance public understanding of climate change and to inspire community engagement in solutions to climate change. For example, the UCT branch of Engineers without Borders and the Environmental and Process Systems Engineering Research Group have worked with the Abilimi urban garden scheme in Khayelitsha, near Cape Town, to install a bio-digester. The digester provides a complete waste cycle, with organic waste used to produce valuable manure and cooking gas, and acts to show the wider community how the technology can provide a sound and easily implementable renewable energy solution.

According to Professor Mark New, Pro-VC for Climate Change and Director of ACDI at the University, "much of what needs to be done in Africa on the climate issue is political and economic…it is important that the research community works to provide the best evidence, appropriate to the African situation, for political and economic decision-makers. There are exciting research and education challenges in climate and development in Africa — and a responsibility to take them on."

CONCLUSION AND SUMMARY

This paper has described the challenges, tensions, risks and opportunities associated with the so-called "third mission" where universities move beyond their classical roles of teaching and research to actively engage with their socioeconomic and political environment.

It has been demonstrated that universities in the Global North preferentially engage with industrial stakeholders, while universities in the Global South extend their engagement beyond industrial stakeholders to address pressing social problems.

The risk has been identified that an asymmetric focus on industrial engagement may lead to a shift of the centre of gravity away from teaching and fundamental research and may result in the degradation of the university to an extended, externalized research facility for industry.

Two examples cited from Africa demonstrate how the university community is using its community engagement activities to involve a significant number of relevant stakeholders in addressing the developmental issues of the continent. Here universities are providing the knowledge and the appropriate responses for communities that are exposed to rapid, unexpected changes such as epidemics and the consequences of climate change. In addition to providing relevant technological and policy solutions, they are also using these activities to develop the curriculum and establish new transdisciplinary fields of research.

In conclusion, it should be noted that the tension between the three missions of the university should be carefully managed and that a key criteria for the success and relevance of the third mission is the way in which it contributes to the development and renewal of the curriculum and the research agenda.

REFERENCES

Bloch, E. (1985). *Das Prinzip Hoffnung*, Suhrkamp, Frankfurt am Main.

Dell, S. (2010). "SOUTH AFRICA: Decline in PhD numbers a major problem," *University World News*, 22 August 2010, p. 1.
http://www.universityworldnews.com/article.php?story=20100820150736361

Jüngel, E. (2000). *Unterwegs zur Sache: Theologische Erörterungen 1*, Mohr-Siebeck-Verlag.

Laredo, P. (2007). "Toward a third mission for Universities," paper presented at the *UNESCO research seminar for the Regional Scientific Committee for Europe and North America*, 5-6 Paris 2007
http://portal.unesco.org/education/es/files/53913/
11858787305Towards_a_third_Mission_universities.pdf/
Towards_a_third_Mission_universities.pdf

Stellenbosch University, Faculty of Medicine and Health Sciences (2012). *Referencing electronic information*.
http://sun025.sun.ac.za/portal/page/portal/Health_Sciences/English/Centres%20and%20Institutions/Ukwanda_Centre

Thompson, N. (2013). "The end of Stanford?" *New Yorker*, 8 April 2013, p. 1
http://www.newyorker.com/online/blogs/elements/2013/04/silicon-valley-start-ups-and-the-end-of-stanford.html

U.N. Millennium Declaration (2000). 55/2 United Nations Millennium Declaration. 8th plenary meeting, September 2000.
http://www.un.org/millennium/declaration/ares552e.htm"

University of Cape Town (2013). *Referencing electronic information*.
https://www.uct.ac.za/about/initiatives/acdi/

CHAPTER

The Impact of Technology on Discovery and Learning in Research Universities

James J. Duderstadt

oday, our world has entered a period of rapid and profound economic, social and political transformation driven by knowledge and innovation. Educated people, the knowledge they produce and the innovation and entrepreneurial skills they possess have become the keys to economic prosperity, public health, national security and social well-being. It has become apparent that economic strength, prosperity and social welfare in a global knowledge economy will demand a highly educated citizenry. It will also require institutions with the ability to discover new knowledge, to apply these discoveries and transfer them to the marketplace through entrepreneurial activities.

Yet, the fundamental intellectual activities of discovery and learning that enable these goals are being transformed by the rapid evolution of information and communications technology. Although many technologies have transformed the course of human history, the pace and impact of digital information technology are unprecedented. In little more than half a century, we have moved from mammoth computer temples with the compute power of a digital wristwatch to an ecosystem of billions of microelectronic devices, linked together at nearly the speed of light, executing critical complex programs with astronomical quantities of data. Rapidly evolving digital technology, so-called *cyberinfrastructure*, consisting of hardware, software, people and policies, has played a particularly important role, in expanding our capacity to generate, distribute and apply knowledge (Atkins, 2003). It has become an indispensable platform for discovery, innovation and learning. This technology is continuing to evolve very rapidly, linking people, knowledge and tools in new and profound ways, and driving rapid, unpredictable and frequently disruptive change in existing social institutions. But since cyberinfrastructure can be used to enhance learning, creativity and innovation, intellectual span and collaboration, it presents extraordinary opportunities, as well as challenges, to an increasingly knowledge-driven society.

Clearly, today cyberinfrastructure continues not only to reshape, but actually create new paradigms for science and engineering research, training and application in science and engineering, and increasingly also in the humanities and arts. The availability of powerful new tools such as computer simulation, massive data repositories, massively ubiquitous sensor arrays and high-bandwidth communication are allowing scientists and engineers to shift their intellectual activities from the routine analysis of data to the creativity and imagination to enable them to ask entirely new questions. New paradigms are evolving for the sharing of scientific knowledge, such as the open knowledge movement and powerful search engines. Globalization is a particularly important consequence of the new forms of scientific collaboration enabled by cyberinfrastructure. Cyberinfrastructure is allowing scientific collaboration and investigation to become increasingly decoupled from traditional organizations (e.g., research universities and corporate R&D laboratories) as new communities for scholarly collaboration evolve.

New paradigms are rapidly emerging as well for learning and education, as well as innovation and professional practice such as open knowledge resources (e.g., Wikipedia, MIT's OpenCourseWare initiative and Google Books), online education supported by social networking (e.g., Massively Open Online Courses or MOOCs), open learning initiatives (e.g., Carnegie Mellon's cognitive tutor technology) and immersive learning environments (including massively multiplayer gaming). The challenge for discovery and learning is to use cyberinfrastructure as a platform for enhancing knowledge communities and for expanding their scope and participation unconstrained by time and distance by stressing the interconnection between learning about, learning to do and learning to be, eventually becoming a member of a community of practice (Brown, 2000). To quote Arden Bement, former NSF Director, "We are entering a second revolution in information technology, one that may well usher in a new technological age that will dwarf, in sheer transformational scope and power, anything we have yet experienced in the current information age" (Bement, 2007).

THE FUTURE OF DIGITAL TECHNOLOGY

A Personal Observation

In the early 1970s, while I was working in the area of nuclear systems at Lawrence Livermore National Laboratory, I was allocated daily computing time on their CDC 7600, then the fastest computer in the world at 10 MFLOPS (one million floating-point-operations-per-second, the standard unit for measuring computing speed). Today, my colleagues are running their simulations of nuclear reactors on the TITAN computer at Oak Ridge National Laboratory at a speed of 16 PFLOPS. Hence, over the past four decades, computation speeds have increased over a billion-fold. In fact, most characteristics of this technology are continuing to evolve exponentially at rates of 100 to 1,000 fold per decade. We are already developing our nuclear system computer software for the anticipated delivery of an exaFLOP super-computer in the next five years, so the trend continues.

This is one of the big reasons for the continued surprises we get from the emergence of new applications — the Internet, social networking, big data, machine learning — appearing in unexpected ways at an ever faster pace. We have learned time and time again that it makes little sense to simply extrapolate the present into the future to predict or even understand the next "tech turn". These are not only highly disruptive technologies, but they are highly unpredictable. Ten years ago nobody would have imagined Google, Facebook, Twitter, etc., and today nobody really can predict what will be a dominant technology even five years ahead, much less ten!

Fortunately, universities have been able to adapt to such rapid technological change in the past because they have functioned as *loosely coupled adaptive systems* with academic units given not only the freedom, but also the encouragement, to experiment to try new things. It is at the level of academic units rather than the enterprise level where innovation and leadership will occur. Why? Because academic programs are driven by learning and discovery, by experimentation, by tolerance for failure, and by extraordinarily talented faculty, students and, particularly, staff. Most academic institutions have intentionally avoided the dangers of centralizing these activities and instead focused on maintaining a highly adaptive academic culture.

Moore's Law

Although most characteristics of cyberinfrastructure, e.g., processing power, data storage and network bandwidth, continue to increase at an exponential pace described by Moore's law, various components of the technology do eventually encounter limits and saturation that require major technology shifts. For example, VLSI processors and memories are approaching the limits of miniaturization and hence processing speed. In the near term, devices are exploiting multiprocessor architectures, with dozens of processors on a single chip (and millions of processors in supercomputers). But other constraints, such as power requirements, will soon require new technologies such as DNA storage and quantum computing.

Similar evolution continues to occur in how information is processed. For example, companies such as Google and Amazon are built around data, analysing and extracting information and knowledge from large data centres (or clouds). Here, scale truly matters, with increases of factors of ten in storage and processing speed regularly required and achieved to meet market requirements. Similarly, data concepts have shifted to larger, more abstract structures such as entities, concepts and knowledge, that require enormous increases in data storage and processing speed. They also require more sophisticated software for data processing to enable rapid searches for abstract concepts through petabytes of data.

The Human Interface

One of the most rapidly changing characteristics of this technology involves the human interface. Although we look back at the transition from text to image to video to 3D immersive displays, there are other characters such as mobility, size and context that also change rapidly. For example, the development of software agents that rely on natural interactions such as speech and context awareness are already transforming both mobile phones (e.g., Apple's Siri) and interfaces with the physical world (e.g., Google's efforts to insert computing into eyeglasses to assist in context analysis). The use of intelligent agents or assistants (IBM's Watson) can make us look better than we really are by anticipating and completing tasks that are not fully defined, although this raises an interesting set of policy and legal issues since even the most intelligent agents can make mistakes because of faulty information or incorrect assumptions based on inaccurate data. The question of what intelligent agents do on your behalf and liability issues are unresolved questions. Similarly, there is great interest in the evolution of the Internet into a network of objects such as ubiquitous sensors, the rise of contextual data and the ability to do predictive models of individual behaviour. The need for accessibility raises the issue of digital inclusion in the broadest sense. How does one design technology to assist physically challenged individuals, aging populations, those with limited literacy skills and, indeed, provide a global population of 10 billion with robust digital access.

Although the rapid evolution of information and communications technology is driving much of the change in the activities of the university, it is important to consider this from a much broader perspective, including legal issues (patents, copyright), policy (local, national, international) and social issues (access and accessibility, equity, interoperability, sustainability and resilience). For example, students and faculty need appropriate technology scaffolding for their academic pursuits (e.g., cyber-infrastructure). But they also need a broader systems understanding of cyber-infrastructure because of the major disruptive changes this technology will drive in learning and discovery.

The Next Big Paradigm Shift

So what are the early warning systems for the next major paradigm shifts? What does one look for? During the 1980s, a modest computer network, NSF-net, was developed to connect scientists to supercomputer centres, only to find that people did not want to use supercomputers but rather to communicate with one another. This led within a few years to the Internet, another technology that changed the world. Google spun out of the Page Rank search algorithm created by a Stanford research project to develop digital libraries (Levy, 2011). Facebook was started even more modestly by a group of students seeking to digitize and distribute the picture book Harvard created for entering students (Kirkpatrick, 2011).

So where do you look for these surprises? Do you look at the research labs on college campuses? Do you look at Harvard dormitories for what students are doing before they drop out? Do you try to spot the next Bill Gates, Mark Zuckerberg or Larry Page? Do you have any tracking systems? Industry participants usually respond that they first sense such possibilities when activities characterized by hyper exponential growth break free of the campuses, e.g., the Internet, Google and Facebook. Similarly, they look for interesting students and faculty members that they can break free of the campus culture. Their success model is based on what escapes rather than what stays inside academic institutions.

From industry's viewpoint, the elephant in the room is knowledge creation, not knowledge dissemination, which is the role of the research university. The challenge is to become more focused on knowledge creation, integration, synthesis and dissemination, or perhaps more abstractly, DIKW: *data, information, knowledge and wisdom*. One needs to use cyberinfrastructure together with tools that enhance creativity and then broaden access through libraries, search tools and push models in education.

As a framework, one can begin by observing that the fundamental activities of the university are organized into knowledge communities – those that engage with knowledge and discovery. (Brown, 2000) The extent to which the university facilitates knowledge communities should be the basis for its merit. Today, people can work together in four quadrants: same/different —

time/place. One can build a rich connection between people, information and tools. The work of these knowledge communities supported by a cyberinfrastructure platform can now be done in new workflows that go through space-time quadrants in different ways. Cyberinfrastructure now allows tools, data, experiments and other assets to support online knowledge communities, making these functionally complete in any of the four quadrants, that is, with all the resources necessary to handle knowledge flow. Using the scaffolding of cyberinfrastructure, one can dramatically reduce constraints of distance and time. This creates a major disruption in how knowledge work is done, expanding significantly the degrees of freedom.

POSSIBILITIES, GAME-CHANGERS AND PARADIGM SHIFTS

New Paradigms for Learning and Teaching

So, what are the opportunities presented by cyberinfrastructure for learning and teaching, for example, Massively Open Online Courses (MOOCs), cognitive tutor systems or Carnegie Mellon's Open Learning Initiative. Some believe that today higher education is on the precipice of an era of extraordinary change as such disruptive technologies challenge the traditional paradigms of learning and discovery (Friedman, 2013). They suggest that new technologies could swamp the university with a tsunami of cheap, online courses from name-brand institutions, or adaptive learning using massive data gathered from thousands of students and subjected to sophisticated analytics, or even cognitive tutors that rapidly customize the learning environment for each student so they earn most deeply and efficiently, entirely without the involvement of faculty.

But are these really something new or rather simply old wine in new bottles? After all, millions of students have been using online learning for decades (estimated today to involve over one-third of current students in the United States). There are many highly developed models for online learning, including the UK Open University, the Western Governor's University in the United States and the Apollo group's global system of for-profit universities. Adaptive learning has been used in Carnegie Mellon's cognitive tutor software for years in secondary schools and more recently in the Open Learning Initiative. Many of the buzzwords used to market these new technologies also have long established antecedents: Experiential learning? Think "laboratories" and "internships" and "practicums"… and even "summer jobs"! Flipped classrooms? Think "tutorials" and "seminars" and "studios". Massive markets of learners? Many American universities were providing free credit instruction to hundreds of thousands of learners as early as the 1950s through live television broadcasts!

Of course, today's MOOCs do have some new elements, aside from the massive markets they are able to build through the Internet and their current practice of free access (Waldrop, 2013). They augment online broadcasts of canned lectures and automated grading of homework with social networks to provide teaching support through message boards and discussion groups of the students themselves. Their semi-synchronous structure, in which courses and exams are given at a specific time while progress is kept on track, allow them to augment online broadcast of canned lectures and automated grading of homework with social networks to provide free teaching assistants through message boards and discussion groups. Here one might think of MOOCs as a clever combination of UK's Open University (online education) and Wikipedia (crowd sourcing of knowledge)! Furthermore, MOOCs, like the far more sophisticated Open Learning Initiative, are able to use data mining (analytics) to gather a large amount of information about student learning experiences. When combined with cognitive science, this provides a strong source of feedback for course improvement.

Certainly the MOOC paradigm is characterized by a powerful delivery mechanism. But it is just one model. It is much more important to focus on improving learning by integrating emerging technology with research about how people learn. There are also other models to explore and much richer collaboration opportunities to share. Through knowledge creation, we need to embrace new paradigms as a community. Automated assessment and evaluation could turn the whole education business upside down because we will have access to massive data sets that potentially will give us some insight in not how we deliver content but rather how people learn.

Of course, many of these efforts are driven by the exploding global needs for higher education that creates gigantic markets. For example, to meet the needs of its population, India would have to build thousands of new universities just to handle its current number of secondary school graduates. But here is where new paradigms such as MOOCs come in, since these can handle courses for 100,000 or more students at a time by using a combination of online and social networking technology. Of course, there remains the need for rigorous assessment of learning effectiveness, but some of the efforts to apply data mining and analytics to the massive data collected by these online efforts may be a key to evaluation.

What about the role of credentials? While there has been recent exploration of providing college credit for MOOCs on a highly selective basis, it is more likely that an alternative certificate or badge system will be used to certify that learning goals have been achieved. One might even consider micro-credentials with a time value, that is, a student would receive a certificate that would be valid until they take the next test. But students who might like a MOOC may be different than those who respond to tutor or that pedagogy or certain structure on content. Customization for individual need is required to meet huge opportunity space in this knowledge area. The learner is the customer. It is not just about the learning or how to push it out, but rather how will they learn with this technology? How can this be structured to address different learning styles since good classroom teachers have this capacity to adapt teaching methods to the students?

It is likely that MOOCs are a disruptive technology, and that analytics on learning data holds considerable promise. But it is also very important to separate the fundamental character of a college education from the specific resources used to achieve that, e.g., courses and curricula, textbooks and course notes, faculty and laboratory staff, and, of course, the complex learning communities that exist only on university campuses. After all, MOOCs are marketed as <u>courses</u>, not as a college education. We must remember that the current university paradigm of students living on a university campus, completely immersed in an exciting intellectual and social physical environment and sophisticated learning communities, provides a very powerful form of learning and discovery. MOOCs are interesting, but they are far from the vibrant, immersive environment of a college education, at least as we understand it today (Brown & Duguid, 2000).

There is also a big difference between the perspective of the providers of MOOCs and the students who are their consumers. Right now, we are watching the providers figure out what they are going to do, with strong investments from the venture capital community and for-profit education providers suggesting that at least some people believe they might become very rich from these gigantic educational markets. Furthermore, today's MOOCs are aimed primarily at individuals, not communities. There is a huge challenge thinking about what they will mean in the university, and whether the second-tier institutions can use off-the-shelf MOOC courses and do something with them to reduce cost or bring in new kinds of students. But there are many questions. What happens to faculty governance issues? What about copyright issues? Who owns these courses? Are all of the professors going away, replaced by MOOC broadcasts from star teachers and using crowdsourcing to grade and answer questions?

Finally, we should remember that this new paradigm is being launched by several of the most elite and expensive private universities in America (e.g., Stanford, Harvard and MIT) using both the Internet and social media, as well as their powerful brand names to build mammoth markets for their MOOC companies (Udacity, Coursera, EdX) in an effort to eventually create new revenue streams to subsidize the rapidly rising costs of more traditional, highly expensive education on their own campuses. A related concern is that the intense media hype given these new learning paradigms has put enormous pressure on public colleges and universities from governing boards and state governments attempting to reduce the costs of college education, even at the sacrifice of educational equality. It would be tragic if technology-based paradigms such as MOOCs were to drive even greater inequities in higher education.

NEW PARADIGMS FOR RESEARCH AND SCHOLARSHIP

Is the Paradigm for Basic Research Really Changing?

Are the paradigms characterizing research and scholarship paradigms also shifting with emerging technologies? Certainly the language of research is changing to embrace concepts such as clouds, data mining, convergence, etc. If you subscribe to the view that there is a paradigm shift from hypothesis-driven to data-correlation-driven discovery, then the culture of scientific and engineering discovery and innovation is changing as a result of access to data, computational technology and social networks. We are going to need new models for sharing data, software and resources such as computational technology.

But is the way in which research is conducted changing? What about global competition? Is the world of facilities-intensive big science, such as high-energy physics, sustainable when it requires sending faculty and students to the only places capable of conducting the research (e.g., CERN), resulting in a list of authors longer than substance of the papers? Are we moving to a wiki world where crowd sourcing of amateurs becomes important for scientific research? How important is the role of research and scholarship within universities? Do we need to tweak tax laws so that the translational research characterizing earlier paradigms, such as Bell Laboratories, begin to reappear as part of the knowledge ecosystem?

Universal Access to Knowledge and Learning

Ironically, while we generally think of cyberinfrastructure in terms such as terabit/sec networks and petaflop supercomputers, the most profound changes in our institutions may be driven not by the technology itself, but rather by the philosophy of openness and access it enables — indeed, imposes — on its users. Of particular importance are efforts to adopt the philosophy of open source software development to create new opportunities for learning and scholarship for the world through *open educational resources* by putting previously restricted knowledge into the public domain and inviting others to join in both its use and development (Atkins *et al.*, 2007).

MIT led the way with its OpenCourseWare (OCW) initiative, placing the digital assets supporting almost 2,000 courses into the public domain on the Internet for the world to use (Vest, 2004). Today, hundreds of universities have adopted the OCW paradigm to distribute their own learning assets to the world, with over 15,000 courses now available online. New resources, such as

Apple's iTunes U, are providing global access to such open educational resources.

To this array of open educational resources should be added efforts to digitize massive quantities of printed material and make it available for search and eventual access. For example, the Google Book project is currently working with a number of leading libraries (26 at last count in 35 languages) around the world to digitize a substantial portion of their holdings (22 million volumes in 2013, with a goal of 30 million by 2020), making these available for full-text searches using Google's powerful internet search engines. (Google, 2013) A number of universities (84 thus far) have pooled their digital collections to create the Hathi Trust ("Hathi" means "elephant" in Hindi), adding over 400,000 books a month to form the nucleus (currently at 11 million books, with 3 million of these already open for full online access) of what could become a 21st century analog to the ancient Library of Alexandria (HathiTrust, 2013; Kelly, 2006). While many copyright issues still need to be addressed, it is likely that these massive digitization efforts will be able to provide full text access to a significant fraction of the world's written materials to scholars and students throughout the world within a decade.

We should add into this array of ICT-based activities a few more elements: mobile communication, social computing and immersive environments. We all know well the rapid propagation of mobile communications technology, with over 4 billion people today having cell-phone connectivity and 1.2 billion with broadband access. It is likely that within a decade the majority of the world's population will have some level of cell-phone connectivity, with many using advanced 3G and 4G technologies.

Finally, the availability of new learning resources, such as massively open online learning (MOOC) consortia (Udacity, Coursera and EdX), cognitive AI-based tutor software (Carnegie Mellon's Open Learning Initiative) and immersive learning environments similar to those developed in the massively player gaming world (World of Warcraft and Second Life) are providing resources that not only open up learning opportunities for the world, but furthermore suggest new learning paradigms that could radically challenge and change existing higher education paradigms.

What do we know about the effectiveness of these technology-based approaches? Where are the careful measurements of learning necessary to establish the value of such forms of pedagogy? Thus far, promoters have relied mostly on comparisons of performances by both conventional and online students on standard tests. The only serious measurements have been those that Ithaka has conducted on the learning by cognitive tutor software in a highly restricted environment (Bowen *et al.*, 2012).

Of course, it eventually comes back to the questions of "What is the most valuable form of learning that occurs in a university…and how does it occur?"

Through formal curricula? Through engaging teachers? Through creating learning communities? After all, the graduate paradigm of *Universitas Magistrorum et Scholarium* involving the interaction of masters and scholars will be very hard to reproduce online...and least in a canned video format!

As William Bowen, former president of Princeton and the Mellon Foundation and a founder of Ithaka, suggests, it is time to "Walk, Don't Run" toward the use of cyberlearning. We need lots of experimentation, including rigorous measurement of education — before we allow the technology tsunami to sweep over us! (Bowen, 2013)

CHANGE AND THE UNIVERSITY

History provides many examples of the ability of the university to adapt to change. Five centuries ago some suggested that the medieval university would not survive the printing press since people could learn by reading books rather than attending lectures. More recently, a decade ago, MIT's Open-CourseWare initiative to place the digital assets for all of their courses, 2,000 in number, in the public domain stimulated similar fears this would sink the universities and create a $2 trillion for-profit education economy. But, once again, universities floated through this technology turn without major change.

In fact, the university today looks very much like it has for decades — indeed, centuries — in the case of many ancient European universities. It is still organized into academic and professional disciplines; it still bases its educational programs on the traditional undergraduate, graduate and professional discipline curricula; and the university is still governed, managed and led much as it has been for ages. We can always explain this by falling back on that famous quote of Clark Kerr: "About 85 institutions in the Western World established by 1520 still exist in recognizable forms, with similar functions and with unbroken histories, including the Catholic Church, the Parliaments of the Isle of Man, of Iceland and of Great Britain, several Swiss cantons, and...70 universities" (Kerr, 2001).

But, if one looks more closely at the core activities of students and faculty, the changes over the past decade have been profound indeed (Duderstadt, 2003). The scholarly activities of the faculty have become heavily dependent upon digital technology — rather cyberinfrastructure — whether in the sciences, humanities, arts or professions. Although faculties still seek face-to-face discussions with colleagues, these have become the booster shot for far more frequent interactions over the Internet. Most faculty members rarely visit the library anymore, preferring to access digital resources through powerful and efficient search engines. Some have even ceased publishing in favour of the increasingly ubiquitous digital preprint or blog route. Student life and learning are also changing rapidly, as students bring onto campus with them the skills of the net generation for applying this rapidly evolving technology to their own interests, forming social groups through social networking technology (Facebook, Twitter), role playing (gaming), accessing web-based services, and inquiry-based learning, despite the insistence of their professors that they jump through the hoops of the traditional classroom paradigm.

In one sense, it is amazing that the university has been able to adapt to these extraordinary transformations of its most fundamental activities, learning and scholarship, with its organization and structure largely intact. Here one might be inclined to observe that technological change tends to evolve much more rapidly than social change, suggesting that a social institution such as the university that has lasted a millennium is unlikely to change on the timescales of tech turns, although social institutions such as corporations have learned the hard way that failure to keep pace can lead to extinction. Yet, while social institutions may respond more slowly to technological change, when they do so, it is frequently with quite abrupt and unpredictable consequences, e.g., "punctuated evolution".

It could also be that the revolution in higher education is well under way, at least with the early adopters, and simply not sensed or recognized yet by the body of the institutions within which the changes are occurring. Universities are extraordinarily adaptable organizations, tolerating enormous redundancy and diversity. It could be that the information technology revolution is more of a tsunami that universities can float through rather than a rogue wave that will swamp them.

Admittedly, it is also the case that futurists have a habit of overestimating the impact of new technologies in the near term and underestimating them over the longer term. There is a natural tendency to implicitly assume that the present will continue, just at an accelerated pace, and fail to anticipate the disruptive technologies and killer apps that turn predictions topsy-turvy. Yet, we also know that far enough into the future, the exponential character of the evolution of Moore's Law technologies such as info-, bio- and nano-technology makes almost any scenario possible (Kurzweil, 2005).

However, here we should take heart with a note of reassurance provided by Frank Rhodes in his Declaration for the Millennium crafted in the III Glion Colloquium:

"For a thousand years, the university has benefited our civilization as a learning community where both the young and the experienced could acquire not only knowledge and skills, but the values and discipline of the educated mind. It has defended and propagated our cultural and intellectual heritage, while challenging our norms and beliefs. It has produced the leaders of our governments, commerce, and professions. It has both created and applied new knowledge to serve our society. And it has done so while preserving those values and principles so essential to academic learning:

the freedom of inquiry, an openness to new ideas, a commitment to rigorous study, and a love of learning.

"There seems little doubt that these roles will continue to be needed by our civilization. There is little doubt as well that the university, in some form, will be needed to provide them. The university of the twenty-first century may be as different from today's institutions as the research university is from the colonial college. But its form and its continued evolution will be a consequence of transformations necessary to provide its ancient values and contributions to a changing world." (Rhodes, 1999)

Acknowledgements: Much of the material for this paper was provided by a workshop at the University of Michigan sponsored by the National Science Foundation in October of 2012 to assess the impact of rapidly evolving information and communications technology (i.e., cyberinfrastructure) on the activities of discovery, learning and innovation. This workshop convened an unusually diverse group of thought leaders from multiple disciplines and venues to consider the changing nature of learning and discovery in broad terms, spanning learning at all levels and discovery for all forms including research, development, innovation, invention, design, and creativity. The complete discussion sessions of this workshop were captured using multiple HD camera and sound technology and can be found at: http://specular.dmc.dc.umich.edu/Atkins/

REFERENCES

Atkins, Daniel E. (chair) (2003). *Revolutionizing Science and Engineering Through Cyberinfrastructure.* Report of the National Science Foundation Blue-Ribbon Advisory Panel on Cyberinfrastructure. Washington, DC: National Science Foundation.

Atkins, Daniel E., Brown, John Seely & Hammond, Allen L. (2007). *External Review of the Hewlett Foundation's Open Educational Resources (OER) Program: Achievements, Challenges, and Opportunities.* Menlo Park, CA: Hewlett Foundation, February 2007.

Bement, A. L. (2007). *"Cyberinfrastructure: The Second Revolution".* Chronicle of Higher Education, January 2007.

Borgman, Christine L. (chair) (2008). *Fostering Learning in the Networked World: The Cyberlearning Opportunity and Challenge.* Report of the NSF Task Force on Cyberlearning. Washington, D.C.: National Science Foundation.

Bowen, William G., Chingos, Matthew M., Lack, Kelly A. & Nygren, Thomas I. (2012). *Interactive Learning Online at Public Universities: Evidence from Randomized Trials.* Ithaka, 22 May 2012, available on the ITHAKA website: http://www.sr.ithaka.org

Bowen, William G. (2013). "Walk Deliberately, Don't Run, Toward Online Education", *Chronicle of Higher Education,* 25 March 2013; See also Bowen, William G. *Higher Education in the Digital Age.* Princeton, NJ: Princeton University Press.

Brown, John Seely & Duguid, Paul (2000). *The Social Life of Information*. Cambridge, MA: Harvard Business School Press; see also Thomas, Douglas & Brown, John Seely. *A New Culture of Learning*. San Francisco, CA: Thomas and Brown.

Duderstadt, James J. (chair) (2003). *Preparing for the Revolution: Information Technology and the Future of the Research University*. Washington, D.C.: National Academy Press; see also Duderstadt, James J., Atkins, Daniel E. & Van Houweling, Douglas. *Higher Education in the Digital Age: Technology Issues and Strategies for American Colleges and Universities* (2002). Westport, CT: American Council on Education and Praeger Publishers.

Friedman, Thomas L. (2013). "Revolution Hits the University". *New York Times*, 26 January 2013.

Google Books (2013). http://books.google.com/

HathiTrust (2013). http://www.hathitrust.org/

Kirkpatrick, David (2011). *The Facebook Effect: The Inside Story of the Company That Is Connecting the World*. New York: Simon & Schuster.

Levy, Stephen (2011). *In the Plex: How Google Thinks, Works, and Shapes Our Lives*. New York: Simon & Schuster.

Kelly, Kevin (2006). "Scan This Book!" *New York Times Sunday Magazine*, 14 May 2006.

Kerr, Clark (2001). *The Uses of the University*. 5th Edition. Cambridge: Harvard University Press.

Kurzweil, Ray (2005). *The Singularity Is Near: When Humans Transcend Biology*. New York, NY: Viking Penguin.

Rhodes, Frank H.T. (1999). "The Glion Declaration: The University at the Millennium", in *Challenges Facing Higher Education at the Millennium*. Phoenix, AZ: American Council on Education and Oryx Press.

Vest, Charles M. (2004). "Why MIT Decided to Give Away All Its Course Materials via the Internet". *Chronicle of Higher Education*, 30 January 2004.

Waldrop, M. Mitchell (2013). "Campus 2.0". *Nature*, Vol. 495, 14 March 2013.

CHAPTER 8

Can the IT revolution lead to a rebirth of world-class European universities?

Patrick Aebischer and Gérard Escher*

THE DIGITAL REVOLUTION

We have reached a critical moment in time when the digital revolution — brought on by ubiquitous personal, mobile and affordable information devices — is challenging the historical missions of education and research; a challenge for our universities that constitutes a disruptive force and an opportunity for world-class European universities.

This IT revolution has given rise to a new generation of minds and novel technologies, both bound to impose new educational paradigms on our universities. In education, the iconic manifestation of the digital disruption is the MOOCs (Massive Open Online Courses). And, in research, the IT disruption is represented by MOORs (Massive Open Online Research projects), which feed on open access science, collaborative research and the development of simulation-based research. Both MOOCS and MOORS, whose impact and challenges are the subject of this paper, are undoubtedly changing the face of education and research — a change that should be welcomed and nurtured to ensure the future of the European academic tradition.

A long History of Online Education, and then a Tsunami

Computers, information technologies and online/off-site technologies have been biting at the edges of education for over 50 years: Computer-assisted Instruction was introduced in 1960; Computer-Based Learning was all the rage in 1980; Educational telematics appeared in 1988; followed by Online Education (1993); e-learning (1993); open learning (1995); the Virtual University and Learning Management Systems in 1999; and, for Switzerland, a national Virtual Campus in 2000. Yet, all these initiatives were only modestly successful. In 2008, the first recognizable massive open online course was developed in Canada (Massive Open Online Courses, 2013), and then a Tsunami hit in late 2011: one on-line class, "Introduction to artificial intelligence", by Sebastian Thrun at Stanford University, attracted 160,000 students of whom 22,000 completed the course. Of these there were 420 students with perfect scores — and legend has it that none of these students were from Stanford.

One short year later, a number of world-class universities integrated MOOCs in their portfolios, and thus acknowledged the impact of online education on the academic landscape. In this first year, MOOCs had a great start: rigorous backing by academic leaders, seamless technical capacity, strong technical platforms and amazing media coverage. The momentum of this online learning is considerable: in this first year over 3 million students have enrolled in MOOCs at Coursera — one of the leading platforms — with over 60 participating universities.

What happened this time that was different from the attempts over the past 50 years to harness IT for education?

A phase transition: a new generation of learners

We argue that this tidal wave of MOOCs is different because we are experiencing a new generation of minds in a particular context, and not only novel technological advancements; a *phase transition* that has been brought about by the confluence of economic, demographic and technological factors. With the crisis in tuition costs and student debt, there are necessary economies of scale to be made. There is also a crucial need to accommodate the growing demand in higher education: the number of students enrolled in higher education around the globe is forecast to more than double to 262 million students by 2025. Half this growth will be in China and India, which plan to build thousands of universities. Lastly, recent IT trends, including high bandwidth, social networks and cloud computing, are facilitating this transition. Global Internet Device Sales (PCs, smartphones, tablets) have exploded: there were no more than 150 million devices sold in 2000, and the sales are estimated to reach 2.5 billion in 2016. In 2015, the G-20 countries alone will have over 2.5 billion consumer broadband connections. We have definitively entered a mobile, hyper-connected world.

But while it is true that the technology has matured to a critical point — Internet, mobile access, bandwidth and novel IT platforms are taken for granted — we are also in the presence of students with a completely new mindset, the "Facebook and iPhone" generation, made up of digital natives. For this generation, IT technologies have become the central, normalized means with which to interact socially, to gather news and information … and to learn.

MOOCS

Things take longer to happen than you think they will and then they happen faster than you thought they could.

Ruedi Dornbusch (MIT)

Novel Features of MOOCs

We summarize the main new features of MOOCs in the following way:

1. Open access: the content of MOOCs is freely accessible ("free" as in "free beer");
2. Personalization: the content is segmented in short modules, typically consisting of short videos, quizzes and assignments; this segmentation allows for adapting speed to individual learners;
3. (massive) Synchronization: the student is an empowered participant: learning tasks are crowd-sourced, grading is done by peers (and everyone is a peer), discussion forums lead through the course module by module.

Having tens of thousands of students in your class makes teachers reinvent teaching. The enthusiasm, both from teachers and from students, is real. The best knowledge produced in our universities is sent out for free, because it is the right thing to do. And there is a lot of experimenting and variety at this stage. For the moment, providers of MOOCs make their courses available to anyone — there is no admissions process. Similar to an online video game, anyone can begin, but you then have to master levels that can prove very difficult. "For the 10% who get to the end, the learning is real" (Allen, 2013).

Networking between students, a trademark of the MOOC experience, is a crucial feature. It's "rubbing minds via the computer", in the words of Coursera co-founder Daphne Koller. Though important, student engagement in a MOOC forum is not (yet) widespread: the median percentage of students — taking only the best students — who contribute more than one post is 21.7, with a range of 10% to 68% across all Stanford MOOCs (Manning & Sanders, 2013). Grading by peers is another important — and controversial — MOOCs feature. In one careful analysis, student grading appears to be as accurate as grading by teachers or TAs (Lewin, 2012).

Impact on teaching

Enlarging the student base. MOOCs broaden the impact a university has by recruiting from a student population unable or unwilling to spend a full-time studentship on a physical campus. The first impact is clearly on lifelong learning or continuing education, especially continuing education in technical fields — over 40% of the students of the first MOOCs in machine learning course were already employed in the software industry. Likewise, for EPFL's top hit in MOOCs, "Functional Programming Principles in Scala", about 45% of the 10,000 students who took the final exam already had a Master degree (and 5% had a PhD). This first MOOC was a fantastic experience: "More than classes, these are vast networks of knowledge," says Martin Odersky the course instigator (Perrin, 2012). Incidentally, with about 50,000 registered students, and 10,000 final exams, this MOOC also holds a record completion rate of 19.2% (Parr, 2013).

The fever has spread from IT subjects — where MOOCs where born — to social sciences and humanities. Professor Mitchell Duneier (Princeton) says, "I had more feedback on my ideas in [Introduction to Sociology] than during my whole career." And Professor Al Filreis (U Penn) calls his class "Modern and Contemporary American Poetry," with 36,000 students enrolled and 2,000 students completing the course, an "outreach for poetry" (Lewin, 2012).

Improved teaching: A seemingly paradoxical impact of MOOCs. Since professors invest a great amount of energy to prepare these courses, where they are "judged" by the entire planet, the quality of the course material is very high. Do not be mistaken, MOOCs are not replicating in-class instruction. MOOCs — even in the absence of formal credits — are, in fact, less "laid back" than traditional courses, with continuous testing and strong involvement of faculty. MOOCs might even have a positive effect on in-class teaching, since lecturing can be moved out of the classroom. When given the choice, students will indeed opt for the online version of a course and transform the classroom into a site of active-learning; this has been called the "flipped-classroom", where students come to class better prepared and teachers can then engage in active interactions. This, of course, will also entail a major effort by faculty.

Teaching as a research object: MOOCs are also a valuable source of data for pedagogical research. We will learn a lot from the massive data on learning we can collect to answer questions like: What are students confused about? How do they go about solving their problems? We should however acknowledge a lack of hard evidence today to produce the best courses. As a collateral effect, MOOCs will also surely transform the textbook industry, with professors making their "traditional" textbooks freely available to students, like Martin Odersky did in his MOOC on Scala.

In short, teaching becomes suddenly attractive with worldwide exposure for the teachers, course materials are of excellent quality because there are scrutinized by thousands, and students contribute to the teaching material. Finally, traditional, on-campus students seem to like the additional flexibility and adaptability of having an online course.

European Angle

Specific European angle: There are few European universities among the early adopters of MOOCs. On the Coursera Platform there are (as of June 2013) 11 universities (all top tier). As example, the University of Edinburgh has published a first report on its MOOC experience (MOOCs@Edinburgh Group, 2013). A recent survey (Kolds, 2013a) at the first European MOOC Stakeholders Meeting at EPFL indicates that universities in 13 European countries have started MOOCs, on Coursera or edX platforms, or national ones. MOOCs adoption is faster in the U.S. since it is linked to the intense discussion on cost containment. In Europe, student fees still play a minor, albeit increasing role in university budgets; so the pressure to adopt a "mass model of instruction" for economic reasons is weaker. We solicit Europe to seize this chance and develop a crop of MOOCs that build on our strengths, in the tradition of exchange and mobility, of open and free access to education. European universities, by developing their *brand* of MOOCs — while still sharing global platforms — can build on these pillars:

1. The **"global ladder of opportunity"** (Gordon Brown): Europe's best universities can be proud of their courses and can contribute to "build a better world through knowledge," with generous access and good credentialing for all;

2. A rich **landscape of cultures**: Europe can build on its rich history and long tradition in the humanities; there is no risk of uniformity through massive courses; on the contrary, students will benefit from various approaches in social sciences and humanities. Europe, we think, has a lot to offer in the area of digital humanities (see below);

3. A **variety of languages**: Europe should make use of the richness of languages, build strong partnerships with continents that are close to us, namely Africa;

4. **Good framework conditions**: thanks to public support of our universities, and to the existence of Europe-wide initiatives like ECTS (transfer of credits between universities), Bologna (common degree structure) and ERASMUS (student mobility program), we can maintain a world-class university system. However the excellence — or reputation — of the MOOC providing institution will play a decisive role.

Problems & Challenges

Many questions remain open: the credits to attach to the courses; the openness of platforms; the ownership of course material and student data; ways to verify the identity of students; the business model (a conundrum for all stakeholders: platforms, teachers, students, universities); standardization and accreditations; completion rates.

1. **Drop out rates**: MOOCs have been launched with an exploratory, some may say zealous, spirit: there aren't many formal requirements for students who get to peek in and then decide to complete courses or not. The ease of non-completion in online MOOCs can be viewed as an opportunity for risk-free exploration (Koller *et al.*, 2013). This analysis indicates that in 2012, the typical Coursera MOOC enrolled between 40,000 and 60,000 students, of whom 50 to 60% returned for the first lecture. Of these around 15 to 20% submitted an assignment for grading. Of this group, approximately 45% successfully completed the course and earned a Statement of Accomplishment. In *fine*, roughly 5% *of the students* who signed up actually completed the course.

2. **Managing both internal & external students**: Universities are not bare "information-dispensing" enterprises, but, unless universities respond to the rising tide of online courses, new players will emerge to displace them, or so thinks Wikipedia founder Jimmy Wales (Coughlan, 2013). The *boring* university lecture might be the first casualty of the rise in online learning in higher education (Coughlan, 2013), since professors can be freed from "grading and repeating the same lecture." However, the synchronous existence of onsite and online student groups will require major redesign of courses to guarantee the vital "organic" link between these online and on-site activities. Students also typically fear the loss of direct contact with a professor.

3. **The workload frightens teachers**: MOOCs are demanding for students and for teachers. MOOCs will test both the loyalty of faculty to their institution, should for-profit platforms arise, and reduce the need for faculty to teach entry-level courses (often of "massive *onsite*" nature) because universities in the second and third tier will likely succumb to the pressure of "buying" excellent quality MOOCs provided by first-tier universities. With faculty generally reluctant to teach what they do not own, recognizing MOOCs from other universities will also put university governance, especially presidents, to the test. In addition **flipped classes** are difficult to set up and require deep rethinking of one's course than the MOOC per se. For our on-campus students, watching MOOCs in small teams is an ideal solution.

4. **Plagiarism** is widespread and will require a better understanding of the MOOC student population and their motivation. This is a crucial question to resolve in the likely event that eventually, students will be credited if they successfully follow a MOOC.

5. **Intellectual property (IP) and privacy issues.** Students criticize the fact that their "pedagogical data" and academic performance are owned by the platforms. Indeed, legal issues are a growing concern, notably concerning the IP of course content, the security and pri-

vacy of data storage and the possibility to reuse contents with university partners and networks.

EPFL — Strategy & Experience

Better be an Actor than a Spectator: In its first year of MOOCs activity, EPFL (Ecole polytechnique fédérale de Lausanne) reached out to 150,000 students with five MOOCs. The geographic repartition of the students was variable, and depended on the offered course: 20%-50% from Europe, 20%-35% from the Americas, 15%-30% from Asia and 3%-16% from Africa. To date, 21 MOOCs (EPFL, 2013) are produced or in production, including 10 in French. Four are on edX and 17 on Coursera.

Why invest in MOOCs? The main objectives of our MOOC strategy:

1. **Visibility** and outreach: Enhance EPFL's global reputation; be a member of leading platforms (Coursera, edX); reach out to science-minded citizens; and be a promoter of MOOCs in Europe.
2. Engage **on-campus teaching:** ameliorate first-year teaching; introduce flipped classrooms; optimize courseware (we have set up a small production team with professional video/audio skills). MOOCs are a complementary tool for on-campus education. Indeed, students appreciate MOOCs that are based on on-campus classes.
3. Create opportunities for **continuous technical education.** The demand is there: most students were postgraduates in the first batch of MOOCs. This is also a potential source of revenue.
4. Building networks in Europe and Africa, notably RESCIF (Réseau d'Excellence des Sciences de l'Ingénieur de la Francophonie), a network of technical universities of the Francophonie, and EuroTech: network for postgraduate education in Europe.

MOOCs are a unique tool for building networks in countries that have leap-frogged from no technology to the mobile world. First collaborations on MOOCs within RESCIF start in Autumn 2013, with invited faculty from African universities to our MOOC studio to produce first year level MOOCs (in physics and programming), and later a "lab-work" MOOC on Microcontrollers, a course run with a network of local instructors in over 50 universities covering 10 African countries.

Governance and implementation at EPFL: MOOC strategy is a <u>management issue for the university as a whole</u>. A steering board (provost, vice-presidents and Deans) oversees the process. An editorial committee controls quality, approves courses and allocates budgets, and synchronizes teaching calendars. Finally, a **Center for Digital Education** with a MOOC studio has been created, which supports course development and delivery, and engages in research in learning and data analytics. The production process at EPFL is illustrated in the figure above.

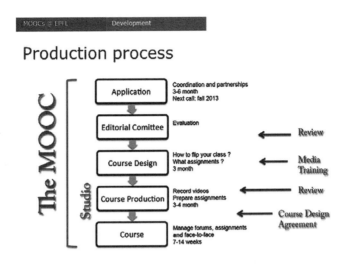

MOORS

Global Context: open access and collaborative research

As MOOCs challenge our teaching habits, MOORs (Massive Open Online Research projects) are shaking up the research enterprise itself. They are fueled in particular by the irreversible irruption of the "open access ethic" on the scientific-political scene, by the rise of collaborative and/or citizen-oriented research projects, and by the *invasion* of digital methods in the humanities and medicine.

Open Access: ArXiv, an open on-line archive for electronic preprints of scientific papers (mostly in the fields of mathematics, physics), owned by Cornell is already 22 years old, and today boasts 834,189 archived pre-prints, at a submission rate of over 7,000 per month. **PLOS,** the Public Library Of Science, founded in 2000 in California, is a nonprofit open access scientific publishing project. It launched its first journal, *PLOS Biology,* in October 2003 and publishes seven journals, all peer reviewed, as of April 2012. **Frontiers,** a Swiss initiative launched by Henry and Kamila Markram of EPFL in 2007, is a web-based publishing platform that offers semi-automated submission and processing, interactive peer-review, and open access publishing of research articles. 5,000 articles were published in 2012 at Frontiers and the number doubles every year. Nature Publishing Group (McMillan) acquired a controlling stake in the company in 2013. Outsell, a consulting firm, estimates that open-access journals generated $172m in 2012, up 34% from 2011. This is still a small fraction of the $6 billion generated by journal subscriptions, but open-access is clearly taking off.

Collaborative research: The second leg of the MOORs revolution is a slew of projects aiming at developing more collaborative, participative research. As a sample, three such projects are presented here. Reproducible Research (http://reproducibleresearch.net) is an online initiative to help researchers publish papers and data in a reproducible way (for anyone), thus improving research quality. The Polymath blog (http://polymathprojects.org) is a collective endeavour to launch massively collaborative mathematical projects. Citizen Science (http://www.scientificamerican.com/citizen-science) presents research projects involving teams of scientists (and curious amateurs) collaborating across continents.

Digital Medicine and Digital Humanities: Inspired by the Human Genome Project with its promise of individualized treatment, and by increasing pressure by society on the health system in terms of cost and demographics, traditional medicine will no doubt undergo a profound transformation towards *digital* medicine. MOOCs and massive data are impacting also the humanities and social sciences. For many years now, a flurry of small-scale projects have brought together scientists from humanities and IT engineers, but now a wave of ambitious digitization — national libraries, historic collections, anything ever published or written — is deeply transforming the access to our past, the understanding of the present, and projections into our future.

Simulation-based research

The IT revolution — notably in supercomputing capacity — has brought the field of computer simulation to the threshold of a new era: realistic, interactive, real-time simulations. **Simulation-based research** is developing as a "Third line of research", complementing theoretical and experimental science. Particle physics (CERN) with grid-based participative super-computing, and Neuroscience are fields where simulation-based research is expected to finally permit the integration of the data deluge and fragmentation into realistic models. In Neuroscience, the emblematic MOOR is the **Human Brain Project** (*www.humanbrainproject.eu*), a Europe-wide, 1 billion Euro research consortium of 134 institutions in 23 countries that aims at building a simulation-facility permitting to simulate the human brain in development, ageing and disease. EPFL houses its coordination and simulation facility.

Big data leads to simulation science, and this will disrupt and transform the way we do research. Experimental data will continue to be generated at a tremendous volume, but in addition there is the data deluge coming from all of our monitoring devices — from smartphones to satellites. Big Data will impact curricula, with emphasis on mathematics, computation and disciplinary knowledge. It will also change the way we organize research, with the development of "big science" projects, based not just on single labs, but on large-scale, ad-hoc consortia with armies of mobile researchers.

Europe should continue to bet on simulation and systems science. It has already started with the EU "Future Emerging Technologies (FET) Flagship" initiatives, where the core strategy is integration of information, knowledge and know-how through simulation. The FuturICT proposal, integrating ICT, complexity science and the social sciences, was a finalist of the competition, and the Human Brain Project, whose ambition is to integrate experimental and clinical data about the brain in models through simulation, was a winner. Simulation science will become a strong component of science in this century and Europe is well positioned.

CONCLUSIONS

If Europe intends to continue to be competitive in the international economy, our schools need to ride the tidal wave of open access learning and research. As George Siemens, a Canadian innovator in the field, writes, "Much of today's economy is knowledge-based. In a knowledge economy, we need to be learning constantly. Universities have failed to recognize the pent-up demand for learning as the economy has diversified and society has become more complex and interconnected. As a consequence, the Internet has contributed by creating a shadow education system where learners learn on their own and through social networks. MOOCs reflect society's transition to a knowledge economy and reveal the inadequacy of existing university models to meet learner's needs," (Kolt, 2013b). **It is time to harness the potential of this shadow educational system found in social media and citizen-based initiatives, or be left behind.**

But MOOCs and MOORs should be approached as a key to opening the door of novel forms of online education and research. According to Bonnie Stewart, "MOOCs are a symptom of change in higher education, not its source....So if we are to envision a future for higher education that values more than the bottom line, we need to get beyond the illusion of the simple divide between markets and education as we've known it. If we close ourselves off to the possibilities of open, online learning, it's not marketization we undermine, but our own capacity to experiment with new models for higher education" (Steward, 2013).

Massive online education and research will transcend the boundaries of our institutions. MOOCs and their kin will be, for most students and researchers, "booster shots of education" needed to expand their minds or enhance their credentials for jobs. Let us practise massive online academia with a "let's do it" spirit, understanding that we will evaluate things while we are doing them. As Europeans, looking at international rankings of our universities can be depressing. But if we play our strengths right and engage the IT revolution cleverly, European world-class universities will once again be among the best.

* *We thank Michael Mitchell for his help in editing the manuscript*

REFERENCES

Allen, D. (2013). An online college revolution is coming. http://www.washingtonpost.com/opinions/an-online-college-revolution-is-coming/2013/07/26/62f21720-de9c-11e2-b2d4-ea6d8f477a01_print.html

Coughlan S. (2013). "Jimmy Wales, Boring university lectures 'are doomed'." http://www.bbc.co.uk/news/business-22160988

EPFL (2013). MOOC List. "MOOCs de l'EPFL." http://moocs.epfl.ch/page-92640-fr.html

Kolds (2013a). Session 1: "Tour d'Europe". (European MOOC Summit, EPFL, June 2013). http://www.slideshare.net/Kolds/tour-europemoo-cssummit

Kolds (2013b). "Disruptor, Saviour, or Distractor: MOOCs and their role in higher education". http://www.slideshare.net/Kolds/u-of-wisc-moo-cs

Koller, D., Ng A., Do, C. & Chen, Z. (2013). Retention and intention in Massive Open Online Courses: In depth. http://www.educause.edu/ero/article/retention-and-intention-massive-open-online-courses-depth-0

Lewin, T. (2012). "College of future could become one, come all." http://www.nytimes.com/2012/11/20/education/colleges-turn-to-crowd-sourcing-courses.html?pagewanted=all

Manning, J. & Sanders, M. (2013). "How widely used are MOOC forums? A first look." https://www.stanford.edu/dept/vpol/cgi-bin/wordpress/how-widely-used-are-mooc-forums-a-first-look/

Massive Open Online Courses (2013). Wikipedia. http://en.wikipedia.org/wiki/Massive_open_online_course

MOOCs@Edinburgh Group (2013) MOOCs @ Edinburgh 2013: Report #1. http://hdl.handle.net/1842/6683

Parr, C. (2013). "Not Staying the Course". http://www.insidehighered.com/news/2013/05/10/new-study-low-mooc-completion-rates

Perrin, S. (2012). "More than classes, they are vast networks of knowledge". http://actu.epfl.ch/news/more-than-classes-they-are-vast-networks-of-know-7/

Stewart, B. (2013). "Moving beyond a binary view of MOOCs". http://www.universityaffairs.ca/moving-beyond-a-binary-view-of-moocs.aspx

PART III

•••••••••••••

Cost, Price and Value

CHAPTER 9

Who is responsible for providing and paying for higher education?

Luc E. Weber

INTRODUCTION

H igher education (HE), more than most other goods or services, can be provided either by the public sector or the market. It can be also paid for either by the State (the taxpayers or lenders) or by private interests (individuals, business or other private sources, e.g. foundations). This flexibility is rather unique. Even if is true that no goods or services are 100% public or private, some are basically public (e.g. foreign affairs, defence, fire brigade, etc) and paid for consequently by the taxpayers — or by borrowing — whereas others are mainly private (durable goods, hotels and restaurants, banking, etc) and bought in the market.

This high degree of manoeuvrability with respect to the provision and financing of HE explains the great variety of solutions from one country to another worldwide (with, nevertheless, some established patterns, according to the continent or region). It is not surprising, under these conditions, that the most adequate arrangement for the provision and financing of HE remains in many countries the source of intense political discussion.

This variety of solutions takes many forms; the most relevant are the proportion of the Gross National Product (GNP) spent by a country for Higher Education and the relative share paid for by the State. Table 1 illustrates the situation in a few countries with the sole purpose of showing these differences.

In a time of rapid change, when HE is facing increasing political and business pressure, as well as increasing financial difficulties, the Glion Colloquium

Table 1: National effort for HE and share paid for by the public sector in 2009

	Brazil	Chile	Denmark	Finland	France	Germany	Japan	Korea	UK	USA
HE/GDP in %	0.8	2.5	1.9	1.9	1.5	1.3	1.6	2.6	1.3	2.6
% paid by the State		23.4	95.4	95.8	83.1	84.4	35.3	26.1	29.6	38.1

Sources: *Education at a Glance 2012*, OECD, Paris 2012.

provides a good opportunity to revisit once more the basic principles that could guide policy-makers. Indeed, the fact that the provision and financing of HE allow so many different institutional solutions does not mean — by a long shot — that all solutions are similar, considering the fact that HE is expected to contribute to reaching the supreme objectives of a society and in satisfying two — in general opposed —economic criteria, which are the efficiency of provision, as well as the policy effectiveness, and equity of provision and financing.

In the first part of this chapter, we shall stress that HE has not only a beneficial return for individuals, but has also a collective one, which justifies the fact that it is a public responsibility. We shall also show, from another point of view, that the particular economic characteristics of the service HE provides mean that the effort of studying is not only beneficial to the students themselves, but also to the entire society. In other words, the action of studying induces external benefits. We shall try in the second part to draw from these two findings answers to the questions regarding who can or should provide HE and who should pay for it. We shall conclude that, even if the degree of freedom is large, some solutions are better with regard to efficiency and effectiveness, as well as equity. The reminder of these basic principles can (should) help policy-makers to revisit the policies implemented in their countries and show what strategies can improve them.

WHY IS HIGHER EDUCATION A PUBLIC RESPONSIBILITY?

We shall briefly show from two different angles of views why, in addition to being a good investment for individuals (higher expected income, lower vulnerability to unemployment, richer life), HE is a public responsibility, meaning that the State must have and implement an HE policy. We shall limit ourselves to highlighting two arguments (Weber, 2005).

The collective and individual benefits of higher education

National constitutions describe the highest (supreme) objectives pursued by a nation. Let us quote, for example, article 2 of the Swiss Confederation's Constitution (1999):

Art. 2 Aims

1. The Swiss Confederation shall protect the liberty and rights of the people and safeguard the independence and security of the country.
2. It shall promote the common welfare, sustainable development, internal cohesion and cultural diversity of the country.
3. It shall ensure the greatest possible equality of opportunity among its citizens.
4. It shall be committed to the long-term preservation of natural resources and to a just and peaceful international order.

In substance, the Constitution identifies as supreme objectives of the country the promotion of the common welfare of the people. Common welfare comprises two totally different notions. The first one is material or economic, and therefore tangible. HE is essentially an investment for individuals and the community, which generates individual, as well as collective benefits. The second dimension points at basic societal principles. It refers to these intangible qualities that are also crucial for people's well-being, like the respect of fundamental rights, freedom, tolerance, security and justice, in other words citizenship.

In an era in which economy and finance play a role of overwhelming importance, it is extremely important never to forget that the welfare of a population depends not only on material welfare (in other words on economic growth), but also on many other important intangible values. One concrete consequence of this is that it would be bad policy to drive the HE system exclusively according to the views of the economy and finance. Education and, in particular, HE should also contribute to the satisfaction of these other immaterial objectives, which contributes to individual and collective welfare. This means in concrete terms that:

- Teaching and learning should be focused not only on transmitting professional knowledge, but also geared to developing a broader culture and critical thinking.
- Besides the disciplines more or less directly serving the economy, such as natural sciences, engineering, computer sciences, spoken languages, law and management, universities should also promote philosophy, history, archeology, literature, political sciences and political economy to prepare students not only to work in business or administration, but also to become active and thoughtful citizens (at national and world levels).

But the fact is that it is more difficult to secure the necessary resources to develop or even maintain these "softer" disciplines in a period when globalization is exerting huge pressure on countries to remain competitive and in a time of financial crisis and slow growth. A country's competitiveness depends on the flexibility and dynamism of its business sector and on a light and efficient public sector, but it also depends strongly on the quality of the whole education sector and, of course, the efficiency and pertinence of research. In the short term, some disciplines contribute to a country's competitiveness more than others. But the situation is different in the longer term. There is therefore a trade-off between what seems to be good policy in the short run and what is correct in the long run. Obviously, if the market was free to choose, it would be largely biased in favour of short-term success. Thus, the public sector has a major responsibility to secure a correct balance between the short- and long-term goals of Society and to protect those disciplines that contribute to the immaterial objectives that are important for better citizenship.

The specific economic nature of higher education

Another way to respond to the question of who should provide and pay for higher education is to look at the particular economic characteristics of HE. HE is what economists call a mixed collective good. This means three things:

- First, up to a certain limit, an increasing number of students can benefit from higher education provision without significantly increasing the total cost of provision. One aspect of this can be seen in the important difference of the staff-students ratio from one country to the other, without necessarily impacting significantly on quality. This characteristic might become more important with the development of distance and online learning, because this allows the spread of the cost of preparing a course over a much larger number of students;
- Second, higher education is the source of external benefits, which means that the whole community benefits from the study effort made by students, even those citizens who have not been in any tertiary education institution;
- Third, the providers of higher education service can reserve them for beneficiaries satisfying some conditions. These conditions can be either financial, that is paying a given fee, or qualitative, in particular, the capacity to study. These criteria can even be positive when, for example, a special effort is made to enrol students from disadvantaged families, regions or ethnical groups; but they can also be restrictive, for example if the level of fees becomes a barrier to entry or when restrictions are imposed against, for example, a specific ethnic group.

WHO SHOULD PROVIDE AND PAY FOR HIGHER EDUCATION?

The huge diversity of HE systems across the world turns around the institutional response given to three questions:

- Who is providing higher education? The public sector? A private not-for-profit institution? Or a for-profit one? We are voluntarily ignoring the fact that the organization of production can differ from the organization of the provision. The State can, for example, be responsible for the provision and subcontract it to private organizations: depending on the definition we are using, this might, for example, be the case in England where HE institutions are private, but still significantly financed by the Higher Education Founding Council, which is nothing less than an arm of the Ministry of Education.
- Are there distinct differences of quality related to the type of provider? In more concrete terms, are the public institutions better or worse than the private ones?
- Who is paying? Is studying entirely free of charge or should students pay a fee, and, if so, what should be the level of these fees? Low, moderate or high enough to cover entirely the cost of provision? Moreover, do students receive financial help to cover the fees and/or for their cost of subsistence and study expenses? And from whom? Upon which criteria (their merit or on the basis of some interpretation of the right to study)? And, do they have to reimburse this support afterwards? Finally, who is eventually paying for the total study cost (subsistence costs and fees) for students who do not receive any financial help? The students themselves, who have to work to pay for studying? Their parents? Their grandparents? Or an even larger group, usually within the family? Or, alternatively, do they have to borrow from a specialized institution or even a bank?

Obviously the responses given to these three questions impact on individuals and on Society. We shall now very briefly compare a few distinctive HE systems worldwide and try to draw a few conclusions regarding their efficiency and quality, as well as equity.

Provision

The comparison between systems worldwide regarding who provides HE reveals amazing differences. While private institutions play an important role in some developed countries like the U.S. and Japan, they are still not a serious alternative to public institutions in Western Europe.

Western Europe, where the concept of Universities has been widely developed since the 16th century, counts only a small number of private institutions, even not-for-profit ones (apart perhaps from institutions in the U.K. which are categorized by the OECD as "government-dependent private institutions" (OECD, 2012, p. 252). There are only a few exceptions to this. An important private sector developed in Portugal at the end of last century in response to the slow reaction of the public sector to absorb the demographically and income-related increase of the student numbers. Austria introduced, 12 years ago, a policy promoting the development of a private sector, but its success is relatively modest as only 2% of students study in private accredited universities. Switzerland has many private institutions, but, apart from IMD which is one of the best World business schools, these institutions are not really visible and offer teaching programs in a limited numbers of disciplines, strongly related to business.

In the United States, the German Humbolt University model strongly inspired the development of the higher education system in the 19th century, which became highly successful thanks to public, but even more, to private not-for-profit institutions. It is also in the U.S. that the concept of excellent private teaching colleges developed.

More recently, in post-communist Eastern and Central Europe, the number of private higher education institutions mushroomed — after the transition — in response to the strong demand, in particular for business studies, but also to provide an alternative to a public system which was obsolete and slow to change.

The situation remains quite fluid in the developing world, despite the fact that the World Bank is pushing hard for the development of a private sector, considering rightly that it is the only way to increase the capacity of the sector, but neglecting the fact that the main limitation is the lack of qualified teachers.

Quality

The crucial question of quality is basically an efficiency question, but we find it easier to address it separately. As we all know, there are — everywhere — good, satisfactory and poor institutions, and this more or less independently of who provides or produces the service, the public sector or private institutions. Two cases are sufficient to make the case. At first sight, in countries like the U.S. and Japan, where a strong private sector coexists alongside the public sector, there are good to excellent public as well as private institutions, as well as poor ones. The situation is quite different in Eastern Europe: most of the private institutions that were created after the transition to more liberal regimes are basically mediocre or poor institutions. The level of requirements for students is low and the teaching staff is often insufficiently qualified or dedicated to its responsibilities because they are teaching in many institutions. Finally, before it became a requirement for participation in the Bologna process, the institutions were, for a very long time, not subject to any independent evaluation or accreditation. In conclusion, experiences in different countries tend to prove that the quality of institutions depends only slightly on the ownership status. But, the experience of Austria, which introduced a serious system of accreditation for private universities and programs, shows that today it is not easy to develop from scratch a strong private university sector.

Financing students' studies

The financing of studies, fees in particular, is the other source of large differences between systems. Roughly, fees vary between an order of magnitude of US$100 a year in many European higher education institutions — in particular in Northern Europe — to approx. $50,000 a year in a couple of not-for-profit American universities. Moreover, fees are almost continuously increasing in countries like the US, in private institutions as well as in public ones. This is, rightly, raising serious questions of access. Paradoxically, apart from England, which follows the American model of rapidly increasing fees to compensate for the decreasing willingness of the State to pay for higher education, the situation in continental Western Europe is hardly changing. Even in countries like Germany where modest fees of approximately $1,000 a year have been introduced in a few States (Länder), some States have already abolished them after a change of political majority. Students' fees are even lower in France and there is no willingness to increase them today, although the State is currently in a difficult economic and financial situation. Considering that the fees' question is, almost everywhere, politically very sensitive, it is certainly useful to reconsider the arguments for and against fees in terms of efficiency and equity.

Efficiency

The first and main argument which explains why the level of fees tends to increase greatly in countries traditionally levying fees is that they are an important source of revenue for universities and are increased precisely because the public sector cannot or does not want to increase the financial means allocated to HE. This is obviously the case in the U.S. and in England. Many are however wondering if this policy really brings all the expected additional funds as they suspect the public sector is taking advantage of this increased private contribution to reduce its own. This argument has been strongly put forward by opponents of fees in Germany.

The second argument is that studying is an investment for students, which will bring them more interesting jobs, higher salaries and lower vulnerability to unemployment. Economic studies in general demonstrate this quite clearly, although some also show that it is no longer the case in a few countries with a very high proportion of graduates and probably also graduates in disciplines that are mainly recruited by the public sector.

The third point is that levying fees stimulates the sense of responsibility of both the buyers and providers of education services: students are encouraged to work more effectively to avoid unduly prolonging their stay in a higher education institution, and institutions and teachers are reminded by the students that they have to deliver a good education for the fees the students are paying. Some will argue that good behaviour is a given with teachers being civil servants and with students eager to learn; unfortunately, such an ideal world does not exist, and the price is an effective way to bring more responsibility into the system.

However, the positive private return on investment of longer studies does not justify the proposition that students pay for the full cost of their studies. We have seen in the first section that there are at least two solid arguments against it.

- First, the effort made by students preparing a grade will not only benefit them, but will also benefit all those who have not had the opportunity to study, as it contributes to increasing the general level of skill and knowledge of the entire community.
- Second, in today's knowledge society, investments in human capital are becoming increasingly important compared to investments in tangible capital, such as transport. The private and public sectors and Society as a whole increasingly need qualified people to master the increasing complexity and rapidity with which the economy is changing and to continue innovating in order to remain competitive and to face numerous challenges like sustainable development, internal and external security, political stability and social justice. Therefore, it is shortsighted to charge those studying for the benefits accruing not only to them as well as those accruing to the entire population. This is unfortunately what happens in those private institutions charging very high fees. Being private, they have to balance their books despite public support clearly inferior to the support accruing to public institutions. However, unless training in these institutions is so much better that it compensates for the smaller number of students who can afford to pay, the State has to develop a generous system of grants to make sure that potential good students can also gain access to these institutions, along with the children of more privileged families.

Equity aspects

These efficiency arguments are rather technical and do not retain much attention among the public. The population, and particularly students — paradoxically more so in the regions where there are no or only small student fees — are more sensitive to the equity dimension of students' fees and measures to alleviate their impact on the possibility for students to go to Higher Education. This question has two dimensions.

The first is politico-philosophical. Is higher education, like liberty, freedom of speech, the right to elect and be elected, and basic education, a fundamental social right that should be granted to all citizens? If it were, it could be claimed that every citizen would have the right to study in a higher education institution, whatever his or her capacity to benefit from it and to succeed. To pretend that higher education is a fundamental right is an exaggeration: due to inequalities at birth and/or during childhood, not all adolescents or mature people have the wish and the capacity to successfully follow higher education studies. The real problem that has to be addressed is the risk of barriers to access due to financial or other reasons. The valid equity objective is that no one who has the capacity to engage successfully in higher education should be prevented from doing so. And, if they do not have the necessary financial means to do so, they should be helped, either by receiving a non-refundable grant or a grant refundable later on, when their earnings reach a specified level (Australian and English systems). Alternatively, they should be able to get credit at a very low interest rate. Avoiding barriers to access requires more than mere financial measures. Policies should be put in place to identify those who are capable, but might not be interested in continuing because it is not in the family culture or because their family is expecting, for example, that they take up work as soon as possible in a family business, and to encourage and help them to consider longer studies. Such policies are all the more justified for a Nation in that they contribute to bringing into higher education the greatest possible number of potentially capable students.

The second argument is that — contrary to widespread opinion — free access does not contribute to the expected distributional justice. On the contrary. This erroneous opinion is understandable because fees — if no financial help is provided — are a real burden for students from low-income groups. But, in reality, the opposite is true because: mainly for cultural reasons, the proportion of students originating from the low-income group remains, despite all the efforts made, much lower than those from the middle- and high-income groups. The fact is that there is a correlation between the level of education of the parents and the education ambitions of their children. Therefore, the politically desired income redistribution from the "rich" to the "poor" goes in the opposite direction because the members in the low-income group pay taxes (sales tax or VAT, sometime also income tax), thereby participating in the provision of free (or almost free) higher education for the children of better-off people, who will themselves hold, later on, positions where they are likely to have a higher income throughout their professional life and will be less subject to the hazards of unemployment. To put it more bluntly, workers, whose children leave school at the age of 15-16 are — although modestly — paying for youngsters from middle- or high-income groups, who could much more easily pay for their studies and will most probably earn much higher salaries throughout their working lives. It is only if the proportion of students is the same — whatever the social background — that this undesired income redistribution will end. It is therefore surprising that low- and middle-income groups are so strongly opposed to student fees.

As already mentioned, the fact that student fees are justified on many grounds does not mean they should or can be set at record highs. The principles developed above teach us clearly that only part of the cost of providing a good college or university education should be paid for by the direct beneficiaries, the rest being the responsibility of the public sector for the good of the entire community. This responsibility should clearly be respected by public institutions. But it is also necessary for private universities to pay attention to this as they are part of a system that contributes to the improvement in well-being of the whole country. The best solution is for the State to put in place a generous system of grants to support capable students wherever they study, in a public or private institution.

CONCLUSIONS

We have argued that almost all solutions are possible for the provision and financing of HE. Does this mean that the shape of a national HE system has only a limited impact on its efficiency and quality, as well as equity? Comparisons are difficult because the context is never the same for historical, cultural, political and financial reasons. In particular, we have seen at the beginning that the national global investment effort in HE (public and private), as well as the proportion paid respectively by the State and by private interest, differs greatly from one country to the other. But, even if money plays an important role for the efficiency, quality and equity of the system in place, it is in no way the only determinant of performance. The characteristics of the system also play an important role.

The main purpose of this chapter was to revisit the pros and cons of public vs. private provision and financing. Basically, HE is a public responsibility: it is profitable for a Nation to invest in HE for reasons of efficiency and equity. For the State, it is a continuation of its responsibility to provide elementary and secondary education, as well as professional education. The difference is that State involvement is very broadly considered as an obligation for the first two levels to guarantee that all children have access to basic education, whatever their origin and the income level of their parents. It is coherent to argue that HE is also, somehow, a fundamental right, providing it is made clear that this right is restricted to those who have the ability to study in a higher education institution. The efforts by many countries for political and philosophical reasons to encourage too many young people to go to college is eventually counterproductive as it contributes to increasing the number of failures or impacts negatively on the quality level of higher education institutions.

The fact that Higher Education is a public responsibility is not an argument against the development of a strong private sector, quite the opposite. The main justification is that a developed private sector contributes to increasing the total capacity of the system, which is particularly useful when the State does not, or only slowly, responds to an increased demand of higher education due to demographic reasons or increased expectation from students. Moreover, private investments in higher education also increase the responsiveness of the HE sector to changing needs. It does not follow from these two very positive arguments that a private sector has developed in all countries. It very much depends on the cultural tradition and the circumstances. For example, a private sector developed extremely rapidly in East and Central Europe when these countries abandoned communism and a centrally planned economy. However, in particular in developing countries, there is a real danger that private institutions meet the same constraints as the public ones, the lack of qualified teachers-researchers. Moreover, there is also a risk that many potential students cannot afford to pay the fees levied by private institutions.

On the other hand, there is no guarantee that all private institutions pay enough attention to quality. If in the U.S. there are more private not-for-profit universities than public ones among the best world universities, the poor quality of private institutions is a real preoccupation for the public authorities in many countries. This is certainly the case in Eastern Europe for the reasons we have seen, but it is a risk for developing countries if they do not pay attention early enough to this matter.

The fact that higher education is a public responsibility does not prevent or forbid either public institution from levying fees. However, for public higher education institutions, levying fees should remain an additional source of revenue and should certainly not justify a reduction of the financial support of the State. For private institutions, it is obviously a crucial source of financing as they are less or not at all subsidized by the Public sector.

However, as a matter of principle, fees should remain reasonable as higher education not only directly benefits those in the system, but the whole community. If this principle can be respected in public institutions, very little encourages private ones to respect it as they have to break even or even want to make a profit. The public sector is in most cases not capable of regulating fees, but, as a compensation, it can develop a generous system of student grants to prevent any barrier to entry. There is otherwise a danger that access is restricted, which raises an equity issue. Alternatively, there is a risk of pushing students into a very dangerous path of being deeply indebted at a young age, forcing them to reimburse large sums in their early years of professional and family life. Sensitivity to this equity argument varies strongly from one region to another, Europe being more sensitive than the Americas, Oceania and Asia.

Finally, the main conclusion of this chapter suggests that social sciences and, in particular political economy, offer a solid framework to compare and evaluate HE policies and systems worldwide, and especially the two key questions: who is providing them (the public sector or a private organization — for profit or not-for-profit)? And who is paying for it (the State or private interests)? The fact that numerous solutions are feasible could, at first sight, give the impression that this framework (set of analytical tools) is of little use. This is far from true. These principles offer a solid framework enabling us to compare and evaluate HE policies and systems. They focus upon what counts most for any policy and organization: first, the efficient use of scarce resources in order to maximize the realization of the expected objectives and, second, doing so in the most equitable manner or even contributing to a better distribution of income and wealth.

They derive their analytical power from the fact they are focused on the two most crucial questions raised by any policy or organization: how efficiently and equitably do they satisfy the expected objectives?

REFERENCES

Swiss Confederation Constitution (1999). *Federal Constitution of the Swiss Confederation* of 18 April 1999 (dating basically from 1848).
    http://www.admin.ch/org/polit/00083/?lang=en
OECD (2012) *Education at a Glance 2012*, Paris
Weber, L. (2005) "Nature and scope of the public responsibility for higher education and research." in Weber & Bergan (eds) pp. 29-43, *The Public Responsibility of higher education and research*, Council of Europe higher education series No.2, Strasbourg

CHAPTER 10

How and where are dominant funding models steering HE & Research?

Howard Newby

INTRODUCTION AND CONTEXT

We are living in a time of great economic uncertainty where governments are providing our universities with less resource, yet at the same time expecting to exert greater influence, through increasing regulation and a more and more forensic focus on impact and value for money. At the same time, the world is facing a set of grand challenges that research-intensive universities, working with industry, are in a unique position to solve.

Focussing on examples from the United Kingdom, the European Union and the United States of America, I will reflect on the present funding environment, in particular for research, and explore the clear push we are seeing from funders to drive research in a more top down and programmatic way, putting a premium on multi-disciplinarity and collaboration. The nature of the funding environment and, more importantly, the challenges we face as a society mean that links with industry and business are increasingly essential. However this traditional relationship must be redefined.

This unique combination of circumstances means that universities have to learn to be more responsive to funders and to look beyond traditional national and subject boundaries. In this way, we can ensure the breadth of expertise and the capacity exists to deliver relevant research in a sustainable way.

The response of universities to the changing demands of research funders is part of higher education's long track record of facing new challenges and finding a way to respond, while remaining true to our mission and purpose. Before I focus on changes to research funding and how these have affected us all, it is worth reflecting on how radically higher education and the influence of its funders, especially in the U.K., have transformed over the lifetime of many of today's academics.

Universities were traditionally rather elite institutions educating only a very small minority of their national populations. As we know, there was then a transition from this elite system to a mass system of higher education. In so far as how higher education was publically provided, this, of course, placed ever-increasing claims upon the public purse. As the need for these resources grew, so governments began to examine the purpose of this investment. If one adds into this the growing recognition over the last 20 years that higher education is an important component of global economic competitiveness, then one produces the circumstances for a radical change in the relationship between universities and the state. This can perhaps best be summarized by stating that it was once the role of governments to provide for the purposes of universities, but it is now the role of universities to provide for the purposes of government. It can be argued that governments increasingly regard universities as delivery agents for public policy goals. This, we will see, is particularly true of research funding.

And now, in the 21st century, it could be argued that we find ourselves given the role of transforming education. It is our responsibility to educate, engage, empower and energize the next generation of problem solvers. It is research universities that drive a robust international and collaborative research agenda designed to identify, invent, test and deploy solutions designed to address the formidable challenges that we all face. At the same time we must build both disciplinary depth and trans-disciplinary breadth of research and education, connecting the science, engineering, technology, mathematics, social sciences, arts and humanities disciplines in service to society. And finally we need to assess the need for societal action, to transmit authoritative information to stakeholders and then take ownership of the process of transition of knowledge to application, working in new partnerships.

How we carry out these responsibilities is clearly driven by the funding environment, and specifically the research funding environment, that we face.

The funding environment that we see across the E.U. and the United States, whilst obviously exhibiting clear differences, also has many similarities. Public funding from governments for research, while decreasing and being unpredictable, is being driven by what I will call the grand challenge agenda. As we will see, in order to access public funding, research must help answer questions in areas of strategic and societal importance, more than ever before. Increasingly there is a realization that the traditional relationship with business and industry must change. Arguably this relationship should evolve into a more peer-to-peer nature, stressing collaborations in areas of joint interest rather than the traditional customer-supplier relationship in which business procures graduates and intellectual property from universities.

I will draw out these themes by looking at the U.K., Continental Europe and the U.S. in more depth.

THE U.K.

In the U.K., investment in universities generally and their research in particular, has grown on the back of expectations about the transforming power of higher education and the contribution of research-driven innovation to the economy. Universities have grown enormously in number and size in the past 20 years and expansion has arguably placed the system, at least in part, in the role of service-provider with the resulting impact on the distribution of resource, activity and outcomes. Whilst universities in the U.K. remain autonomous institutions, increased public investment, both through grants and fee income, has made them more visible and more accountable. Meanwhile, many research fields have grown, diversified and matured to an enormous extent. Within the U.K., public perceptions of research outcomes have changed from discovery to utility, reflected particularly in the overt objectives of policy instruments.

In the U.K. there is a strong tradition of research in all subjects, and most of the U.K.'s long-term, curiosity-driven and strategic research is carried out in HE. The U.K. continues to punch well above its weight and our research remains the most productive and efficient of all the G8 countries. Crucially, in the current economic climate, the U.K. offers the best value for money. We now rank first among the G8 nations on the number of citations in relation to public spend on R&D.

U.K. HEIs receive billions of pounds annually to fund research. This comes from four main sources:

1. The research councils, who provide grants for specific projects and programs on a competitive basis. The councils also make a contribution to the overhead costs of research, and from 2006 have paid 80% of the full economic cost.
2. The four HE funding bodies, who provide block grants to support the research infrastructure — for example, building and IT costs. When combined with research council funding, this is known as the "dual support system".
3. Charities, which are particularly important in funding medical research.
4. Various other sources, including industry, the European Union and U.K. government departments.

The "dual support system", which combines block grants from the HE funding bodies with research council funding, forms the bedrock of research funding in the UK. This approach is distinctive to U.K. HE and is defined by being highly selective and competitive. Funding through the four U.K. HE funding councils is distributed according to the quality and volume of research measured and assessed periodically through a national exercise (formerly the Research Assessment Exercise, now the Research Excellence Framework – REF). The main feature of this QR ("quality related") funding is that HEIs are free to invest it in accordance with their own strategic priorities. This flexibility of bloc grant funding is much valued by HEIs in that it can support the research areas most important to them, while allowing them to integrate this funding into their own resource allocation systems.

Research council funding is allocated competitively, and is highly selective. The common objectives of these funding councils are to:

- Fund basic, strategic and applied research involving project or program funding.
- Support post-graduate training.
- Support science in society activities.
- Contribute to economic competitiveness, the effectiveness of public services and policy, and the quality of life.

While QR funding promotes freedom within HEIs, the competitive approach to grant funding by the Research Councils promotes discovery that has a clear social and/or economic impact.

The U.K. government recently (2011) launched its Innovation and Research Strategy, setting the direction of travel moving forwards, and giving universities a clear understanding of the government's priorities. What stands out is the very strong push towards collaboration and consortia. There is now a clear set of principles governing the treatment and submission of multi-institutional funding bids, and global collaboration is firmly on the agenda. Importantly the research funding paradigm of funding excellence is here to stay with a strong commitment shown towards that, the Research Excellence Framework, the dual support system and a balance between fundamental and user-led research.

What is clear, again to echo the themes that we see across the E.U. and America, is that there is, and will continue to be a programmatic approach to solving the grand challenges. Research Councils U.K. (2011), in their strategic vision, state that in order to foster economic growth and ensure the prosperity and well-being of the U.K., the strategic delivery of focused research programs, alongside nurturing innovative fundamental research, will be vital. It is recognized that public investment in research is an investment in the nation.

Six major themes, similar to the E.U.'s grand challenges, and America's national goals, have been identified that will provide the framework for all research council funding. These themes are:

- Digital economy
- Energy
- Global food security
- Global uncertainties
- Lifelong health and well-being
- Living with environmental change

A clear strategic goal of the research councils is to maximize opportunities for breakthrough research that crosses discipline and domain boundaries which it is hoped will result in solutions which can be exploited to the advantage of the U.K.

A key element of this is the relationship between universities and industry. Many civic universities traditionally had strong industrial links in the past, forged through a theme of relevance to and their origins in the local economy. Inevitably these particular links have weakened over the last 30 years or so, although wider networks have diversified. Between 1995-07, private research contract income to higher education rose from £170 million to around £300 million. But, at the same time, it fell as a share of total grant and contract income from about 11% to about 8%. To meet the legitimate expectations of wider society, it could be argued that public and private sector partners need a larger stake in a relationship of "mutual confidence". Changing knowledge balances and growing financial accountability will cause the higher education research base to reconfigure its external relationships, with stakeholders inside the U.K. and with international partners in Europe and elsewhere. Such partnerships will not only involve HEIs, but also governments, research funders and other stakeholder bodies, including industry and local and regional policy-makers seeking support for innovation and economic regeneration.

A good example of the U.K. HE infrastructure adapting to this approach is the Research Partnership Innovation Fund, launched in 2012, which supports universities involved in major collaborations with industry on a project-by-project basis. We at Liverpool are a beneficiary of this fund, having recently bid in conjunction with Unilever for funds to support the development of a Materials Innovation Factory on our campus at a total cost of over £40m.

Clearly internationalization will become, if it has not already, a core element of successful research and an integral part of remaining globally competitive. U.K. higher education research works well when it works with partners. However, it will be necessary for those partnerships to be more active than in the past, with clearer strategic investment, engagement and feedback. U.K. researchers must become more mobile between sectors and between countries, and Government must look to stimulate more effective engagement from industry than it does currently. The challenge then for all involved is to iden- tify innovative ways in which the wider academic, commercial and social communities can combine together to deliver useful outcomes.

So, as in America and the E.U., it is clear that there will be many difficult discussions and decisions to be made in the U.K. Increasing selectivity will lead to tough decisions about the future of the research base. Meanwhile uni- versities must do everything they can to access the funding that is available, whether from government, the European Union, industry, charity or other sources. The nature of much of this funding means that we must demonstrate impact and ensure value for money, a drive that is recognized by the weighting given to impact in the REF, the recently launched government "Gateway to research" (a portal to allow access to publically funded research across the U.K.), and the push towards open access publishing. The programmatic nature of this funding ensures that we are expanding interdisciplinary activity and collaboration between a number of stakeholders.

Although there are always uncertainties and challenges with higher educa- tion policy and funding, the relatively stable approach of funders in the U.K. ensures that, at least for the time being, there is a clear direction of travel for research in HE.

EUROPE

In this section I will predominantly focus on the European Union as a funding body and how the direction that they are taking is having a fundamental effect on national governments and universities. If nothing else, the E.U. is worth dwelling on as one of the few funders of research that is looking to increase the amount of funding for R&D. While in one sense, this, by definition, is good news for higher education, the E.U.'s programmatic approach means that universities have to continually respond to changing priorities so that they can access more and more of this funding.

The traditional European model of higher education emphasizes central- ized planning, state control, state funding, little competition and a focus on research and advanced training. However there is starting to be increased competition that is inducing a process of differentiation across universities in many member countries. Some universities are on the way to become truly internationally orientated, research-based universities, while others are devel- oping their strengths in a national or regional context. Others still are focus- ing on their role as teaching institutions. In short, higher education in the E.U. has become more open, more international and more stratified.

This effect is enhanced by the European governing bodies' view that Govern- ment ministries and agencies responsible for science and innovation across Europe need to develop more effective policies to address societal challenges, and to stimulate competitiveness, through intervention in research, education and innovation. Policies to promote knowledge triangle linkages remain problematic. Government bodies increasingly recognize the need to promote excellence by increasing competition for public research and innovation funding, but are confronted by limitations of doing this at a purely national level. More and more, they stress value for money and impact as key funding aims, and look to transnationally coordinated programs and projects as an important channel for achieving them.

In this context, the E.U. is seeking to use its power as a funder to tackle a number of perceived structural problems related to HEIs and research in mainland Europe.

Primarily it is felt that there should be a greater contribution of research and innovation to tackling societal challenges. Although many major societal challenges will have the same profound effects on all E.U. countries, there is still a relatively weak coordinated response at a pan-European level in the field of science and innovation. It can be argued that, to be successful, Europe must stimulate coordinated research aimed at addressing these challenges and improve the way it is transformed into new products and processes.

Likewise, while Europe has a historically strong science base, when it comes to highly cited science or top ranking universities, it often lags behind the U.S. For example, 15% of U.S. scientific publications are among the top 10% most cited publications worldwide, only 11% of E.U. publications fall into this category. Furthermore, the E.U. faces increasing competition from emerging countries. If Europe is to strengthen its scientific and technological performance, and to provide the basis for future competitiveness, it needs to increase its spending — in "Blue Sky" frontier research, in associated infrastructure, in training and education — and to make this spending more effective.

Finally there is insufficient cross-border coordination. Europe's research and innovation system remains constrained by national borders. Research funding is often dispersed, leading to duplication and inefficiencies. In spite of the benefits of coordination, almost 90% of R&D budgets are spent nationally without coordination across countries.

The European Union's response to these problems is captured in Horizon 2020 (European Commission, 2011), its new funding program for research and innovation. By bringing all E.U. research and innovation funding into a single research and innovation framework, it is hoped that participation will become easier, that collaboration will be encouraged, that there will be an increase in scientific and economic impact and that value for money will be maximized.

The programme's objectives are now presented as the broad themes:

1. Excellent Science, to raise the level of scientific excellence in Europe to protect Europe's long-term competitiveness.

2. Industrial Leadership, to make Europe a more attractive location to invest in research and innovation. It also seeks to stimulate the growth potential of European companies, and SMEs in particular.
3. Societal Challenges, to develop new and convincing solutions to today's important societal problems.

And the framework identifies six societal challenges as priorities for funding:

1. Health, demographic change and well-being
2. Food security, sustainable agriculture, marine and maritime research and the bio economy
3. Secure, clean and efficient energy
4. Smart green and integrated transport
5. Climate action, resource efficiency and raw materials
6. Inclusive, innovative and secure societies.

Horizon 2020 follows on from the multiannual Framework Programme, which up until the inception of Horizon 2020 was the E.U.'s main programme for funding research, technological development and demonstration. We are now within the final phase of Framework Programme 7 (FP7 – 2007-2013) and spending is expected to have reached €50bn by 2013.

The Framework Programme has traditionally focused on supporting transnational research collaborations in industrially relevant areas and underpinning E.U. policy-making — although support for research mobility, transnational access to research infrastructure and coordination of national programs has been added over the years. FP7 currently funds around 5% of overall E.U. civil investment in research and innovation (the rest coming from national governments and the private and charitable sectors).

The evaluation of FP6 concluded that it had contributed to increased industrial competitiveness; generated extended networks and strengthened the knowledge infrastructure in Europe. FP6 included world-class projects with the best researchers, contributing to improved researcher mobility, internationalization of research teams, and to Europe performing internationally-competitive research at the frontiers of science and technology in areas of social and industrial importance. The interim evaluation of FP7 has demonstrated that funding is going to leading researchers engaged in high-quality projects and that the new European Research Council has succeeded in funding world-class research and is playing an important role in attracting and retaining research talent within the E.U.

The largest proportion of the current Framework Programme is allocated to specific programs which fund a number of thematic areas relating to challenges, technologies and sectors mostly awarded on a "top-down" basis to cross-border consortia of researchers from academia, research institutes and industry. This has been underpinned by a commitment to supporting demonstrable excellence in research, through competition at a European scale, which in turn has led to word-class outputs.

The Grand Challenge programmes, at the heart of Horizon 2020, such as climate change and the need to pool resources to meet the demands of internationally competitive research, will mean that collaboration, between universities, industry and others, becomes an increasingly frequent part of normal business. The concept that individual E.U. countries might split the agenda seems absurd, but the idea that there should be some specialist hosting of shared, major facilities is a realistic extension of established institutions such as the European Organisation for Nuclear Research (CERN), and the European Molecular Biology Laboratory and the Institut Laue-Langevin. The European Commission's research budget is expected to increase after 2013 and, particularly in light of the current funding environment, U.K. universities will need to continue to work strategically and collaboratively with universities in other E.U. member states in order to maximize their funding opportunities.

It is clear then that through the implementation of Horizon 2020, and the previous Framework Programme, the E.U. is taking a programmatic approach to research funding, while, for universities, operating in a difficult funding environment, the approach to European funding is becoming increasingly important. It is likely that the nature of the grand challenges will ensure that universities look at strategic partnerships in terms of long-term research commitments, rather than only academic exchange and short-term student recruitment mechanisms. These strategic partnerships will increasingly involve industry and measurement of impact will continue to dominate the agenda. However, there is still a need to ensure that "Blue Sky" research is appropriately supported and that the mix with applied research is appropriately distributed, a fact recognized by the E.U. following feedback on its initial announcements around Horizon 2020; we will see to what extent when the budget for the European Research Council is set.

To finish my overview of the impacts of E.U. funding with an aside, underlying all of the factors I've just mentioned will also be the drive for economic efficiency, as European funding continues to bring with it issues around administration (particularly around reporting and the accountability burden) and the reimbursement of indirect costs. Again, the E.U. is responding to feedback on this area, and is now being positive about "simplification", and making it easier for universities to access and manage research funding.

THE USA

Much like the United Kingdom and the European Union, in the USA, the approach of funders is shaping higher education research. It feels like America is at a turning point in its approach. A recent report commissioned by the U.S. Congress — "Research Universities and the future of America" — reflects this view, and I will use it as a basis for discussing the impact of research funding in America. Importantly this report looks forward and the recommendations made indicate the potential for making change in the new world we are in.

In the American ecosystem there is significant diversity among research universities in size, geography and mission. The sector is characterized by decentralization, pluralism (public and private universities), diverse funding sources (endowment, federal, state, tuition), high levels of competition and a hybrid model that includes undergraduate education, graduate study and research in the same place, done by the same people, frequently at the same time. The report argues, as you would expect, that research universities are drivers of renewal and producers of knowledge. They create a pipeline of talent that is upwardly mobile and this in turn creates prosperity. Yet, despite this, America, along with the U.K., has been cutting funding for research as part of its response to the global financial downturn, when it would appear most of the world, especially the BRIICS countries, are increasing funding.

For example, since the report was published, we have seen a process of "sequesterization" introduced in the U.S. since March, with automatic cuts in funding being applied to research as part of wider budget cuts. The National Science Foundation, for example, is slated to lose more than $280m this year, and expects to fund about 1,000 fewer research grants than last year. The National Institute of Health is expected to lose about $1.6bn in funding this fiscal year.

In addition to this, American research universities are also facing other pressures such as record reductions in state funding, erosion of endowments, soaring tuition costs reaching unaffordable limits, and, in some cases, a loss of political and public confidence in the value of university-based research.

Despite this, the expectations for university-based research to produce creative solutions for a growing list of complex problems have never been higher, forcing institutions to be more strategic about applications for research funding.

The report goes on to identify two other key issues in the partnership between federal government, states, business and universities:

1. Business and industry have largely dismantled the large corporate research laboratories that drove American industrial leadership in the 20th century, but have not yet fully partnered with research universities to fill the gap at a time when they need to more effectively translate, disseminate and transfer into society the new knowledge and ideas that emerge from university research.

2. Research universities need to be responsive to stakeholders by improving management, productivity and cost efficiency in both administration and academics.

Importantly, the current approach to funding and policy is having a negative impact on the operations of universities. There has been under-investment in campus infrastructure, particularly in cyber infrastructure, that can lead to long-term increases in productivity, cost effectiveness and innovation in research, education and administration. Universities have to cross-subsidize research from other sources because research sponsors do not pay the full cost of research they procure — an issue not restricted to America. Finally, there has been a burdensome accumulation of federal and state regulatory and reporting requirements that increase costs and sometimes challenges academic freedom and integrity.

The current approach to research universities is fragmented, with no coherent national plan or rational strategy to support university-based research.

What is clear, regardless of government policy, is that the nature of the grand challenges is helping to drive the actions of research-intensive universities. The grand challenge agenda is not unique to Europe. In America it is expressed through national goals:

1. Advances in medicine and health care
2. A sustainable, healthier environment
3. Energy security
4. Improved standards of living
5. Education for our children and adults
6. Enhanced security

To enable impact-orientated research that addresses these significant social challenges the need to increase inter-disciplinary collaboration within and between other universities and with industry is essential, and it is clear that federal funding is driving research in these areas, forcing universities to be more strategic in applying for research funding when faced with a reducing pot.

With federal funding comes a new level of expectation and scrutiny. Accountability measures mandated by the American Recovery and Reinvestment Act of 2009 have placed new demands on universities to ensure they demonstrate quality and value added outcomes of their research. "Quality" and "value" are terms commonly used to rank all types of activities, and research programs are no exception. As has been done with other publicly funded functions, academic research is entering a time of greater political accountability. In this time of increases in performance and results planning and reporting, the scientific and academic leadership are looking for ways to be more responsive, while at the same time mindful that programmatic and funding decisions must be scientifically sound, relevant and responsive to public need — a theme echoed across the U.K. and Europe.

In the absence of a national research strategy, the competition between such disparate universities in the U.S. has begun the trend of consolidating academic research into fewer but larger institutions. It could be argued that as this trend continues, the overall research enterprise loses out. Furthermore the need for universities to use their own resources to subsidize sponsored research contributes to the consolidation of university research into fewer but larger institutions, and benefits those who have larger endowments. It seems likely that a number of universities at the margins will not be able to bear the costs of supporting competitive research efforts. Cuts in state support to universities are not evenly distributed when viewed as a percentage of the overall budget. Many will not have the internal funds necessary to support their academics at a level where they can be competitive for external funds, without which there is essentially no ability to maintain a significant research enterprise.

The central problem, then, which brings the future of academic research into question, is inadequate funding. Simply put, the current size and scope of the academic research enterprise cannot be sustained in the absence of additional financial support. Furthermore, research is among the most complicated aspects of higher education. There are many points of possible failure, making it more difficult for institutions to adjust and succeed. The financial resources of an institution, if high, will tend to favour its structural competitive advantage over an institution dependent on public resource.

On the face of it, it would appear that there are different issues in America to those seen in the U.K. and Europe, with not only major concerns over the approach to funding of research, but also more widely to what appears to the a lack of strategy moving forward. However, there are similarities too. Like the U.K. and the E.U., there is a rising level of accountability. Public funding bodies are ensuring that the research they fund contributes to solving the strategic challenges that are faced. Likewise, the nature of these challenges results in new partnerships being formed, across universities, disciplines and across sectors.

The impact on American universities is clearly profound. With uncertain funding streams and increased global competition, many are facing difficult choices about their future direction. Research continues to be cross-subsidized from other activities, directly affecting the ability of universities to invest strategically. Without a grand unifying plan in sight, somehow a new, more sustainable direction must be found.

CONCLUDING THOUGHTS

In drawing my contribution to a close I want to recap and reflect on the direction in which research-intensive universities are heading. From the three groups that I have cited, the U.K., the E.U., and the U.S., I hope it has been clear that there are many similarities, in particular the expectation by funders of impact from research, the expectation of interdisciplinary approaches to pre-identified themes and the need to engage with industry and other partners outside HE. However, there are also many differences. The lack of a coherent approach in the U.S. compared to a clear direction of travel (like it or not) in the U.K. Increasing funding for research in the E.U., compared to a more austere approach in the U.S. and U.K. These positions become starker as we find ourselves living in a time of economic austerity, where any amount of funding cannot be guaranteed. We are also all living in a time of global competition that is continuing to shape the response of governments and individual universities.

It is clear that we must all strive to demonstrate impact and value as a necessary consequence of spending public money. However, we must also strive to lead the agenda and ensure that, as individual universities, we are able to shape our own futures. Of course this is easier said than done. And even harder than this is the challenge for universities to retain some of their original identities and original raisons d'être in amongst the demands for more impact and a more immediate product. And that challenge is of course to strike the right balance between "Blue Sky" research, where results and impact cannot be predicted, and applied research, that is driven by utility and often by industry. Getting this balance wrong, either one way or the other, will be to the detriment of the sustainability of the research base and to society at large. It is clear that we must all work hard to diversify funding streams so that we can shape our universities as we see fit. The HE sector is being driven in a clear way by the funders and models that they implement. As has been demonstrated, the approach of research funders can be characterized by increasingly becoming more top down, programmatic and with a clear focus on grand challenges that can only be solved by forming collaborative partnerships between disciplines, institutions and industry.

REFERENCES

Department for Business Innovation and Skills (2011). *Funding for EU Research and Innovation from 2014: A UK Perspective.*
https://www.gov.uk/government/uploads/system/uploads/attachment_data/file/32484/11-901-funding-eu-research-innovation-from-2014.pdf
Department for Business Innovation and Skills (2011). *Innovation and Research Strategy for Growth.*
http://www.official-documents.gov.uk/document/cm82/8239/8239.pdf
European Commission (2011). *Horizon 2020 — The Framework programme for Research and Innovation.*
http://ec.europa.eu/research/horizon2020/index_en.cfm
FP7 (2007-2013). European Commission: Community Research and Development Information Service. http://cordis.europa.eu/home_en.html
National Research Council (2012). *Research Universities and the Future of America: Ten Breakthrough Actions Vital to Our Nation's Prosperity and Security*, Washington,

D.C: The National Academies Press.
http://www.nap.edu/catalog.php?record_id=13396
Research Councils U.K. (2011). *Strategic Vision.*
http://www.rcuk.ac.uk/Publications/policy/Pages/StratVision.aspx
The Research Universities Futures Consortium (2012). *The Current Health and Future Well-Being of the American Research University.*
http://www.researchuniversitiesfutures.org/
RIM_Report_Research%20Future's%20Consortium%20.pdf
The Russell Group (2009). *The concentration of research funding in the UK: driving excellence and competing globally.*
http://www.russellgroup.ac.uk/uploads/Concentration-of-research-funding.pdf
Universities U.K. (2010). *The future of research.*
http://www.universitiesuk.ac.uk/highereducation/Documents/2010/TheFuture-OfResearch.pdf

CHAPTER 11

Fault Lines in the Compact: Higher Education and the Public Interest in the United States

Ronald J. Daniels, Phillip M. Spector and Rebecca Goetz

The research university stands as one of the most admired and emulated of American institutions.

Year after year, American universities dominate the international rankings of institutions of higher education. The demand for places in American programs continues to grow, and the quality of matriculating students continues to improve. The prospects for students graduating from American universities continue to strengthen, as measured along dimensions as varied as enhanced lifetime earnings, life expectancy and quality of civic participation. And the research contributions of American universities continue to command scientific recognition and fuel economic innovation and life-saving discoveries.

And yet, in spite of these achievements, the relationship between government and the university in the United States is, in the minds of many commentators, fraught. The points of conflict are many: federal governmental failure to protect the real value of research investment; marked reductions in state support for public universities; non-trivial university tuition increases that have raised vexing issues of access and affordability (and triggered threats of governmental intervention); and highly publicized and acrimonious governance conflicts that have pitted publicly appointed state governing boards against university leaders (on subjects ranging from program priorities, to the use of technology, to cost control and pricing).

There is no gainsaying that throughout American history the role of the university has commanded the attention and intervention of government.

This is to be expected. Under the neo-classical framework, government has a central role to play in addressing a host of market failures involving higher education and in ensuring the Jeffersonian promise of equality of opportunity.

And indeed, over the years, governments and universities had forged a robust and dynamic compact in the United States. Public institutions and instruments have shaped the growth of the modern American university: The federal government has invested over $500 billion in academic research and $1.7 trillion in student aid since 1970, has created and financed a range of grant and loan programs aimed at subsidizing student participation, and oversees a vast system of regional accreditation that seek to address quality and related concerns. State governments — in many cases, aided by federal legislation and support — have founded state public universities and actively supported their activities, providing direct appropriations to institutions as well as grant aid to students. At the same time, our universities have returned countless benefits to the communities in which they reside, anchoring and accelerating the economies in the surrounding areas, serving as an engine for upward mobility and economic advancement, and birthing countless world-altering discoveries for the betterment of humanity.

It is against this backdrop of decades of constructive collaboration, one that has conferred staggering benefits on American society, that the current malaise between university and government is so disturbing.

In this paper, we explore the state of the compact between the government and the university in the United States, and the prospects for constructive reengagement. In the first part of the paper, we discuss the rationales for government intervention in the higher education sector. In part II, we briefly sketch the history of the compact between the government and universities, and the ways in which government has shaped and supported the flourishing of the sector. In Part III, we canvass the sources of the contemporary conflict between the government and higher education, which we argue has been exacerbated by the economic and social impact of the Great Recession. In Part IV, we identify several ideas for institutional and policy reform, while also locating these questions in a broader debate about inter-generational equity and the capacity of government to invest in our future. We argue that, although there is scope for more creative use of policy instruments to redress some of the current tensions between the state and research universities, ultimately a broader and more systematic set of interventions aimed at redressing rising inequality in the United States is necessary.

THE ROLE OF GOVERNMENT

The market for higher education is beset by several frailties — public goods, human capital market failures, information asymmetries and equitable concerns — that demand government intervention.

To be sure, the state has not always produced efficacious regulation in this domain. And yet, this should not be seen as an argument for an end to government's role altogether. One must instead ask how it can intervene in a targeted manner that responds to the risks posed by institutional actors, so the public can obtain the benefits of private initiative, investment and ingenuity in this area without distortion of incentives or danger of abuse.

Public Goods and Positive Externalities. Some share of the benefits of post-secondary education — promotion of research and discovery, inculcation of civic values and economic growth — accrue to the public good and not to individual students alone. This means that without government support, the education and research activities associated with higher education will be under-supplied from a social welfare perspective. Take, for example, basic research activity. Without supplementary funding, it is unlikely that private parties will dedicate a significant amount of their resources to such research, which has grounded much of the industrial innovation and other achievements whose benefits extend far beyond the university itself. Columbia University Provost Emeritus Jonathan Cole estimated that "perhaps as many as 80% of new industries are derived from discoveries at American universities." The widespread social benefits of these research activities provide a clear rationale for government investment.

Wholly apart from its contributions to basic research, universities are among the most powerful engines for economic growth and development. Higher educational attainment has been connected to reduced crime rates, lower unemployment rates and reductions in public spending on assistance and social support programs. One recent study shows that an additional year of average university level education in a country raises national output by a remarkable 19%. The university is also a powerful source for upward social economic mobility for its students and their families (this rationale overlaps with the equity rationale below). For all of these reasons, the state has a prevailing interest in nurturing the sector.

A range of intangible benefits can also be traced to higher education. For example, volunteerism and voting rates are higher among those with bachelor's degrees than high school graduates. Universities also play a central role in advancing civic culture and community cohesion. These non-pecuniary benefits to society provide yet another powerful set of rationales for government involvement.

Imperfections in Human Capital Markets. The state also has a strong interest in intervening in higher education to right failures in human capital markets that constrain the ability of students to finance their education.

Banks are often reluctant to provide private loans to students, due to their inability to secure collateral in the students' prospective human capital, and their difficulty of anticipating students' likelihood of academic success and future economic prospects. In the best of circumstances, banks will charge a risk premium that will often price students — who are reluctant to accumulate substantial amounts of debt at such an early age — out of higher education. This is a particular challenge for students of lower socioeconomic backgrounds, leading to distributional effects. All of these problems lead to suboptimal private lending in higher education, and a need for government intervention to compensate for these failures by reducing the amount students need to borrow.

Information Asymmetries. Since post-secondary education is inherently optional, and potential post-secondary students are of an age where they should be regarded as being capable of making rational and informed decisions regarding the future course of their education, the government should perhaps be wary of exercising a paternalistic role in shaping those decisions. However, there may be some modest scope for government intervention to resolve information asymmetries between students and post-secondary institutions. Accordingly, the state has a role in requiring those institutions that receive public funds to publish information respecting the quality of the entering class, the quality and character of the academic program, student completion rates, faculty research activity and career placement patterns for graduates.

Equity. Given the considerable role that institutions of higher education play as gatekeepers to economic opportunity and professional advancement, the representation of various communities in these institutions and the social consequences of admissions policies must be taken seriously. Most universities are committed to recruiting the strongest possible student body, and the admissions decision is typically merit driven. Even so, universities present a unique capability to remedy persistent and self-perpetuating ethnic or socio-economic imbalances in higher education and society at large. States have an interest in supporting and preserving the unique role of universities as a force for equal opportunity for its citizens, and making sure that all citizens are given a chance to obtain the skills and training that are essential to upward mobility in our knowledge-based society.

THE FORGING OF THE COMPACT

For each of these reasons and in each of these ways, the state has played a fundamental role in shaping higher education in the United States. The compact we know today was forged over time across the sweep of American history: The university did not always act in response to the needs of the state, and the state did not always act in the interest of the university. However, over time, history reflected a dawning recognition of the two institutions' indispensable relationship.

Even before the American Revolution, colonial governments dedicated transportation taxes, sales taxes and other sources of revenue to the founding and maintaining of a college in each colony. The methods and types of institutions varied from state to state, but there was, even then, a commitment to supporting the provision of higher education, and a belief that education was a fundamental state interest.

The relationship only grew stronger during the first century of the republic. One key moment in this relationship occurred in 1862, when Congress enacted the Morrill Land Grant Act, through which the federal government would provide land grants to certain eligible states to support collegiate programs in "useful arts" such as agriculture, mechanics and military instruction. Over the next 30 years, Congress would expand the sweep of the Morrill Act to the entire nation. These statutes set a powerful precedent: they expanded undergraduate colleges into the university model across the United States with multiple programs beyond the liberal arts, and they enlisted the states in an effort to make higher education accessible to groups outside the privileged elites, making them available to the working classes of the period.

The first half of the 20th century saw the emergence of state legislatures as major players in their own right in the funding of higher education: states in the Midwest and the West in particular used tax revenues to fund and grow universities into the tens of thousands of students. The levels and types of support varied considerably from state to state. California, for example, made access to education a priority and charged no tuition, while other states saw higher education as a privilege and kept tuition at public institutions higher. Nonetheless, this area saw the expansion of state support that would eventually lead to the creation of renowned public research universities that operate at the level of private institutions while working to serve a larger segment of the state's population.

The federal government would stake out an even more influential and striking role in expanding access to higher education with the GI Bill in 1944, which guaranteed up to four years of tuition, fees and a stipend at a U.S. institution of higher education in exchange for service in the U.S. military. By 1947, veterans accounted for 49% of college admissions. The increases in enrolments spurred by the GI Bill and continuing through the 50s and 60s led to the acceptance of enrolment-based funding at the state level, allowing public universities to absorb the new students without dramatically increasing tuition levels. The federal government, concerned about the growth of diploma mills and looking to protect veterans and taxpayer dollars, also began making eligibility for funds contingent on accreditation. This program laid the foundation for increasing access and affordability through portable student grants, which would become one of the most important forms of federal support for higher education in the next half of the century.

Soon after the GI bill, two documents set the modern trajectory for the federal government's involvement in U.S. higher education for the next 50 years, one on the issue of research support, the other on funding: Vannevar Bush's Science: The Endless Frontier in 1945 argued for the essential role of federal support for basic research, using competitive grants to universities. Over the next several decades, a host of federal agencies would harness the research talent at universities to create what Clark Kerr would later call the "Federal Grant University" — about 20 institutions received almost 80% of federal research funds. Support for university research is still one of the federal government's most important avenues of support for higher education.

At the same time, the Truman Commission Report on Higher Education chronicled fundamental concerns with equity and access in higher education. Among its influences, the Truman Report would lay the groundwork for future financial aid policies. One of the most historic steps along this path at the federal level was the passage of the Higher Education Act of 1965, and then the amendments to it in 1972, which established direct grants and loans to students. The Basic Educational Opportunity Grant, later renamed the Pell Grant, remains a major source of aid for low-income students. These grants are portable, allowing students to become consumers of education and forcing institutions to compete for their aid dollars. The federal government has continued to raise the maximum grant amount, and spending on the program more than doubled between 2000 and 2010. Many state governments also took steps in this period to make higher education more affordable and accessible to a significant portion of the population through appropriations to institutions and low tuition.

FAULT LINES AND THE GREAT RECESSION

And yet, despite these energetic state interventions in higher education, fault lines have emerged in the relationship in recent years.

One area of very real tension concerns the level of government financial support for higher education. The many reasons for the state to invest in higher education remain as true today as they did in earlier times (perhaps even more so given the rise of the human capital economy), and yet the willingness and/or capacity of government to invest in higher education has waned. On average, state level support for higher education has declined 25% in the last decade, while, in many states, the cuts have been steeper still (National Research Council, 2012). What is more, the level of state support for higher education is significantly lower than it was a few decades ago: in 1990 states spent an average of $9,100 per student on higher education, while in 2011 the number dropped to $6,700 per student, both in 2011 dollars.

A similar (although softer) trajectory can be seen in federal research investment: After the dramatic doubling of government investment in NIH research during the Clinton administration, the real value of support has declined almost 20% in the last decade. As a consequence, the average age of a first RO1 research award has risen steadily, while the success rate for applications has steadily declined. The consequences of this government withdrawal have been profound for our universities and their research mission, as well as the status of the United States as the world's leader in research (and industrial competitiveness): As other countries continue to increase their research expenditures, the U.S. share of world R&D expenditures has declined significantly. All of this has occurred at the precise moment when universities with academic health centres in the United States are also wrestling with significant changes to health care models and declining clinical revenues, making it even more difficult for them to weather these financial shocks.

Another fault line has surfaced around issues of cost and affordability. Universities have raised tuition significantly in recent years: While median family income rose 147% from 1982 to 2007, tuition and fees rose 439% over the same period. The share of income families spend on higher education has risen for decades, and the rise has been sharpest for low-income families, who need to spend about half of their income to send a child to college. Despite efforts by several of the leading American research universities to augment financial aid, and the expansions to Pell Grants and other federal aid programs instituted by the Obama administration, there has been a declining level of participation by low- and moderate-income students in four-year university programs. In 2010, the Advisory Committee on Student Financial Assistance presented a report to Congress on increasing inequality in college access: While total college enrolment had increased over the past few decades, their study found that between 1992 and 2004 enrolment rates of academically qualified low-income high school graduates in four-year colleges decreased from 54% to 40% (Advisory Committee on Student Financial Assistance, 2010).

Still another area of tension has concerned value and innovation. Empirically, the benefits to higher education have clearly been shown (particularly in relation to lifetime earnings and risks of unemployment). However, many have begun to question the objective and mission of a university, and the pedagogical approach of universities, and inserted themselves into academic decision-making. Universities are increasingly viewed as engines of job creation and wealth. More than ever, their essential role as wellsprings of citizenship and social welfare is overlooked. Governors have sought to scale back low-enrolment programs or fields with less perceived utility post-graduation, such as the humanities, and have sought to tie funding to job placement and similar metrics. Critics have also pointed to declining completion rates as evidence that universities may not be accomplishing their fundamental education mission, as well as recent studies that reach a similar conclusion. One recent analysis by sociologists Richard Arum and Josipa Roksa (2011) maintains that

45% of students had effectively made no progress in critical thinking, complex reasoning and writing in their first two years at U.S. colleges and universities. (Notably, two recent studies by the Council for Aid to Education contradict that finding, arguing that there is a significant improvement in students' performance between their freshman and senior years.)

Each of these concerns might have continued to vex the relationship between the state and higher education, but would not have commanded the policy salience they do today, if not for the devastating impact of the Great Recession. In 2008 and 2009, the U.S. labour market lost 8.8 million jobs and total wealth declined by $15 trillion. The median household income fell to its lowest level since 1996, meaning that the recession effectively wiped out the middle class income gains for the last 15 years. The effects of the contraction on the higher education sector have been profound and varied. At one level, the Great Recession placed enormous financial stress on the states' fiscal capacity and constricted their ability to maintain their investments in higher education. At another level, the Great Recession impaired the ability of many families who suffered wealth and income reductions to provide the level of anticipated support for their children's enrolment in university. Finally, universities themselves were directly buffeted by the effects of the Great Recession in the form of significant decreases in private donations, endowment reductions and increased demands for financial aid support.

And although the country has started to recover from the Great Recession, the challenges surrounding the federal government's fiscal pressures continue to impact the sector. For instance, federally mandated sequestration will reduce NIH funding by another 7.8%, the largest cut in its history. The price of attending a four-year public university in the United States will have increased 27% above the rate of inflation across the last five years, even though average family incomes will have actually declined during that period even when adjusted for inflation (Oliff, Palacios, Johnson & Leachman, 2013). Colleges are downsizing: some have cut as many as 200 academic programs, while also slashing funds for instructional staff, library and student services. More and more students are choosing to enrol first in community colleges instead of four-year schools, but these schools also face significant budget cuts. 69% of Americans now feel that college is unaffordable and that there are highly qualified students who cannot gain access to a university education (Immerwahr, Johnson et al., 2010).

All of this in turn has fuelled mounting concern and heightened rhetoric on the part of government officials regarding questions of rising costs, declining completion rates and the value of a college education. State officials in Wisconsin, Virginia, Montana and others have all attacked universities for rising costs and have imposed tuition freezes, even as state spending declines. Florida Governor Rick Scott has proposed charging different rates of tuition for different majors in an effort to drive students towards STEM fields, saying: "If I'm going to take money from a citizen to put into education, then I'm going to take that money to create jobs." North Carolina Governor Patrick McCrory has argued that there is no value to the humanities, and said: "If you want to take gender studies that's fine. Go to a private school, and take it… But I don't want to subsidize that if that's not going to get someone a job." And President Obama has made college affordability one of the centrepieces of his second term agenda, emphasizing that government "can't just keep on subsidizing skyrocketing tuition," and even suggesting that universities would need to keep costs down or lose federal funding.

NEW APPROACHES AND ENDURING QUESTIONS

It may be tempting to dismiss many of these tensions as cyclical, and believe that when the economy rebounds, states will reinvest, tensions will cool, and the earlier equilibrium of constructive collaboration will return.

However, there are reasons to believe that these recent tensions reflect deeper structural issues, and the Great Recession has raised fundamental and vexing questions surrounding the strength, durability and content of the compact between state and university that command attention and resolution.

At one level, addressing the conflict will require renewed federal and state efforts in devising innovative and thoughtful regulatory approaches.

For instance, we must explore new approaches to financial assistance that do a more effective job of addressing market failures and aligning resources to areas of need. One promising set of options that has won favour in recent years involves income-contingent loan repayment programs, through which students pay what they can up front, and contract with the government to defer any remaining payments until they graduate and are working. At that time, they pay any deferred fees as a fixed percentage of their income, an obligation enforced through the tax code. The loans address concerns of liquidity, enforceability and complexity in the current system and the daunting fear of students that they will not be able to pay back loans. This approach to student debt has been popular in Britain and Australia for years; although the United States has offered an income contingent plan for federal loans, it is not widely used by students, many of whom are not aware of their repayment options or are put off by the program's complexity. The Obama administration has taken steps to simplify the process and make information more available to borrowers, and the administration's proposed 2014 budget included an expansion of the option to all borrowers, eliminating the income caps and other barriers that currently make some students ineligible.

We can also do a better job of addressing the scope of states to undermine the U.S. government's expenditure of funds through the opportunistic substitution of federal for state funds. As one example, the 2009 federal stimulus created a $48.6 billion State Fiscal Stabilization Fund that provided direct formula-based grant aid to states to advance essential education reforms. However, 23 states cut spending on higher education in the first year that they received the federal funds. And six of those states slashed spending on higher education while increasing their total state spending, suggesting that rather than using stimulus funds to offset necessary cuts, the grant allowed them to divert education spending elsewhere (Cohen, 2010). We need to explore methods of federal funding that limit the opportunities for this substitution, including rewards to states that increase their spending, directives to states to maintain certain levels of investment to receive federal funds, or the provision of funds to states through competitions that are keyed to appropriate criteria rather than formulas.

And we should seek policy tools to redress the widening gap between the magnitude of state investment in, and state regulation of, higher education. Often, states will provide relatively little in the way of investment in its higher education system, but involve themselves extensively in the internal affairs of its universities. For example, the University of Colorado receives only 4% of its budget from the state (the average public university received about 20%), and finds itself the target of significant and obtrusive regulations and intervention. The state approves and reviews all academic programs, establishes admissions standards and prescribes standards for construction and capital improvement. It is time to start a conversation about the importance of parity in the scope of funding and intervention. This could include incentives for states to withdraw from governance in situations where they have a *de minimis* stake in operational support, or even a national conversation to develop norms and expectations for state regulation in a sector under strain.

And, yet, universities also must shoulder their share of the burden for addressing the tensions in higher education. The call has gone out for universities to reduce tuition and control costs, and they must respond with purpose. Of course, the precise cause of rising costs in higher education is a matter of some debate. One theory blames rising costs on stagnating productivity, and says it is difficult for a labour-intensive industry such as education to substitute capital for labour, and so, as wages rise, so inevitably do costs. Another theory, proposed by Howard Bowen (1980), argues that universities' principal goals are excellence, influence and prestige, and they are prepared to spend whatever is necessary to achieve these goals — in particular, as revenues increase, from tuition, endowments and donations, so unavoidably will expenditures and costs. William Bowen (2012) argues that there are inefficiencies too fundamental to how universities are structured to be easily resolved, including fixed costs such as specialized laboratories and faculty with highly specialized talents.

Whatever the cause, universities cannot remain unstirred much longer to the changes roiling the industry around them. These changes include not only the enormous financial strain in the U.S. economy, with the accompanying calls for higher education to reduce tuition and control costs. It also involves the manifold changes occasioned by the information age: Higher education is famously one of the few industries that until now have managed largely to hold at bay the disruptive and potentially transformative effects of technological development in the information age. Universities have still largely unexplored the opportunities of this age, ones with the capacity not only to reshape and reduce administrative costs and improve services to students, but also expand mission and reach, augment revenue and reshape pedagogy in ways we have never seen before.

And yet, in truth, all of the above approaches can only take us so far. The problems we face are broader than only higher education, and cannot be solved by higher education policy standing alone.

The Great Recession exposed in a profound way the weakening of the middle class in America. Low- and middle-income families were hit the hardest by the downturn, and they have been the slowest to recover. Families in high-poverty areas lost the highest percentage of their wealth and were the most likely to be unemployed during the recession. According to a recent report from the Russell Sage Foundation, Americans are now less socially mobile than the citizens of a number of other countries around the world. A middle-class upbringing is no longer a guarantee of lifetime success, with a third of Americans raised in the middle class falling below the middle class as adults.

For most of U.S. history, higher education was one of the most powerful mechanisms for social mobility in the nation, and served as a powerful counterforce to rising stratification. However, caught in a spiral of rising tuition and declining state investment, compounded by the fiscal effects of the Great Recession, the capacity of higher education to play this role is itself in jeopardy. The historic rate of growth in educational attainment has slowed — the percentage of those under 34 with a bachelor's degree has remained virtually unchanged for decades — and the gap in enrolment rates between students from low- and high-income families has risen steadily over the last 40 years. Only 11% of students from the bottom quintile ever graduate, compared to 53% from the top. Our education system is not helping low-income students reach the same attainment as their higher-income peers.

As economists Claudia Goldin and Lawrence Katz (2008) argue, these trends in educational attainment deeply compound the problems of income equality across the American economy. The Great Recession has only widened this gap, with the college educated recovering more quickly and bearing less of the brunt of the crisis. Those with a college degree actually gained 187,000 jobs from December 2007 to January 2010, while those with high school diplomas or less lost 5.6 million jobs in this period, and another 230,000 during the recovery (Carnevale, Javasundera & Cheah, 2012). More than half of the jobs created during the recent recovery from the recession have gone to workers with a college degree or higher, even though they make up only a third of the labour force.

One of the principal ways to narrow this divide is to invest in pre-K, K-12 education, higher education, training and technology — in short, invest in tomorrow. And yet, the government is ill equipped to take these steps. There is perhaps no greater impediment to addressing the endemic problems plaguing society than the crushing growth in entitlement spending (particularly health care). This fiscal burden is subverting the scope for federal and state investment in education and starving the country of the investments that — at each stage in U.S. history — have nourished a cycle of innovation and growth that has accrued to the benefit of all. The current approach to retirement funding is nothing less than a dramatic inter-generational transfer. To take only one example, the Medicare funding formulas mean that male recipients only paid a dollar for every three received. Because they live longer, the discrepancy is even greater for women.

Without meaningful reform of these sorts of spending pattern, we are tilting our priorities toward consumption at the expense of investment. We are, simply put, forfeiting our capacity to invest in the next generation, in their capacity to create and converse and experiment and innovate. Ironically, universities are better positioned than most to drive the innovations that will bend the health care cost curve, at the very moment when this is leading to disinvestment. Unless and until the core issue of inter-generational equity and, more specifically, entitlement reform is addressed squarely by government, the likelihood that either the federal or state governments will be able to resume their vanguard role in ensuring the next stage of the great American experiment with higher education is dim indeed.

CONCLUSION

Since the founding of the Republic, universities have been a powerful force for upward social mobility and forward economic progress, just as the state has been a powerful force in building and shaping the modern university. For much of our history, this cooperative arrangement has been at the heart of the American experiment and the American dream.

Nevertheless, it is the thesis of this paper that that several forces are conspiring to test the stability and durability of this compact, and pose significant risks to the strength of American higher education and to the country as a whole. To some degree, we believe that the preservation of the compact requires a willingness of government and university to adopt more innovative instruments to ensure alignment of universities with well-established public goals. It also requires energetic public leadership that is aimed at preserving (and, indeed, enhancing) the level of state investment in higher education given the sundry public benefits associated with this sector. But, most significantly, we believe that the durability of this compact cannot be isolated from the broader debates and concerns over growing inequality in the country (which were given particular salience by the wrenching economic losses associated with the Great Recession). Simply put, in the absence of a vigorous and systematic approach to the challenge of income equality in a human capital society, the more likely it is that universities will be saddled with the symbolic burdens associated with the failure to live up to the Jeffersonian ideals of equal opportunity. This is a lesson that stakeholders in modern research universities ignore at their peril.

REFERENCES

Advisory Committee on Student Financial Assistance. (2010). The Rising Price of Inequality: How Inadequate Grant Aids Limits College Access and Persistence. Washington, DC.

Alvarez, L. (2012). Florida May Reduce Tuition for Select Majors. *The New York Times*, 9 December. http://www.nytimes.com/2012/12/10/education/florida-may-reduce-tuition-for-select-majors.html.

Arum, R. & Roksa, J. (2011). *Academically adrift: Limited learning on college campuses.* Chicago, IL: University of Chicago Press.

Atkinson, R. D., Ezell, S., Giddings, V., Steward, L. A., & Andes, S. M. (2012). *Leadership in Decline: Assessing U.S. International Competitiveness in Biomedical Research.* The Information Technology and Innovation Foundation website http://www.itif.org/publications/leadership-decline-assessing-us-international-competitiveness-biomedical-research.

Baum, S., Kurose, C., & McPherson, M. (2013). An Overview of American Higher Education. *The Future of Children 23*, 17-39.

Baum, S., Ma, J. & Payea, K. (2010). Education Pays, 2010: The Benefits of Higher Education for Individuals and Society. *Trends in Higher Education Series*. College Board Advocacy & Policy Center.

Blumenstyk, G., Stratford, M. & Supiano, B. (2012, 5 February). "Obama Aims to Make Colleges Cut Costs". *Chronicle of Higher Education*. http://chronicle.com/article/Obama-Aims-to-Make-Colleges/130673/.

Bowen, H.R. (1980). *The costs of higher education: How much do colleges and universities spend per student and how much should they spend?* San Francisco, CA: Jossey-Bass.

Bowen, W. G. (2012). "The 'cost disease' in higher education: is technology the answer?" *The Tanner Lectures*, Stanford University.

Carnevale, A.P., Jayasundera, T. & Cheah, B. (2012). The College Advantage: Weathering the Economic Storm. Georgetown University Center on Education and the Workforce.

Cohen, J. (2010). The State Fiscal Stabilization Fund and Higher Education Spending in the States: Part 1 of 4. Issue Brief. New America Foundation.

Daniels, R. J. & Trebilcock, M. J. (2005a). Towards a New Compact in University Education in Ontario. In F. Iacobucci & C. Tuohy (Eds.), *Taking Public Universities Seriously*. Toronto, ON: University of Toronto Press.

Daniels, R. J. & Trebilcock, M. J. (2005b). *Rethinking the Welfare State: The Prospects for Government by Voucher*, London, UK: Routledge.

Goldin, C. & Katz, L. F. (2008). *The Race Between Education and Technology*. Cambridge, MA: The Belknap Press of Harvard University Press.

Immerwahr, J., Johnson, J., Ott, A. & Rochkind, J. (2010). Squeeze play 2010: Continued public anxiety on cost, harsher judgments on how colleges are run. *Public Agenda*. http://www.publicagenda.org/pages/squeeze-play-2010.

Kiley, K. (2013, 6 May). Another Liberal Arts Critic. *Inside Higher Ed*. http://www.insidehighered.com/news/2013/01/30/north-carolina-governor-joins-chorus-republicans-critical-liberal-arts.

National Research Council. (2012). *Research Universities and the Future of America: Ten Breakthrough Actions Vital to Our Nation's Prosperity and Security*. Washington DC: National Academies Press.

Oliff, P., Palacios, V., Johnson, I. & Leachman, M. (2013). *Recent Deep State Higher Education Cuts May Harm Students and the Economy for Years to Come*. Center on Budget and Policy Priorities.

Thelin, J. R. (2004a). *A History of American Higher Education*. Baltimore, MD: The Johns Hopkins University Press.

Thelin, J. R. (2004b). Higher Education and the Public Trough: A Historical Perspective. In E. P. St. John & M. D. Parsons (Eds.), *Public Funding of Higher Education*. Baltimore, MD: The Johns Hopkins University Press.

CHAPTER 12

The Challenge of Transition in Public Higher Education

Linda P.B. Katehi

INTRODUCTION

The American Land-Grant University was established in 1863 when President Abraham Lincoln signed the Morrill Act into law. Setting aside federal land in the individual states for public universities, the idea behind the Act was to make higher education accessible for the first time to the broader American population in a concentrated effort to help the nation grow and develop economically.

Five years later, the University of California was created in Berkeley. Today it is one of the largest and best public university systems in the world, with 10 campuses up and down the state, five health systems, 234,000 students, 19,000 faculty, 190,000 staff, 1.6 million alumni and an annual budget of about $20 billion. President Lincoln's vision, all the more remarkable because he acted on it during one of the worst crises in American history — the Civil War was raging at the time — has come spectacularly true. Today, however, that vision is in jeopardy for a variety of reasons, and university administrators have had to search for creative and unconventional ways to meet this serious challenge.

THE CALIFORNIA STORY

The system of higher education developed in California began to take firm shape in 1960 when Gov. Pat Brown signed into law the California Master Plan, which was developed in large part by Clark Kerr, the former UC Berkeley chancellor who by that time was president of the entire UC system. The plan envisioned higher education for everyone in California who wanted it, with UC accepting the top eighth of eligible students, California State University the top third and the rest to be admitted by the California Community Colleges. In many ways, it was the perfection of Lincoln's vision in the Morrill Act, and the Master Plan has served the people of California remarkably well. It helped propel the state's economy into one of the largest and most dynamic in the world, and today 33% of UC undergraduates come from the community colleges and 25% of UC's graduate students enter from CSU.

However, with declining public investment in higher education occurring throughout our nation, we have been forced to come up with new ways to keep higher education affordable and accessible. Our ability to continue educating our young people and growing and enhancing our economy are dependent on our success.

Anyone associated with higher education knows of the profound changes that have been sweeping through the halls of The Academy, and this is particularly true in our public universities and colleges. The changes are primarily a response to difficult economic circumstances, which have triggered deep cuts around the nation to most public services, including higher education. For fiscal year 2012, for example, state and local funding for higher education declined 7% to $81.2 billion (State Higher Education Executive Officers Association, 2013). Similarly, per-student support declined 9% from the prior year and 150% since 1999; the current rate is less than $6,000 per student in constant dollars, the lowest level in a quarter century. By way of comparison, per student public support in 1999 was $17,000.

The reduction in public funding became most severe in the four years after the start of the so-called Great Recession that began at the end of 2007. That being said, it is important to recognize and acknowledge that the disinvestment in public higher education was under way long before this latest economic downturn. In 1987, for instance, the portion of public university revenues coming from tuition and fees was about 23%. As of 2012, the figure had more than doubled to 47% (State Higher Education Executive Officers Association, 2013). This longer-term trend can be traced to shifting budget priorities driven in large part by the changing demographic patterns in the United States.

In other words, our public universities are competing with a variety of growing demands on taxpayer funds. From increased health care costs for aging Baby Boomers and rising public employee pension obligations to growing prison and infrastructure needs, other budgetary concerns have increasingly taken precedence over higher education funding. In California, 2011 marked the first time since the initial University of California (UC) campus opened in 1869 that the total funds received by UC from student tuition and fees exceeded what it received in state aid (Gordon, 2011). Another even more sobering fact: the California general fund budget now appropriates more money for prisons than it does for the state's two flagship university systems, UC and California State University (CSU) (Anand, 2012).

Nationally, most public universities have faced challenges associated with decreasing public funding. In California, a state with a history of budget deficits, these challenges have been particularly acute.

The UC system lost about $1 billion in state funding from 2008 to 2012, forcing it to cut or eliminate whole programs, lay off staff, furlough faculty and impose repeated increases in tuition and fees.

At the same time, shifts in governance have diffused power inside UC and made it more difficult to move forward on issues and initiatives. Shared governance between the UC Board of Regents, the individual campus administration and Faculty Senate, despite the fact that smaller and smaller percentages of university faculty are tenured and members of the Senate, is one big challenge. We must also accommodate the Student Senate, Staff Assemblies, advisory boards, state and federal advisory boards and more.

As I write this, we have received some short-term financial relief because California Governor Jerry Brown's approved 2013-2014 budget has given the UC and CSU systems their first increase in state funds in four years. Governor Brown's budget appropriates an additional $250 million to both the UC and CSU systems ($125 million each, respectively).

The improved budget picture is due to passage in November 2012 of Proposition 30, which imposed temporary increases in the state sales tax and the income tax on high earners. Most observers credit California college students with helping to turn the election in Proposition 30's favour by working to register large numbers of young voters acutely aware of how the election outcome would affect the costs of their college education.

Because of legislation sponsored by California Assembly Speaker John Perez, Brown's budget also has provisions to create a new "middle-class scholarship" program. Under this measure, students with families making between $80,000-$100,000 a year qualify for a 40% tuition discount; students with families making up to $125,000 a year qualify for a 25% tuition discount; and students with families making up to $150,000 a year qualify for a 10% tuition discount. Families making less than $80,000 receive full tuition waivers through the already existing Blue and Gold opportunity program established by the UC Board of Regents in 2009.

While these new financial guarantees are positive developments, the budget outlook for California's public colleges and universities is still cause for concern. For UC, for instance, only about a fourth of the $1 billion in cuts over the past four years are being restored, even as fixed costs for employee pensions and health benefits continue to rise. Plus, the governor has tied the extra funding to a suggested freeze on tuition over the next four years, which will create new constraints on our ability to fund programs and meet the needs of our students, faculty and staff.

We face even greater challenges because of the evolving demographic makeup of our state and the effect this will have on future state investment. We have six to eight million undocumented immigrants in California, and, by 2020, the majority of the state's high school graduates will be Hispanic, with the majority of those eligible for Pell and Cal Grants. One of two babies born in California is in families eligible for Medicare or Medicaid, adding even more pressure to the state's treasury. It is not hard to see that a majority of college-eligible students will not be able to afford a higher education at our public universities and colleges.

UC Davis already is dealing with many of these challenges. Because of the many grant and scholarship programs available, 53% of our students do not pay tuition. Just under half, 48%, are the first members of their families to attend college. Only 20% of our students pay full tuition. The vast majority, 95% of our students are California residents, paying cheaper, in-state tuition and every year the number of eligible applicants increases by more than 10%.

Given this reality, the need for additional revenues is acute and UC Davis is working hard and creatively to find additional funds on a sustainable basis. Our first-ever comprehensive Campaign for UC Davis is about to reach its goal of raising $1 billion from 100,000 donors, and we will begin a new, more ambitious campaign in the near future.

UC Davis has also taken aggressive steps to improve our technology transfer capabilities.

There is a long history of public universities using research/entrepreneurial growth to address the decrease in public funding (Clark, 1998). In 1980, only 20 universities in the United States housed their own office for patenting and licensing. By the year 2000, 112 more universities had created their own patent and licensing offices, nearly a 600% growth in only 20 years (Geiger, 2006). Similarly, from 1980 to 2004, in a 24-year period, the number of patents issued to U.S. universities increased tenfold — from about 350 in 1980 to about 3,300 in 2004 (Popp Berman, 2008). While this growth is impressive, there is still room for continued expansion. According to a survey funded by Northeastern University, completed by FTI Consulting, and released at a Brookings Institution forum last November, 83% of Americans believe that higher education must innovate for the United States to maintain its global leadership (Northeastern University, 2012).

UC Davis has embraced this potential for growth by starting a new Venture Catalyst program. The program, the product of a comprehensive review of the campus' entrepreneurial potential, pools together a variety of resources from the Graduate School of Management and the local venture capital community to provide a resource to researchers who seek to bring ideas to market.

More specifically, the program provides resources to researchers on campus to improve their existing ideas and start new, well-funded, growth-centric companies. They will do this by working in concert with a variety of centres on campus to provide educational and networking opportunities for researchers to create new companies and products.

The Venture Catalyst program is focused on identifying commercially viable ideas that fall within UC Davis' Intellectual Property Claims, enabling the university to not only advance innovative ideas and inspire innovative research, but also to benefit from the commercial successes of the research it helps advance.

As contributions from the public sector decline, transferring research from the lab to the marketplace will inevitably assume a greater role if major research universities such as UC Davis are going to maintain their strong research efforts. Not only does the opportunity reaffirm the university's commitment to smart, innovative research, but it also works to disseminate these ideas to the larger world and allows the university to continue its course of strategic growth.

Another way we are dealing with declining state aid has been through the emergence of our 2020 growth initiative. The 2020 initiative, a decision reached after 16 months of extensive study and consultation with campus and regional stakeholders, puts the university on a path toward adding up to 5,000 new students by 2020. This growth will be accompanied by corresponding increases in graduate students, faculty, staff and facilities. Even with decreased public funding, measures can be taken to ensure that our campus maintains and continues its mission for excellence. While there are clear benefits for students, staff and faculty, there are also benefits for the region — UC Davis currently generates approximately $7 billion a year in regional economic activity, and provides nearly 70,000 jobs. These impacts will undoubtedly increase under the 2020 Initiative.

THE ROLE OF ONLINE LEARNING

In a much-quoted 2012 article in the *New Yorker* magazine, John Hennessy, the president of Stanford University, famously predicted "There is a tsunami coming" to higher education. Digital technology, he maintained, would transform our colleges and universities in much the same way it has revolutionized other information-based industries such as music, newspapers and book publishing (Auletta, 2012). The question we face as university and college administrators is whether we will cling stubbornly to traditional ways of delivering education to our students or position ourselves in front of the wave and successfully ride it to a new paradigm that enhances what we do and the services we offer students.

Because we are living in an age driven by information and technology, greater numbers of people are coming to the realization that they need the skills that a first-rate public research university can provide. Unfortunately, for many of the reasons discussed above and more, we cannot possibly begin to accommodate all the deserving people who want to learn the skills and knowledge that come, say, with a UC education. Unless we find ways to reach more people, they will go elsewhere and in time our relevancy will diminish.

The fierce push for more online education is indeed a building tsunami and we must not be swept away by it. There is a new industry forming that is already taking advantage of this growing demand for high-level skills and educational content as people increasingly become aware that their ability to have a good life will depend on the skills they will have and the quality of the learning they obtain.

This powerful centre of gravity is taking hold around us. It has been gaining currency at a rapid pace to compete with public universities and colleges. Although this remains a work in progress, the new online providers have learned from the mistakes and shortcomings of the past. Their content will be high quality. Much of it already is. And they understand that completion of a course of study and obtaining a degree will be crucial to this growing market of consumers who want to compete in the global economy.

We have a great many strengths as public research universities, but change at our institutions typically has occurred slowly and deliberately. If we respond to the rapidly growing demand for online education at the same pace with which we usually embrace change, we will study it, we will take our time, we will do it our way and we will be left behind.

According to the 2012 Survey of Online Learning conducted by the Babson Survey Research Group and the College Board, 6.7 million students reported taking at least one online course in the fall 2011 term, an increase of nearly 600,000 students over the previous year. This growth has occurred as overall higher education enrolments have been in decline and the vast majority of higher education institutions still do not offer a Massive Open Online Course, or a MOOC.

At UC Davis, Professor John Owens has started a MOOC, "Introduction to Parallel Computing", through Udacity. This is the first MOOC taught by a UC Davis faculty member and it has attracted more than 15,000 students from around the world. Much work needs to be done regarding course completion and how students can earn credit or certificates of completion, but the potential of such offerings is apparent by the enormous interest they have generated.

If public education leaders don't embrace a sensible and intelligent way to provide more people with the quality of teaching that we now offer in the traditional campus setting, our institutions will continue to face increasing difficulties. Each university must find the correct approach that works best for its faculty, students and staff.

At UC Davis, we held an online education summit in May in order to evaluate existing courses and consider opportunities for expansion and improvement. The vast majority of attendees generally felt that the courses that have been offered at UC Davis were impressive and well-planned, and maintained a student-centred approach. Positive attributes of the courses were noted: new opportunities for faculty innovation; additional possibilities for improving student-faculty interaction; improved flexibility in course delivery; increased access to impacted courses; and enhanced opportunities for assessment through the abundant data and sophisticated online analytics. Negatives noted at the summit included a lack of understanding of the costs in time and money for development and training; a lack of resources to ensure that students, particularly those who are unrepresented and underserved, can succeed in the digital environment; and a cumbersome course approval process.

Even as faculty and administrators at some universities are resisting the use of online teaching, the tsunami that Stanford's John Hennessy said was coming to higher education is gaining speed and moving even more powerfully than many could fully anticipate. It requires us to wisely and expeditiously develop our own products and our own markets. With the demand and the market for these types of courses likely to grow and pick up speed, the challenge becomes reacting appropriately. We must recognize the potential and appeal of online learning even as we buttress and project forward in a positive way the benefit of educating students on campus.

Better coordination with community colleges and high schools is one appealing possibility. We can offer more online courses to students planning to attend UC Davis, for instance, enabling them to graduate more quickly and spending and borrowing less to do so. Instead of relying on others to provide online content and make it available, we should embrace the idea of providing the content ourselves. Finding our own solutions is far preferable to having them imposed on us by our governing boards or by elected legislators and governors who are, understandably, responding to pressure from constituents who want the high-quality educational content we currently provide to a small portion of the public.

It is preferable to address these issues ourselves, in a deliberative, thoughtful and non-political matter, than to have solutions, however imperfect they may be, imposed on us by outside forces. So, too, must we continue to examine whether we are providing our students the best experience and the optimum environment for their success while they are enrolled in our schools and after. We know that adequate counselling and mentoring would help us improve time to degree matrixes, which in turn would enable us to reduce the actual cost and debt our students must incur to complete their degree.

THE INTERNATIONAL STORY

For higher education leaders in the United States, it is important to recognize that deep cuts to public higher education in California and the rest of the nation are in stark contrast with public funding for higher education in East Asia. While countries in Europe and individual states in the United States have either maintained or decreased funding for public higher education, nations in East Asia have continued to increase public funding for higher education (Varghese, 2010), raising questions about the United States' ability to remain economically competitive.

Japan, South Korea, Singapore, Taiwan and China are four countries that are continuing to expand their funding for public higher education (Organization for Economic Cooperation and Development, 2012).

Relative to the international community, the United States' investment in research and development as a percentage of gross domestic product (GDP) has begun to slide. For the last 30 years, public and private research and development expenditures in the United States have been between 2.5% and 2.8% of GDP (National Research Council, 2012). In contrast, Japan has increased research and development expenditures from 2.8% of GDP in 1996 to 3.3% in 2008, while South Korea has reached 3.5% of GDP (OECD, 2012). Similarly, while annual growth in research and development for the United States and the European Union hover around 5-6%, China's annual growth was an average of approximately 20% for the period from 1996 to 2007 (OECD, 2012).

While U.S. investment in research and development still remains strong, we are losing ground when it comes to historic U.S. dominance of world science and engineering. The high levels of investment made by Japan, China, Singapore and South Korea, among others, are paying off for their economies and for their schools, as the quality and international reputation of their top universities have been rising significantly.

CONCLUSION

This is an exciting time to be an active member of the public higher education academy. While there are many challenges associated with the decline in public funding, especially when the international community is taken into account, public universities can adapt and are doing so.

Institutions of higher education must maintain their historic values and integrity of purpose, but they cannot be oblivious to the changing times. To succeed, public universities must continue to do what has worked in the past, but also actively search for and embrace new solutions. We must seek alternative sources of funding when state funds run short, we must maintain a global perspective, and we must be aware of other, potentially revolutionary, ideas. In doing so, we, as university leaders, will better serve our campuses, our constituencies and — most importantly — our students.

REFERENCES

Anand, P. (2012). *Winners and Losers: Corrections and Higher Education in California.* California Common Sense. Available at: http://www.cacs.org/ca/article/44

Auletta, K. (2012). GET RICH U.: There Are No Walls between Stanford and Silicon Valley. Should There Be? *The New Yorker*, 30 Apr.

Babson Survey Research Group and the College Board (2012). *Changing Course: Ten Years of Tracking Online Education in the United States.* [pdf] Available at: http://babson.qualtrics.com/SE/?SID=SV_4SjGnHcStH5g9G5

Clark, B. (1998). *Entrepreneurial Universities: Organizational Pathways of Transition.* International Association of Universities. Paris.

Geiger, R. L. (2006). "The quest for 'economic relevance' by U.S. research universities".
Higher Education Policy, 19 (4), pp. 411-431.

Gordon, L. (2011). A First: UC Fees Exceed State Funding. *The Los Angeles Times*, 22 Aug.

National Research Council (2012). *Research Universities and the Future of America: Ten Breakthrough Actions Vital to Our Nation's Prosperity and Security.* National Academies Press. [pdf] http://www.nap.edu/catalog.php?record_id=13299

Northeastern University (2012). *Innovation In Higher Education Survey.* [pdf] http://www.northeastern.edu/innovationsurvey/pdfs/survey-results.pdf

Organization for Economic Cooperation and Development (OECD) (2012). *Education at a Glance 2012: OECD Indicators.* [pdf] http://www.uis.unesco.org/Education/Documents/oecd-eag-2012-en.pdf

Popp Berman, E. (2008). "Why did universities start patenting?: Institution-building and the road to the Bayh-Dole act". *Social Studies of Science*, 38(6), pp. 835-871.

State Higher Education Executive Officers Association (2013). *State Higher Education Finance: FY 2012.* [pdf] http://www.sheeo.org/sites/default/files/publications/SHEF-FY12.pdf

Varghese, N. V. (2010). *Institutional Restructuring of Higher Education in Asia: An Overview.* Paris: UNESCO. [pdf] http://www.rihed.seameo.org/mambo/uploadfiles/bali/ir_reform.pdf

PART IV

••••••••••••

Changing Nature and Character of Research Universities: developed countries

CHAPTER

Can the French System support competitive Research Universities?

Alain Beretz

During this symposium, we have addressed the question of the imbalance between educational need and educational capacity. Of course, this question has been asked in France. What are the answers? Are they adequate? Are they specific to the French situation or can they be used in a wider range of countries or systems?

The purpose of this paper is mainly to ask these questions, and only to suggest answers. Although based on the French situation, they might thus have a more general outreach.

A COMPLEX HISTORY THAT GAVE BIRTH TO A SPECIFIC LANDSCAPE

This chapter does not intend to give a detailed historic perspective, but only to summarize some key points in the history of the French higher education system, because it is felt that these historical specificities are important factors for understanding the present situation. For more details on the history of the French higher education system, see Musselin, 2012.

Universities

It is a paradox that French universities are a recent creation. The first universities were created in the late Middle Ages, first in Paris and Montpellier, and then in many other cities. In this respect, French universities share the same roots as the oldest, prestigious British, Italian and Portuguese ones, for example. But their history took a different turn when the Revolution abolished the universities in 1793, because of their analogies with professional guilds. The revolutionary intellectuals wanted to create a new higher education system more targeted towards professional needs.

If Napoleon created universities again in 1805, it was only as a kind of subsidiaries of a nationwide system. This introduced a centrally controlled organization, with one only identified local academic structure, the "faculté" (faculty). The local supervisor is the *recteur* (rector), a government-appointed official, who also has authority over the secondary education system ("lycées"). University professors might also teach in lycées. This system, alongside the "grandes écoles", has been in place for more than 160 years, while, at the same time, universities in other countries were progressively entering into the Humboldtian concept of a research-driven institution.

Then came the big student uprising of 1968. It led to a new law that dramatically altered the old system and provided French universities with characteristics already present in other countries. The degree of strategic and financial autonomy was increased, the governance completely modified, with, instead of the appointed rector, a president and an elected council. However, if "traditional" universities were re-founded, the historical institutions were, in many instances, fractioned into several smaller universities that lost their comprehensive character.

Grandes écoles

Specialized technical military schools existed before the Revolution. The Revolution extended this system of recruitment to all technical administration, and Napoleon enforced this system of "grandes écoles". The purpose was to provide highly qualified personnel to the administration, in defined fields such as: army, mines and bridges, water and forestry, agriculture, veterinary science, education etc.

This system has of course changed through the years, but remains very active. Some of these schools depend on the Minister of Higher Education, but many others on "technical ministries" (Agriculture, Culture, Defence, Equipment, Industry, Justice, Health, even the Prime Minister…) Clearly, research has not been the backbone of these establishments for more than two centuries.

Admission to these "grandes écoles" is by a competitive exam, supposed to provide "republican equality", while the entrance to universities is a vested, unquestionable right if you pass the "baccalauréat", the final exam in secondary schools, which is in fact considered as a university degree. For a critical and humorous look at this strange world, see Gumbel (2013).

A complex sociological and political background

G. Neave (2012) has described the dual presence of universities and "grandes écoles" as that of a "Manichean construct", with, on one side, "a higher education dispensing rigourous technical training and not so less rigorous socialization preparation to state service" and, on the other, a university "given over to the public service of providing mass higher education". Clearly, the system has led to the fact that France is almost the only country were the university is not the place where the economical or political elite is trained. On the contrary, when studying board members of the 40 companies that constitute the main French stock index, the "CAC 40", 84% were graduates from grandes écoles, and just three schools — Polytechnique, ENA and HEC — accounted for 46% of the total (Bauer *et al.*, 1997).

For a detailed sociological analysis of this phenomenon, one should refer to the works of Pierre Bourdieu, who has analysed "strategies of reproduction" that agents or groups use to implement, maintain or improve their social position and especially to his book *The state nobility*, where he focuses on the grandes écoles system as one of the major elite-building systems in France (Bourdieu, 1996). As was proposed by Monique Pinçon-Charlot and Michel Pinçon, the system facilitates the transition process from "classmates" to "caste mates" ("copains de classe puis copains de caste").

The Asterix syndrome

J.-F. Dhainaut (2008), who headed the AERES, the French national research evaluation agency, has humorously proposed that France suffers from the "Asterix syndrome" in the academic field. This "syndrome" is named after a famous comic strip character, hero of the Gallic resistance against the Roman invasion; it is characterized by the belief, held by many French, that their country needs to defend itself against the encroaching foreign (especially "anglo-saxon") cultural influence, just as Asterix fought the Roman invaders. The term indicates an inward, backward-looking way of seeing the world and is also tied up with the French obsession with a "cultural exception".

Dhainaut also thinks that this syndrome is worsened by a "double dichotomy". This dichotomy concerns the missions which constitute our core academic tasks where French universities suffer from internal competition not commonly seen in other countries: 1) for education, a competition with the "grandes écoles" which still attract the best students; 2) for research, a competition with national organizations such as CNRS, which have their own policy.

Conclusion

Elitism and exclusive education tracks are present in many countries. It is beyond the scope of this paper to discuss the relative merits of mass education vs. elite-targeted curricula. But, in most countries, the institutions that train the elite are usually universities developing a Humboldtian model, i.e. which insists on the basic importance of research in the construction of knowledge, while in France these curricula are more organized around the "selection" of brilliant young people.

This short historical summary illustrates that French governments, including in the revolutionary period, believed strongly that higher education was essential for the development of the nation, and this support is still an asset for the higher education system in this country. However Jacobinism and centralized strategies, as well as the dominance of a non-Humboldtian higher education, might be considered as detrimental for the development of world-class research universities in France. Is this a form of "Gallic syndrome", which could lead to a loss in competitivity, or can some of these characteristics be turned at our advantage? This paper proposes a few tracks to answer this question.

DEFAULTS AND PITFALLS IN THE FRENCH SYSTEM

Jacobinism is impairing autonomy

Autonomy is considered as one major factor of the competitivity of research universities. However, in France, some still see autonomy as totally contradictory with the national responsibilities of the republican institution. France's Jacobin state is based on two fundamental legal principles: vertical centrality and horizontal uniformity. Indeed, French universities already do have legal and administrative autonomy (introduced in 1970, enforced by the 1984 "Savary" law and the 2009 LRU law), but, in this country, autonomy remains a contradictory and relative notion. The strong tradition of centralized national policy is overwhelming, and much of the management is performed, or at least controlled, by central bodies.

Thus autonomous universities are still considered only as relays of national policies. They are seen more or less as monitored units, submitted to multiple and often conflicting evaluations by different bodies (Demichel, 2009).

The EUA (European University Association) has measured the autonomy of European universities in 29 countries (Estermann *et al.*, 2011). France is situated at the top of the "medium low" group of countries for organizational, financial and staffing autonomy, and in the "low" group for academic autonomy (17th in organizational autonomy, 23rd in financial, 28th in staffing, and even 29th and last place in academic autonomy!) Curiously, the low position in these rankings of French institutions is not always perceived as shameful, and has raised much less media activity (or political debate) than the rather modest ranking of French universities in highly questionable league tables such as the Shanghai Jiao Tong ranking. But this historically and politically-determined defect in autonomy could heavily impair the development of competitive research universities in France.

Elite training excludes Humboldtian values

Curricula in the "grandes écoles" highlight a series of differences with international counterparts that can be considered as major drawbacks. I can identify at least three of these differences:

Ranking the students is still considered as a major tool, instead of achievement evaluation. Admission in these schools is already through a competitive exam leading to ranking; there are usually no interviews. The question of the abrogation of the graduation ranking at the ENA (Ecole Nationale d'Administration) (at the end of the curriculum) started a major national debate in media and in political circles, that ended up…in a status quo! This means that this ranking will still prevail over interviews and profiling of candidates when hiring them for the "top" of the French administration, i.e. the three great bodies of the State: Court of Auditors, General Inspection of Finance and the State Council.

Research was, until recently, only a secondary issue in the grandes écoles. The national certification agency for engineering schools (CTI) until recently had very negative remarks for engineering schools where the ratio of engineering graduates going on towards a PhD was "too high". Indeed the rate of French engineers with a PhD is very low compared to other countries.

The role of high school ("lycées"): The high school system still has its roots in the Napoleonic system, which means that it was, in part, designed to funnel the best students towards the "grandes écoles". Therefore, pedagogical and evaluation methods are culturally much closer to the grandes écoles system than to a research-driven education paradigm.

A high number of universities

The French university landscape is very composite. In 2011 there were 340 institutions supervised by 11 different ministries, plus the private sector — 13 private (religious) universities and 70 private technical schools. Thus the ministry of higher education and research supervises only about 70% of the students (Piozin, 2012). Among those there are 81 universities, 3 technical universities and 2 national polytechnic institutes.

This high number is due both to the splitting of the historical universities in 1970, but also to the more recent founding of smaller regional universities in towns were there was no academic tradition, very often as the result of the pressure of local politicians.

Although all these universities claim excellence, the lack of academic comprehensiveness and the very heterogeneous levels of achievement in research clearly create important gaps in reputation, prestige and achievements. But, officially, all French university diplomas remain equivalent.

Specialized, disciplinary universities

The 1970 reform in universities has had many positive results. The most constructive was to introduce a new political structure that would, in theory, favour autonomy. Considering the French background, this was indeed a major improvement of this law, often named after the brilliant minister of the time, Edgar Faure. This strong incentive on autonomy is often overlooked (see above). However the major defect of this reform was to split the older universities into smaller, specialized universities; usually they were cut in two or three, for example restricted to experimental science or humanities, or law and business. This yielded universities that lacked the critical mass and transdisciplinarity that are key assets of any modern comprehensive institution.

This unjustified disciplinary specificity is not only a handicap for the students and an obstacle for research, it can also fuel a sterile and counterproductive interdisciplinary competition. For example, it leads even to the paradoxical standpoint that only universities specialized in humanities could defend this endangered section of science. A recent position paper of the League of European Universities shows precisely that the promotion of the humanities is, on the contrary, optimal in comprehensive research-intensive universities (Van den Doel *et al.*, 2012).

The university is not the main player in public research

Research in France is split between national research organisms such as CNRS or Inserm, on one hand, and the universities on the other hand. Until recently, science policy was mainly steered in these organizations' headquarters. However in recent years, the universities have constantly increased their role and visibility. Recent legal changes have sought to place the universities "at the centre of the research system". Nowadays, a majority of the research organizations' money and personnel is housed within universities. However the co-existence of differing procedures, structures or regulations makes the everyday life of the researcher rather complicated, and also blurs the visibility and the corporate image.

ADVANTAGES AND ORIGINALITIES IN THE FRENCH SYSTEM

A strong research base

When the collaboration of universities with research organizations is effective and sincere, especially through a smooth implementation of "joint laboratories", jointly supervised by both partners, this system becomes a key asset for both partners. This mechanism produces a powerful and rather flexible tool for research, including basic research budget and full-time researchers' positions; 85% of CNRS national co-publications originate in laboratories held jointly with universities. A study by Carayol and Matt (2004) has shown that combination of full-time researchers (for example, employees of CNRS or Inserm) and teach-and-research positions (university professors) in the "right" proportion within labs (approximately an equal share) induces a high performance in terms of publications.

Invest for the future: a public endowment

The "excellence initiative", the main action of the "investing for the future" call for projects, is aimed at the emergence of large academic centres, globally competitive on a worldwide scale. This major investment for French research and development was funnelled through direct competition between institutions, and judged by an international jury. In this respect, France is one of the few countries where science funding has seen a "cash boost" intended to stimulate long-term research efforts (Editorial, 2010).

Eight locations now share a grant of €7.7 billion — which they use in programs they specifically designed. The money is part of the €35 billion "Investments for the Future program" — also known as the Big Loan, because the money was raised on the financial markets — launched in 2010 to help spur the economy in the wake of the financial and economic crisis. It should be stressed that most of this money is allocated as capital, and the grantees can only spend the yearly interest. This new form of "public endowment" is very original, and makes the procedure quite different from the German *Exzellenzinitiative*, which uses a more classical granting procedure.

A strong incentive for site organization

Creating an avant-garde of 5 to 10 major universities able to attract the best researchers and students has been a key target of the French government's science and higher education policy. The plan remains controversial because it puts an end to our egalitarian tradition in higher education.

Unfortunately, our government is still convinced that one of the goals of this initiative (and one of its best indicators of success) will be the presence of French universities at a very high level in university rankings such as the Shanghai Jiao Tong rankings. Because of this "ranking syndrome" that has historically plagued the French university system, attention to these league tables has been much too high in this country, where they are unfortunately perceived by the authorities as a relevant proxy for evaluating the results of their policies.

A stronger political impact

Although there is still progress to be made, in a very stiff and traditional polit-ical society, the cause for universities is now rather popular in the Parliament, ministries etc. Many former university presidents have held key advisory posi-tions in the government or high administration. Higher education and research are now part of the debate before elections, which they were not a few years back (see, for example, Butler, 2012).

WHAT SHOULD BE DONE? — QUESTIONS TO BE ANSWERED

At this stage, are we able to answer the question in the title of this paper: "Can the French System support competitive Research Universities"? During the Glion symposium, one of our colleagues, a fine connoisseur of the French higher education system, answered to this question with a blunt, somehow provocative " No!" I proposed a more optimistic answer: "Yes, if..." Yes, French universities have assets, and they can continue to be forefront players, if, and only if, they are allowed to progress in three aspects: financial support, technical and structural support, political support.

Autonomy

Although autonomy is now a major, unquestioned condition for progress (Aghion *et al.*, 2007), French universities still have a long way to go towards autonomy. In some academic circles, the validity of this concept will trigger vio-lent debates, some even seeing university autonomy as contradictory to individ-ual academic freedom. The French tradition of universities as a public service (which I strongly support) is not, as some still try to demonstrate, an obstacle for this evolution. We should look for examples in Scandinavian countries where a highly dedicated public service has attained a very high degree of autonomy.

Financing

French universities, as a public service, depend, to a very wide extent, on pub-lic funds. Most of their workforce are public servants. Thus one of the ques-tions asked during this symposium takes a great importance: is a globally com-petitive research-intensive university sustainable on public funds? Three points might be addressed when looking at the French situation:

Quantitative aspects: Everything should be done to increase the percentage of GDP spent in higher education and research. France, with its high expec-tations, only shows an average EU performance in this field, as seen from the OECD data (OECD 2013).

Where should this increase come from? The French tradition would go for an increase of the yearly budget of universities. But other sources are possible. Student fees in France are very low: however, the student fee question is so politically hot that it might not be tackled before long.

Private donors are starting to support universities through recent foundations. But even when these foundations are successful (which is the case for the university of Strasbourg), this source of funding yields at this time only a very small percentage (1-2%) of the yearly budget.

Qualitative aspects: The "public endowment" is a very interesting mechanism that combines competitive financing with a stable situation that allows long-term planning, which is a prerequisite for a sound university strategy. France has paved the way in this field with the "investing for the future" plan.

Global image

The universities have to cast a more positive image in French society, which has, for centuries, not considered them as elite institutions. Also, we have to work in order to increase the image of our graduates, especially the PhDs. In France, only 13% of researchers working in companies are PhDs, while 52% are engineers. Clearly, the question is not to fuel a competition between two systems. The real challenge is to have everybody in this country admit (opinion leaders, journalists, parents and the students themselves) that there are numerous pathways to the top, and that a modern society should consider universities as one of its greater values.

Concentrations-mergers

One often asks if the trend towards greater concentration is desirable, inevitable — or what? Does size matter, or, on the contrary, as some like to put it, "small is beautiful"?

The French situation is a good case study of a general policy encouraging local networks, federative institutions and even mergers, such as the one we conducted in 2009. The "investissements d'avenir" financing scheme has also been designed as a strong incentive for such mergers. Research-intensive universities have been the key players in this competition. However this type of evolution still faces much opposition, especially because of the uneven geographical distribution of the "big" universities, and the fear of creating "academic deserts" or second-class universities, which both oppose the notion of a public service fostering equal access to higher education.

Our experience in Strasbourg shows that mergers or alliances are positive tools for progress. They can be powerful mechanisms to meet some of our specific challenges, such as academic fragmentation, or the blurred corporate identity of academic institutions. But they can only be successful if a strategic goal remains the main incentive. Our merger was not an opportunistic response to a call for projects; it was a deliberate, slowly matured, bottom-up initiative, which in fact first raised negative remarks from national authorities. Mergers are also not made to solve budgetary problems or to please governments and administrations; they are only successful if built upon a genuine academic ambition (Goedegebuure, 2012).

REFERENCES

Aghion, P., Dewatripont, M., Hoxby, C., Mas-Colell, A. & Sapir, A. (2007). "Why Reform Europe's Universities?" Bruegel policy brief Issue 2007/04, http://www.bruegel.org/publications/publication-detail/publication/34-why-reform-europes-universities/

Bauer, M., Bertin-Mourot, B. & Thobois, P. (1997). *Radiographie des grands patrons français: les conditions d'accès au pouvoir*. Paris Montréal, l'Harmattan.

Bourdieu, P. (1996). *The State Nobility: Elite Schools in the Field of Power*, Polity Press.

Butler, D. (2012). "A question of science. Nature quizzes the French presidential frontrunners on research policies". *Nature* 484, pp. 298–299

Carayol, N. & Matt M. (2004). "Does research organization influence academic production? Laboratory level evidence from a large European university". *Research Policy*, 33, pp. 1081–1102

Demichel, F. (2009). "L'autonomie et l'état Jacobin". Paper presented during the colloquium: Les universités au temps de la mondialisation/globalisation et de la compétition pour l'excellence, Paris, Université Paris-8, 11-13 May 2009, http://www2.univ-paris8.fr/colloque-mai/Communications/Demichel_(autonomie).html

Dhainaut, J.-F. (2008). "Universités: comment surmonter le syndrome d'Astérix?" http://www.aeres-evaluation.fr/Actualites/Actualites-de-l-agence/L-editorial-du-president-Universites-comment-surmonter-le-syndrome-d-Asterix

Editorial (2010). "In times of crisis". *Nature Structural & Molecular Biology* 17, 259.

Estermann, T., Nokkala, T. & Steinel, M. (2011). "University Autonomy in Europe II The Scorecard". Brussels, European University Association, http://www.university-autonomy.eu/countries/france/

Goedegebuure, L. (2012). "Mergers and More: The changing tertiary education landscape in the 21st century". HEIK working paper 2012/01.http://www.uv.uio.no/english/research/groups/heik/heik-working-paper-series/2012/heikwp2012_01.html

Gumbel, P. (2013). *France's got talent: the woeful consequences of French elitism*. (Kindle book); In French: *Elite academy : enquête sur la France malade de ses grandes écoles*, Denoël.

Musselin, C. (2012). "Brève histoire des universités". In Forest F., editor, *Les universités en France: Fonctionnement et enjeux*. Publications de l'Université de Rouen, pp. 13-25.

Neave, G. (2012). *The evaluative state, institutional autonomy and re-engineering higher education in Western Europe*. Palgrave Macmillan.

OECD (2013). Education at a Glance 2013: OECD Indicators, OECD Publishing. http://dx.doi.org/10.1787/eag-2013-en

Piozin, E. (2012). "L'environnement institutionnel". In Forest F., editor, *Les universités en France: Fonctionnement et enjeux*. Publications de l'Université de Rouen, pp. 27-45.

Van den Doel, H.W. *et al.* (2012). "Social sciences and humanities: essential fields for European research and in Horizon 2020". LERU advice paper, http://www.leru.org/files/publications/LERU_AP_11_SSH_Essential_fields.pdf

CHAPTER 14

Contemporary challenges for the Swiss – and the continental European – university system

Antonio Loprieno

A SLIGHT DISCOMFORT

These are very interesting times for university education at the world level, and Switzerland is indeed no exception to this generalization. The importance of higher education in our societies and our economies is being constantly stressed, universities enjoy a higher level of institutional autonomy worldwide than was the case even a few years ago, and a more intense dialogue between academia and society at large causes a higher number of stakeholders to take an interest, and sometimes even to make an investment, in our institutions. In Switzerland, the 12 research universities — a definition which includes the 10 universities supported by the Cantons and the two federal Schools of technology in Zurich and Lausanne — have generally seen their budgets increase in the last 10 years to a much higher degree than other state-funded institutions; they have gained a substantial degree of decisional autonomy from their respective political governance; and they have been the object of sometimes very substantial private donations (the energetic EPFL more than any other Swiss university, but the recent investment of CHF100 million by the UBS bank in the School of economics at the University of Zurich shows that private involvement in institutions of higher education can be seen as a more general national reflection of a global trend.

Yet, the evolution of our university system (in Switzerland as much as in its neighbouring countries) is also affected by a slight malaise, or discomfort, which I think has to do with the evolution in the understanding of what I would call the *societal mandate* of an academic institution. As our universities become richer, they also become less sanguine about their place in our society. I detect several forms of this slight malaise both within academia and in Swiss society at large:

1. The first aspect is a general contraction of the presence of *humanities and social sciences* in our academic — and frequently also social — texture. This also applies to "soft" aspects such as the involvement of universities in social and political discourse. While a move towards empirical research is indeed a general characteristic of the history of science, and therefore of the academic institutions for which science is the basic value, one cannot refrain from wondering whether the generally felt "crisis of the humanities" does not imply, at least in part, a renegotiation of the very role of the university as a mirror of society's intellectual change (and exchange).

2. The second aspect concerns what is sometimes felt to be a *utilitarian* drive in our academic environment. Partly because of an increased attention devoted to the issue of students' time-to-degree, partly because of a closer modelling of academic curricula upon the needs of the job market, partly because of increased sponsoring, a more or less broad segment of Swiss university culture feels that we may be currently betraying the mere educational function (*Bildungsauftrag*) inherent in a primarily state-funded understanding of higher education.

3. The dramatic appearance of indicators of overall institutional performance (rankings, ratings, etc.), reliable or unreliable, legitimate or illegitimate as they may be, has underlined the primacy of research in global *academic competition*. A certain number of university stakeholders feel that focusing on the empirically measurable performance of an educational institution automatically implies devoting a lesser attention to teaching, and generally speaking to the "soft", more impalpable and culturally-driven aspects of university education.

4. The last form of malaise is specifically continental and concerns the philosophical change from a *cumulative* to a *sequential* view of academic curricula — what is usually labelled as "Bologna reform". Many members of the academic community (not only in the humanities, but also in medicine, engineering and applied sciences) feel uncomfortable about a break of solidarity between the Bachelor and the Master education that has been brought about by the Bologna reform and resist *de facto* this evolution by maintaining a mono-dis-

ciplinary view of university education, whereby curricula at the Master's level ideally represent a more or less direct sequence of the corresponding undergraduate program at the same institution.

'SPECIALIST' OR 'GOOD CITIZEN' ?

This potential renegotiation in the understanding of the role of universities in Swiss society is the result of a conflict that has emerged in the last 15 years between two readings of the educational mandate of the university. In the German-, French- and Italian-speaking tradition, "academic formation" (in spite of the different connotations of the German words *akademische Bildung* as opposed to French *formation universitaire* and Italian *cultura universitaria*) is generally considered to be a more or less flexible receptacle of knowledge and competence acquired through academic training. In other words, a close link is perceived to exist between *Bildung* and *Ausbildung*, the latter representing the ideal path in order to reach the former state: what we study at the university is cumulatively acquired and prepares us *paradigmatically*, i.e. by choosing one particular discipline as a model of the world, to a professional activity in a higher stratum of society. While there is no absolute overlapping between socially relevant *Bildung* and academically transmitted *Ausbildung*, the *educational offer* unilaterally conceived by your professors becomes the key to your own social and professional future.

In Western Europe, and probably in Switzerland more than in other countries, this model has been dramatically challenged in the last generation by a fundamentally different understanding of the role of universities at the global level, an understanding which is rather based on the Anglo-Saxon model of higher education. In this model, *Bildung* and *Ausbildung* are ideally covered by two different segments of the academic life: college (or undergraduate) *education* vs. university (or graduate) *training*. The former provides the intellectual frame and the social context (including its potential stratifications) of your life project; the latter prepares you in a systematic way (graduate *school, school* of medicine, *school* of engineering, etc.) for your future professional activity, whether in an academic or in a professional environment. The ideal professorial model is also different for the two academic stages: on the one hand, you expect your college professors to *inspire* you for life; on the other hand, you expect your graduate instructors to *inform* you in a competent manner. At the end of your academic experience, you may end up being well educated but poorly trained, or poorly educated but extremely well trained — something very unlikely in the traditional European academic encyclopedia.

The question mark I put in the title of this paragraph mirrors the transitional dialectic between these two models in the contemporary Swiss university system. We have come to realize that the historically predominant continental model no longer corresponds to the structure and the behaviour of the global academic market, and, to a certain extent, that it does not correspond to the expectations of many of our stakeholders (research peers, industry, etc.) But the lukewarm implementation of truly modular curricula at our universities shows that we are not yet ready to productively digest the effects of the Anglo-Saxon dichotomy between an undergraduate education founded upon *values* (of the *Bildung* type) and a graduate education founded upon *contents* (of the *Ausbildung* type). We find ourselves in a transitional state in the history of our understanding of what a university should be; a moment of trial and error caused by the radical change that has affected the relationship between society and academia in Switzerland (and perhaps in other European countries) over the last 15 years.

FROM THE LOGIC OF EMINENCE TO THE LOGIC OF EXCELLENCE

During this period, our universities have experienced a functional evolution that has challenged both their place in society and their internal organization. This evolution affects three domains of the personal and of the institutional sphere: (a) governance, (b) identity, (c) administration. I shall now briefly describe them by linking them to three ideal states of transition.

Governance: from confederation to republic. Traditionally, European universities, particularly in the German-speaking world, used to think of themselves basically as virtual constructs consisting of aristocratically led small units (institutes, seminars, chairs, etc.), each of them revolving around individual forms of leadership and each of them pursuing an autonomous intellectual or scientific agenda. In this "confederate" view of academic governance, there was little need of cohesion between the different units, institutional governance being usually soft and delegated *de facto* to the political level. What has happened in recent years is a gradual development of corporate governance for universities as compound entities, with a more coherent corporate identity, a relationship with the political power based on checks and balances, but with a lesser autonomy at the level of the single academic units. Bottom-up processes are usually framed within a "republican" approach to academic decision-taking, with relatively coherent mid-size units (departments, schools) replacing the old, decentralized small-size units.

Although the most abundant share of the budget of Swiss universities and federal schools (around 80%) still derives in one way or the other from the public purse, the former hegemonic role of the state tends to be replaced by governing bodies (university councils, advisory boards, etc.) characterized by the presence of a variety of stakeholders. It is fair to state that within the university's community, this development is accompanied by considerable reservations both in terms of the representativeness of the internal government of the university as "republican experiment" (rectorate, presidency, etc.) and of the — usually politically chosen — members of the external governing board (council). The solidarity between the culture of the university and its governance is a matter of sometimes intense debate.

Identity: from "corporation" to "association". While a "corporative" view is usually characterized by the awareness of membership as belonging to a particular *social* class or *professional* group, in associative thinking the predominant feature is culturally driven *identity*. The second major recent development in the Swiss university landscape is precisely the emergence of stronger institutional identities, following once again the model of the English or American academic experience. While in the traditional European approach (what has come to be known as the Humboldt type of university, although Wilhelm von Humboldt himself would probably turn in his grave if he saw what his name has come to be associated with) academic identity was founded upon the corporative belonging to a disciplinary horizon (*Fach*), combined with an underdeveloped institutional identity, the latter now occupies the centre of a university's self-understanding and self-presentation. Thus, Swiss universities find themselves on their way from *universitas* to *university*: although in principle the same word, the Latin term implies a higher commitment to the *diversity* of scholarly or scientific endeavours, while the English term stresses the *unifying* factors at the institutional level. It is not surprising that this development appears to be most advanced at institutions such as the federal schools of technology (ETH and EPFL) and programmatically compact universities (such as the University of St. Gallen), but less advanced at traditional full-fledged universities (such as in Zurich, Basel or Geneva), where institutional marketing tends to still be successfully challenged by disciplinary interests and where societal stakeholders (including sponsors) are more inclined to link their name to individual projects or research areas than to large scale, university-wide endeavours.

In general, the current Swiss university culture tends to de-emphasize the professorial *status* as such and to privilege instead the academic *career*. This has led in many instances to a revision of the traditional status-based selection process for appointment to the professorial rank in favour of a flexible selection process with the possibility of tenure-track appointments.

Administration: from "club" to "business". The third development affecting the Swiss academic landscape is what I would call the "controlling turn" affecting institutions of higher education. What I mean by the use of this term is that current university administration is confronted with the expectation — shared by political decision-makers and many segments of civil society — that the university should be administered at the same level of efficiency, reliability and transparency that is characteristic (or is thought to be characteristic) for business-like enterprises. Perversely, the understandable wish by both taxpayers (and their representatives) and academic peers to be transparently documented about all aspects of the management of a university automatically leads to an increase of the often chastised "administrative costs". In general, the complexity of institutional decision processes obliges university leadership to adopt a bipartite behaviour: on the one hand, university leadership needs to make sure that there is enough "free space" (and free money) in the system to allow for potential excellence to emerge, on the other hand, it has to guarantee a maximum of accountability to conveniently represent the position of the institution among its stakeholders. This of course generates in many members of the academic community the (correct) impression that in the "confederate" era of autonomous units, the administration was far less pervasive than under modern "republican" governance. The concept of "running a university", which in Switzerland would have been unheard of until 20 years ago, now makes our system of higher education còmpare favourably with the hegemonic Anglo-Saxon model, whereas in other European countries a centrifugal administration is still often viewed as a guarantee against the loss of academic freedom.

A typical phenomenon of the controlling turn in Swiss university life is the emergence of institutional "strategies" designed to forecast and guide the development of a university in the years to come. The choice of this concept, derived from the military (and the corporate) world, suggests that the endeavours of a university in the years to come need to be presented as plausible within a sustainable conceptual as well as administrative frame. Here too the dilemma is clear: while future investments, especially in terms of infrastructures, must be carefully prepared and usually require a long (and often politically steered) executive process, scientific evolution per se cannot be foreseen — not to speak of individual excellence. Institutional strategies, therefore, tend to be taken as a textual genre aimed at convincing stakeholders rather than at guiding the university leadership's decisions.

On the one hand, it is certainly correct that the academic market now operates at the global level; on the other hand, Swiss universities are confronted with the specific challenge that their immediate neighbours, from which a vast portion of their academic personnel is recruited, prove more resistant to the evolutions in terms of governance, identity and administration that I just touched on. Academic competitiveness is not something absolute, but is always expressed within a specific geographic, cultural or disciplinary horizon. In a small and diverse academic landscape such as ours, the challenge is not trivial.

SOCIAL MANDATE AND PERSONALIZED BIOGRAPHIES

To sum up, one can say that in recent years the Swiss academic community, whose performance compares rather well at the global level, has experienced the emergence of new challenges that have somewhat shaken its conceptual and emotional foundations. The predominant model of Swiss university has distanced itself from the traditional administratively decentralized, professorially driven and state controlled institution to reach a higher level of stakeholder diversity, corporate identity and executive efficiency. The price paid to sustain this evolution is a certain neglect of the *social mandate* of the university in favour of a higher attention devoted to the needs of a variety of *personalized biographies*: research rather than teaching, social media rather tutorial assistance, lifelong learning rather than extension classes, logos rather than *lógos*.

Focus on research, personalized instruction, global understanding of the role of the university in society: these seem to be the main features — and the main challenges — of contemporary Swiss academic landscape. In many respects, this evolution dovetails quite well with the demographic expectations of our knowledge society: Switzerland does not produce nearly as many graduates as its academic as well as professional system would need. Thus, the more rapid pace of adoption of an Anglo-Saxon model of higher education in Switzerland in comparison with its neighbours will probably maintain a high degree of innovativeness and may turn out to be its strongest competitive advantage in the years to come.

CHAPTER 15

A Research University for both Academic Excellence and Responsibility for a sustainable future — does the Swedish model work?

Eva Åkesson

INTRODUCTION

Sweden has for a long time been spared from armed conflicts and major disruptive social problems. During the past decades, we have gone from a homogeneous state to an increasingly diverse and diverged country. In an international comparison, Sweden looks in many ways like a very attractive country to live and work in, as recently highlighted in *The Economist* magazine (2013).

Sweden and the Nordic countries (except Iceland) stand out among other E.U. countries with relatively strong growth and sound public finances. The success of the Swedish model is reflected in a number of aspects, such as an economic policy focused on making work more profitable and reducing social exclusion, growth and structural reforms, as well as measures to improve education and employment opportunities.

Various reports show that Sweden is holding up relatively well internationally in terms of average citation rates: Sweden currently ranks seventh, with a large number of nations close behind. On the other hand, a bibliometric analysis from the Swedish Research Council shows that Sweden's production of breakthrough research has fallen below that of Denmark, the Netherlands and Switzerland over the last 10-20 years (Karlsson, 2010).

All in all, Swedish research is maintaining high quality, but its international importance is tending to decline — clearly a worrying trend. According to OECD's Education at a glance (2012), the number of today's young adults in Sweden who will complete a tertiary-type A (largely theory based) education over their lifetime is just below the OECD average, but far behind our Nordic neighbours.

At the same time, according to the Global Creativity Index (2011), Sweden is proven to be one of the world's most creative countries. The index measures the technological knowledge of the population and the capacity, competence and openness to new ideas. These parameters are summarized in the form of three Ts: technology, talent and tolerance. In the latest studies Sweden ranks as the most creative country. We end up in fifth place in terms of technology, ranked second in terms of talent and seventh in terms of tolerance. But past success is no guarantee of a glorious future.

From the middle of the 20th century, the Swedish university sector evolved rapidly, and during the latter part of the 20th century and early 21st century higher education in Sweden continued its expansion. Many new university colleges were founded and student numbers soared. The political objective was that everyone should have the opportunity to study at university. Today this aspect of higher education has somewhat ceased, and the volume of expansion has decreased slightly in recent years. During the 2011 autumn semester, 363,000 students studied at undergraduate and graduate level in Sweden. This was 6,000 fewer than in 2010 (Kahlroth & Amnéus, 2012). In the past few years, new institutions have been created mainly through mergers between existing universities. Examples of mergers that have taken place in recent years: 2010 — Linnaeus University was established when the University of Kalmar merged with Växjö University; the most recent merger dates from 1 July 2013 when the University of Gotland merged with Uppsala University. Today there are more than 50 colleges and universities in Sweden of different sizes and with different orientations, offering a wide range of education in various fields.

Sweden is currently ranked second in the U21 rankings latest survey of 50 national higher education systems worldwide (U21 Ranking of National Higher Education Systems, 2013). When it comes to institutional rules, education, innovation and infrastructure linked to the growing importance of information technology and the "knowledge society", Sweden takes the lead. This is pointed out in, for example, the World Bank Knowledge Economy Index 28 (2012) and INSEAD business school's Network Readiness Index (n.d.)

Since 2006 Sweden has a new government with high ambitions for the research and higher education sector. Autonomy as a general concept, combined with quality and performance and a utilitarian aspect, have been some of the guiding principles in creating a new policy for higher education in Sweden.

As a result, the past few years have been a turbulent time with several reforms which in a major way have influenced the development of research and higher education. The prerequisites have changed substantially, and several variables, external as well as internal, will affect us in the near future. The prerequisites for research and education in Sweden have recently changed through a number of governmental reforms such as two major Research and Innovation Bills (Government Bill, 2008 & 2012), the Autonomy Reform (2010) and the reform of higher education due to the Bologna process (n.d.), as well as the new national Quality Assurance System. The introduction of tuition fees for international students in 2011 is another element that contributes to changing the environment for higher education. It is clear that the Swedish government wants to invest in research, but how should we invest, and what are the possible effects of this high pace of reforms? In this paper we aim to discuss how these recent reforms have affected the higher education sector.

IMPRESSIVE AMOUNTS OF NEW MONEY
BUT MANY STRINGS ATTACHED

Since 2008, the government has made major investments in research at Swedish universities. This increase in funding has occurred despite the global financial crisis that took off in 2008. Every four years, the Swedish government presents a Research and Innovation Bill, which outlines the government's priorities for the coming years. The bill "A boost for research and innovation" was presented in October 2008 (Government Bill 2008/09:50), a few weeks before the global financial crisis was triggered with full force. It was an increase in appropriations of SEK 5 billion for the period 2009–2012. The direct funding to universities was to be raised and allocated according to a new system, in which quality should determine how much funding each university or college would receive. Quality was to be measured by two factors — publications/citations and external funding. Investment in research in areas of strategic importance for Swedish society and business was also introduced, as well as a new model for innovation where the utilization and commercialization of research would be stimulated.

Since the Second World War, Swedish basic research has in principle been financed in two ways: through direct appropriations to the university and by competitive grants channelled through the Research Council. One part of the reform was the introduction of a third, major way of funding: strategic research areas. A large part of the five billion (SEK 1.8 billion) in the research bill was deposited in what was meant to be a permanent annual increase in funding for research in a number of strategically important fields, often quite narrowly defined and pre-selected by government based on undisclosed criteria. The strategically important areas of concern identified were mainly in medicine, technology and climate research. This has been criticized for being too narrow a perspective, and that the humanistic and social scientific field was under-represented.

Four years later, in 2012, a new Research and Innovation Bill was presented (Government Bill, 2012/13:30). Surprisingly to most, the amount of new money for research was about the same size as in 2008. The investments included an increase of resources for research and innovation of about 4 billion until 2016, in order to strengthen Sweden's position in the long term as a leading research nation. Among other things, a particular focus on life sciences was implemented. With the increase of 5 billion presented in the previous research and innovation bill, this provided an increase of approximately 9 billion in eight years.

The government submitted its approach to research and innovation policy for the period 2013–2016, and believes that increased funding for research and knowledge-intensive innovation is an important instrument for the improvement of the quality of Swedish research. High-quality research can contribute to the welfare of citizens, social development, economic competitiveness and sustainable development. In the bill, the government stated that measures aimed at the quality of research and utilization of research-based knowledge need to increase.

Furthermore, the funding for international recruitment of scientists engaged in high-quality research was increased. The government estimated that Sweden generally had a low international recruitment of researchers compared to many other countries, which was, and is, a clear gap in the Swedish research system. This concerns particularly the recruitment of established, foreign, high-level researchers. As a part of the efforts to strengthen the quality of Swedish research, a system should be created for international recruitment of scientists with great potential.

Moreover, funding for research infrastructure should be increased. Research infrastructure refers to large research facilities, databases, bio banks or large-scale computing analysis centres and modelling resources, for example. These resources are often critical in order to conduct high-quality research. As the infrastructure becomes more extensive and costly, it is necessary to develop them jointly at a regional, national or international level, according to the government. One prominent example of this is SciLifeLab, a collaboration between four universities in Stockholm and Uppsala (Stockholm University, Karolinska Institutet, the Royal Institute of Technology [KTH] and Uppsala University), where advanced technical know-how and state-of-the-art equipment is combined with a broad knowledge in translational medicine and molecular bioscience.

The Research and Innovation Bill from 2012 places a greater focus on the "excellent individual", and can to some extent be seen as a reaction to the criticism of the previous bill. The government now makes an effort to paint with broader brush strokes, but retains a high degree of political control.

While major funding is spent on research in strategic research areas, research and development in industry have declined these past years. According to Statistics Sweden's (SCB) assessment (2011), investment in research and development increased in 2010, both in academia and the public sector, but business spending on research and development fell relative to 2009. The assessment shows that companies reduced their investments in Sweden from SEK 79.4 billion to SEK 77.8 billion between 2009 and 2010. In the business sector, spending on research and development declined the most in the manufacturing sector.

The emerging picture is thus ambiguous. Spending on research and development seems to increase in the higher education and public sector, while companies reduce their development costs. It is thus most important to monitor this development, and increase the collaboration between higher education institutions and the business sector.

Another aspect of governmental funding is the difficulties for the universities to control their strategic process. Since a large part of their funding comes from governmental appropriations, higher education institutions don't have full control over their own resources and funding. A large proportion of university funding is external and more than 50% of research revenues come from external funding. The investments in research are positive, but what we see are controlled investments, and the balance between external funding and basic grants is lacking.

It also remains to be seen whether international recruitment of top-level scientists is the right way to go. Maybe it could be more appropriate to pick promising young scientists with potential. The aspect of increased funding of research infrastructure and the aspiration to develop them jointly at regional, national or international level are a wise suggestion. Research collaborations such as SciLifeLab are good examples of the advantages of such a system.

UNIVERSITY GOVERNANCE: GREATER FREEDOM FOR WHOM?

In 2010, a governance reform called "The Autonomy Reform" was presented, and entered into force in January 2011. The aim of the reform was to increase the freedom of publicly funded universities and other higher education institutions within the framework of the current governmental format. In the bill the government presents proposals and makes assessments involving extensive deregulation of internal organization and teaching positions. The general regulatory framework for financial administration that government agencies are required to comply with should be reviewed to better meet the conditions of universities and colleges.

The initiative to give greater freedom of self-determination to publicly funded higher education institutions was an important matter of principle in view of the fundamental task of institutions of higher education to be an independent and critically reflective force in the development of society. Also, giving higher education institutions greater freedom and responsibility to adapt to their own situation and needs will benefit the quality of their activities. Greater freedom of action is a prerequisite for enabling higher education institutions to run their activities successfully in a competitive international sector.

The Swedish Association of University Teachers (SULF) has examined in a survey the changes that have been made, and are being made, as a result of the autonomy reform. The report concentrates on issues related to teaching positions and organization. The largest changes due to the reform occurred in smaller colleges, both in terms of employment arrangements and other organizational matters (Samuelsson, 2011).

The Association of Swedish Higher Education (SUHF) also studied the effects of the autonomy reform, and concluded that a comparison of teaching positions and employment schemes displays a broad range of variations between institutions and different interpretations of the same concept. The report gives a mixed picture, which is not surprising, since it is now possible to go different ways (Samuelsson, 2012).

Some variation and diversification can be a good thing, as higher education institutions can use the autonomy reform as a way to promote themselves as attractive workplaces. It is time for higher education institutions to roll up their sleeves and seize the opportunities for change that the autonomy reform offers. Others believe, on the contrary, that the autonomy reform has not led to any significant changes, and the question is whether the universities have really dared to use their space for autonomy.

In summary, the outcome of the autonomy reform so far has been that no one is satisfied. For those looking for more autonomy, not enough has been made. Universities are still authorities and a part of the state, with the obligations that involves. Others argue that the collegial governance has weakened as an outcome of the reform.

THE BOLOGNA PROCESS: UNFINISHED BUSINESS

The Bologna process is another reform that has affected Swedish higher education in recent years. The process based on the Bologna Declaration aims to make Europe a coherent higher education area.

Sweden was one of the last countries within the Bologna family to implement the three-cycle system (bachelor, master and PhD). Decision-makers in Sweden discovered relatively late that we needed concrete reforms in order to meet the guidelines. Once that became clear, the Bologna process encouraged a major reform of higher education in Sweden. The bill, known as "New World — New University", came into effect on 1 July 2007 and brought about changes in the Higher Education Act and Higher Education Ordinance. Within the second cycle, a new two-year master's degree has been introduced. With the introduction of a three-cycle system, all degree descriptions have been reviewed and the degrees have been placed at either first, second or third level. In contrast to most other countries, the consequence of the reform in Sweden has been an extension of the study period.

The new degree descriptions are based on the expected learning outcomes of students and are related to the Qualifications Framework of the Bologna Process. These are formulated for general qualifications (i.e., Bachelor's, Master's and PhD) and professional qualifications as objectives under three headings: knowledge and understanding, skills and abilities, and judgment and approach. Universities in Sweden have the autonomy to establish programs and decide the specific field of specialization and establish more precise requirements within the framework of the national qualification description. So, even though Sweden was one of the last countries to implement the three-cycle system, it carried out the reforms quickly and thoroughly.

One ambition with the Bologna Process is to promote a shift from teaching to learning, from input to outcome. Such a shift was welcomed by most teachers and students in Sweden. The Bologna Process is also seen as an opportunity to leverage further educational reform; to enhance pedagogy, assessment and quality assurance. A positive outcome of the Bologna Process is how it widens the perspective of education, from emphasis mainly on knowledge as the learning outcome to competence and skills. As an example, Uppsala University has developed a variety of master programs and has a stronger focus on internationalization. There is no external accreditation or validation prior to the start of a university program, with the exception of professional qualifications. The validation is performed by the universities' internal quality assurance systems. However, all programs are evaluated periodically by an external quality assurance agency.

QUALITY ASSURANCE SYSTEM: IS SWEDEN AHEAD OF THE PACK, OR DIGGING ITS OWN HOLE DEEPER?

In early 2000, Sweden had a program evaluation system that would look at the prerequisites, processes and outcomes of higher education. The system received a lot of criticism from the sector. It was said to have a one-sided perspective focusing on prerequisites only, not being predictable, clear or transparent. A simpler system was developed, which was based on key indicators, but this attempt failed due to massive criticism from the sector.

A system for quality assurance was then developed by the Swedish Higher Education Authority (HSV) in cooperation with the sector of higher education. This was not endorsed, and instead yet another evaluation system was developed, the governmental bill "Focus on knowledge – quality in higher education", presented in 2010 (Government Bill, 2009/10:139). In the bill, the government proposed that the emphasis of the national quality assurance system for higher education institutions must change to meet the new requirements imposed by the objectives of greater freedom, internationalization and high quality. The government argued that Sweden needs a quality assurance system which strengthens the incentives to achieve high standards of performance in training. Universities with high-quality teaching should be rewarded through increased funding.

The new system of evaluation was launched in 2011, despite the fact that the head of HSV, the University Chancellor, resigned in protest at the new system. In the new system, four criteria are used for evaluation: students' final theses, surveys of previous students, institutions' self-evaluations and students' experience. But the majority of evaluation decisions are made mainly on the basis of students' theses, which has drawn criticism from the SUHF and the European Association for Quality Assurance in Higher Education (ENQA) panel, among others (Myklebust, 2012).

An important point is that the evaluations focus on results. What is considered to be results are how well the program meets the requirements set out in the Higher Education Act and the degree descriptions. Educational institutions are in the new quality assessment system responsible for analysing the conditions and processes that form the basis for the educational outcome.

Evaluations of the current system will be implemented in four-year cycles (instead of the previous six-year cycles) and result in a judgment on a three-point scale. Another new feature is that the evaluations shall provide the basis for a part of the government's resource allocation to universities and colleges (Järplid Linde & Sundkvist, 2012). Also, Higher Education Institutions can have their right to award degrees retracted if they do not comply with the demands.

Where the attention was previously focused on the prerequisites, it now centres exclusively on results, with sanctions and rewards, and we have already seen some of the effects of this. In the first round of evaluations that was reported in April-May 2012, 262 education programs were evaluated; 66 of these programs, corresponding to approximately 25%, were found to have "poor quality". One can ask oneself if this really reflects the reality. The model for evaluation has many critics. The experiences from Uppsala University show that cross-border and more applied courses fall out of the framework for the model of evaluation. The new system of quality assessment has been debated vociferously. Some critics mean that it has a one-sided emphasis on results, which penalizes cross-border and more applied courses. We risk a return to more discipline-based teaching, reversing the achievements made over the past 10–20 years. A more balanced system is needed, which also takes into account the prerequisites and processes. In addition, the ENQA has not given a green light to the Swedish quality assurance system. It is very problematic to have a quality assurance system that is not internationally recognized.

The report from the ENQA (2012) said that the European Standards and Guidelines for Quality Assurance in the European Higher Education Area's (ESG) first principle was that external quality assurance should build on the results of internal quality assurance. But the Swedish system "takes no account of institutions' arrangements for internal quality assurance, except at the very margins".

The report added that while a basic principle of ESG was that quality assurance systems should lead to enhancement, the Swedish system made no recommendations for improvement. Also, the extent to which the new system was prescribed cast doubts on the operational independence of the reviewer. The system is not aligned with the fundamental principles of ESG. In the view of the Review Panel, there are weaknesses inherent in the system that make it possible that unreliable judgments will emerge, even on the narrow and reductive basis intended.

Still, there is a positive side to the new quality assurance system. There is a greater focus on the expected learning outcome and on the examination papers, and the processes of evaluation have raised consciousness about quality and increased quality awareness. The discussions and debate will continue, and hopefully result in some amendments.

TUITION FEES: REVERSING INTERNATIONALIZATION?

Free education and the public good have long been central concepts of education in the Nordic countries, but now we see how tuition fees primarily for non-European students are being introduced. First out in the Nordic countries was Denmark in 2006. Sweden introduced tuition fees for the autumn semester in 2011. The message from the government was that Swedish universities must compete internationally with quality, not with free education. The government also promoted the idea that tuition fees for students from countries outside the EU/EES would give the universities the opportunity to work more strategically with recruitment of these students.

Sweden is a small economy, extremely dependent on international trade and openness to inflows of talent and knowledge. As a small country, with a small native language, it is not realistic to make Sweden the first choice for students looking for education on an international market. That is why the possibility of accepting a number of international students without tuition fees was so important.

In the report from the Nordic Council of Ministers "Tuition fees for international students" (2013), tuition fees for international students (non EU-countries) in the Nordic countries and how the charges affect the number of students have been analysed. The report shows that Denmark lost a large number of students when fees were introduced, but the numbers began to rise again after two to three years. In Sweden, the number of students was reduced from 8,000 to 2,000 when fees were introduced. Norway and Iceland have no tuition fees and in both these countries, the number of international students from countries outside the European Union has increased over the past five years. It indicates that students choose to study in Norway and Iceland, as a result of tuition fees in Denmark and Sweden. In Finland, a pilot project is under way with fees for 41 programs from 2010–2014, and they await the outcome of the pilot project before deciding whether to start using tuition fees or not.

It is clear that Sweden has not gained from the introduction of tuition fees. The new system was introduced too fast, and the application systems have not been adapted to the current situation. The universities today may not have separate admissions, or quotient groups, for students from outside the European Union, which results in a slow admission process. A greater flexibility is required to enable rolling admissions and faster processes. Another issue is the lack of access to more scholarships. We need a real handshake between business and government and a cohesive generous scholarship program to attract talented students to Sweden. These are all issues that must be dealt with immediately.

Another aspect that limits Sweden's attractiveness (and that of other European countries) for international students is the current set of rules for receiving a student visa or a residence permit. The rules and regulations related to visa applications are complicated and unclear. The rules vary between member states of the E.U. and make it difficult, or almost impossible, for those who are not E.U. citizens to move from one member state to another. The European Commission has recently presented a proposal (2013) which aims to make it easier and more attractive for non-E.U. national students, researchers and other groups to enter and stay in the E.U. for periods exceeding three months, and the Commission hopes for the new rules to take effect as of 2016. The proposal includes clear timelines for national authorities to make decisions on applications. It will also provide increased opportunities for overseas students and researchers to access the labour market during their stays and facilitate their mobility within the E.U.

It is most important to remove barriers to international mobility. Only then can we compete for the best teachers, researchers and students. Increased internationalization is an important factor in achieving improved quality in research and education. Reducing bureaucratic hassles for overseas students who want to study and do research in Europe is one step forward.

CONCLUSION

The conditions for higher education in Sweden have changed through the Autonomy Reform, the Bologna process, two research bills, a new quality assurance system and the introduction of tuition fees. Are these reforms measures that will provide academic excellence and take responsibility for a sustainable future? Are they beneficial to Sweden, and does the Swedish Model really work?

One reaction to the recent changes has been summarized in the manifesto for dialogue about Swedish education in 2030 by the Association of Swedish Higher Education (2013). With the manifesto, the Association of Swedish Higher Education wants to establish a dialogue with decision-makers and moulders of public opinion. The core of the manifesto is the question of how higher education in Sweden is to develop academic excellence, while taking responsibility for and contributing to sustainable development in Sweden. This initiative is one way to set the agenda, and to show decision-makers that higher education institutions have an important role in the process of defining, and finding, solutions to the challenges of our society.

The emphasis on research and quality in the recent governmental bills could be seen as a way to take responsibility for a sustainable future. We see large investments in research, while other higher education institutions in the world are scaling down, and we expect to see results from these efforts. However, there are many strings attached to these investments, which may prove to be counterproductive. It is important that the reforms are implemented with long-term goals and political unity. The universities need basic grants in order to strategically plan their activities. The emphasis on certain subjects and areas puts broad universities at risk of impoverishment. The universities have a special role in society, and their activity should involve excellence and breadth, as well as being a critical and questioning voice in society. Investments must be made not only in science and technology, but in the humanities and social sciences. Investments in large-scale infrastructure are positive, but medium-scale infrastructure and interaction with other higher education institutions are also important issues that we must take responsibility for. When it comes to investments in education, efforts must be made to increase the number of students. Sweden is living in its own myth that we are well educated, when in fact we are beginning to fall behind many other countries, including neighbouring Nordic countries.

Regarding the autonomy reform, we would like to see real autonomy, with control over our premises. But we also want to develop the collegial quality culture with a strong student influence. The commitment and potential of our students as agents for change is something we want to take care of and develop.

The quality assurance system must be modified in order to gain legitimacy in the sector of higher education in Sweden, as well as internationally. We must modify the quality assurance system to include a broader definition of quality that takes into account the methods of education to ensure the survival of cross-border and innovative initiatives. Additionally, we need a quality assurance system that is internationally recognized by the ENQA.

The introduction of tuition fees has not been propitious for the higher-education sector in Sweden. Reform was implemented too quickly and needs to be amended in order to make it easier for international students to study in Sweden. The process of internationalization is an important factor in improving the quality of higher education, and the introduction of tuition fees has not been a step in the right direction.

In conclusion, we see a lot of political tampering and focus on details, when what we really need is long-term reforms across political boundaries. Higher education institutions need trust, and to gain that trust we need to show more responsibility with a culture of quality and a broader sense of responsibility.

REFERENCES

Bologna process (n.d). http://www.regeringen.se/sb/d/9267
Education at a glance (2012). OECD indicators, p. 67.
European Commission (2013). "Making the E.U. more attractive for foreign students and researchers", press release, 25 March 2013.
  http://europa.eu/rapid/press-release_IP-13-275_en.htm
  Proposal for a Directive of the European Parliament and of the Council on the conditions of entry and residence of third-country nationals for the purposes of research, studies, pupil exchange, remunerated and unremunerated training, voluntary service and au pairing, 25 March 2013, http://ec.europa.eu/dgs/home-affairs/e-library/documents/policies/immigration/study-or-training/docs/students_and_researchers_proposal_com_2013_151_en.pdf
Finansiering av forskning i Sverige (n.d.) http://www.regeringen.se/sb/d/2470/a/35318
Government Bill (2008). Ett lyft för forskning och innovation. Governmental Bill 2008/09:50 http://www.regeringen.se/sb/d/108/a/113957
Government Bill (2009). Fokus på kunskap: Kvalitet i den högre utbildningen. Government Bill 2009/10:139. http://www.regeringen.se/sb/d/12489/a/142211
Government Bill (2010). Government Bill 2009/10:149. En akademi i tiden – ökad frihet för universitet och högskolor.
Government Bill (2012). Forskning och innovation. Governmental Bill 2012/13:30 http://www.regeringen.se/sb/d/15650/a/201368
INSEAD business school's Network Readiness Index (n.d.)
  http://www.weforum.org/issues/global-information-technology/the-great-transformation/network-readiness-index
Järplid Linde, Karin & Sundkvist, Maria (2012). Högskoleverkets system för kvalitetsutvärdering 2011-2014, Rapport 2012:15 R.

http://www.hsv.se/publikationer/rapporter/2012/
hogskoleverketssystemforkvalitetsutvardering20112014.5.8b3a8c21372be32ace8
0007663.html

Kahlroth, Marie & Amnéus, Ingeborg (eds) (2012). Universitet & högskolor: Högskoleverkets årsrapport 2012.
http://www.hsv.se/download/18.8b3a8c21372be32ace80003121/1210R-universitet-hogskolor-arsrapport.pdf

Karlsson, Staffan (2010). Den svenska produktionen av högt citerade vetenskapliga publikationer. Vetenskapsrådets lilla rapportserie 1:2010 www.vr.se/download/18.1ada9fde1266f78be66800015/Rapport+1.2010.pdf

Myklebust, Jan Petter (2012). Quality assurance regime fails to meet European standards, *University World News*. 6 May 2012.
http://www.universityworldnews.com/article.php?story=20120503164105608

Samuelsson, Marie-Louise, Universitetsläraren (2011). Autonomireformen berör främst mindre högskolor

Samuelsson, Marie-Louise, Universitetsläraren (2012). Ett otal anställningsformer resultatet (2012).

Statistics Sweden (SCB), 2011. Press Release, 23 August 2011. Satsningar på forskning och utveckling 2010.
http://www.scb.se/Pages/PressRelease____319353.aspx

Swedish National Agency for Higher Education: Review of ENQA Membership (2012)
http://www.hsv.se/download/18.1c6d4396136bbbed2bd80002238/HSV_review-ENQA-Criteria-Report-April2012.pdf

The Association of Swedish Higher Education, SUHF (2013). "The future starts now -Manifesto for a dialogue about Swedish higher education in 2030".
http://www.suhf.se/nyheter-press/nyheter/manifest-2013

The Economist (2013). "Northern Lights", 2 February 2013.

The Global Creativity Index (2011). "Creativity and Prosperity".
http://martinprosperity.org/media/GCI%20Report%20Sep%202011.pdf

Tuition fees for international students, Nordic practice (2013).
http://www.norden.org/en/publications/publikationer/2013-516

U21 Ranking of National Higher Education Systems (2013).
http://www.universitas21.com/article/projects/details/152/u21-ranking-of-national-higher-education-systems

World Bank Knowledge Economy Index 28 (2012).
http://info.worldbank.org/etools/kam2/KAM_page5.asp

CHAPTER 16

Human capital, the oft forgotten key challenge for universities

Sijbolt Noorda

"So how's your poor dear wife?" asks the not-quite-superannuated ice queen of Personnel Department, now grandly rechristened Human Resources for no reason known to man...

(John le Carré, *A Delicate Truth*, 2013)

THE STRATEGIC VALUE OF HUMAN RESOURCES

A university without faculty is like a bicycle without wheels. It won't get you very far. I know this is a matter of course, forcing an open door. Yet, precisely because it is obvious that universities without teachers and researchers are just empty shells, it strikes me that, when we talk and write about the future of the university, human capital rarely is a hot topic. Its strategic value usually is underestimated by university leadership, while in reality and mutatis mutandis the topic is relevant to all Higher Education Institutions.

At closer look, it is evident that the quality of teaching and researching is immediately linked to the quality of the women and men doing it. Everyone who is even slightly familiar with university realities knows a good number of positive and negative cases illustrating this point. And every insider knows that recruitment of faculty is a core responsibility in any university. If you cannot hire the right kind of academics, the future of any school or department is at risk. Yet it is a rare theme in strategic documents and not too often discussed in a comparative way, in international conferences or in university management studies outside the circle of HRM specialists. One of the laudable exceptions is IMHE/OECD. Since 1994 they have produced a series of reports on academic staffing and related issues, and organized meetings on these themes, like the international conference on "Trends in the Management of Human Resources in Higher Education" in Paris in August 2005.

Why is it that we are in general so silent on such a key issue? I see three explanations. Human capital is very much seen in terms of hiring and firing, promoting and demoting, in other words in terms of in-house responsibilities of individual institutions or departments. Secondly these responsibilities are usually to a large extent stamped and framed by national traditions and preferences, legal frameworks and salary arrangements. And, last but not least, the labour market of academics is usually seen as a typical buyers' market where individual employers with their reputation and buying powers are champions. Under these circumstances, strategic planning and international benchmarking and analysing are seen either as too simple and straightforward, or too complex to approach or bring under control.

Nevertheless, this paper questions the wisdom of underestimating human resources as a strategic theme and a welcome topic for international exchange and comparison. I shall be asking three questions that are largely within the control zone of individual institutions and, in my view, are and should be relevant to anyone in university leadership positions: 1. Are you certain that in 10 years time you will (still) be able to recruit the junior faculty you need? 2. Are you satisfied with the career dynamics of your senior faculty? 3. And, last but not least, how about the balance between individual faculty's career interests and collective interests of departments and schools?

FUTURE RECRUITMENT OF JUNIOR FACULTY

Will you in 10 years time be able to recruit the junior faculty you need? The most popular answer to this question may very well be "it depends". The domain of human resources is quite differentiated, difficult to predict, and subject to many external and internal forces, some of which are hard, many soft. It is a domain that is largely beyond control by individual parties. It cannot easily be steered by individual employers. So let's just wait and see? That's certainly not good enough. But, then, what can we do? How can individual universities make sure that they will be able to recruit the junior faculty they need, in terms of numbers and of competences? Or at least raise the probabilities that they can, by doing what is in their powers to shape and stimulate.

In answering this question, three topics seem to be relevant: 1) the success of graduate education; 2) its value on the labour market; and 3) talent scouting and development of junior faculty.

Universities — research universities above all — are among employers in the enviable position that they teach and train their new blood. In German there is a fine label for this activity: *Nachwuchsförderung*, hard to translate because it combines the notions of support, patronage, improvement and pro-motion of the next generation. It is one of the main uses of graduate education to cater to the needs of Higher Education and Research itself. These days in almost all cases the academic teaching and research professions demand a doc-toral degree as minimal entry requirement. It is graduate education (the sec-ond and third cycles of the Bologna model) that should generate new genera-tions of aspiring academic teachers and researchers.

To be able to successfully do so obviously two requirements should be met: graduate education must attract a good number of incoming graduate students possessing the desired competences (a), and graduate programs must bring forth a good number of PhDs fit for a career in academia (b). In the interest of future staff quality performance, it is essential that new generations of capable PhDs continue to be available for and interested in a university career. We shouldn't forget that this is by no means certain. Past results are no guarantee for future successes. Long years of preparations for an academic career may in some or even in many fields be seen as a much too risky investment of time and energy.

IS GRADUATE EDUCATION ATTRACTIVE FOR QUALIFIED STUDENTS?

Attracting undergraduate degree holders to graduate education all the way to the doctoral degree depends on the combined force of three factors: the degree will open up attractive career perspectives in terms of labour market value (preferably in more than one sector of the market for holders of graduate degrees) (x), the study path will be doable and affordable in practical terms (y), and, last but not least, alternative options will not be way more attractive (z).

Some of these factors function in a different way in different disciplines, all of them function very differently in different settings, cultures and countries. In a country like Germany where a doctoral degree implies social status gains also outside academia, factor x clearly has more positive weight than in a country like The Netherlands where a doctoral degree only counts in the world of Higher Education and Research, and in a limited number of research-intensive companies. On the other hand, the early introduction in The Neth-erlands in the 80s of relatively many full-time and well-paid assistant-researcher positions for the large majority of doctoral students has clearly diminished the negative side of factor y. The impact of more attractive alter-natives in the labour market (factor z) explains why in fields like law and busi-ness, interest in doctoral studies is usually low.

It's no use going on to describe specific conditions in various settings. The point simply is that universities should not rely on past performance but make sure that graduate education is an attractive option in the early career deci-sion-making process. It is of enormous importance that universities develop strategies — alone and in association with colleagues — to enhance the appeal of graduate education in order to convince qualified students that graduate education is worth its high opportunity cost, above all for the talented ones whom universities would like to attract to it.

SUCCESSFUL COMPLETION OF GRADUATE PROGRAMS

One would think that all serious research universities would understand the need for optimizing and profiling their graduate education. For some, however, this is a fairly recent interest. Yet the rewards are clear, in terms of learning outcomes for the participants, but also in terms of well-conceived institutional self-interest. Successful graduate degree-holders will not only be possible candidates for faculty positions in later stages, they will be key alumni and connections in future cooperatives and academic networks.

The need to enhance successful completion of graduate programs has in recent decades led university systems and individual universities to change traditional schemes of master-pupil graduate education. By introducing (specific research masters and) more structured doctoral programs, European universities have tried to do exactly this. In doing so, they managed to close the traditional gap with North-American graduate education. Thus countries like the U.K., Switzerland and The Netherlands have become attractive destinations for internationally mobile graduate students. These examples demonstrate the possible positive impact of well-chosen institutional strategies.

UNCERTAIN LABOUR MARKET PROSPECTS FOR PHDS

The main reason I am bringing the topic of graduate education up is, however, a slightly different one. Universities are resource-based organizations. As a rule, they spend between 75% and 85% on salaries and wages. Both in teaching and learning and in research, the volume and quality of human capital are key. By far the most important market for universities is the labour market. Maintaining a strong position in this market is therefore essential. This implies that universities must be visible, attractive and strong at the very portals to the upper regions of the job market. Controlling the last station before the border (i.e. graduate education) should be an advantage, not a risk.

This is why the quality of graduate and, in particular, doctoral education, is important. Generally speaking there is a world to be won in this field. Relatively long times to degree and low completion rates clearly indicate this potential gain. These suboptimal achievements should invite universities — individually and in association — to try and make things better.

This is also why universities should take a keen interest in the mechanics of the labour market. And have a realistic, not a complacent, view of their chances and their future in this market. It is by no means certain that the best and brightest of future generations will opt for academic careers. In some cases there is good reason to believe that universities have already lost some of their priority seats. In many areas (in particular Science and Engineering) U.S. doctoral programs attract many foreigners resulting in growing total numbers of doctorates, while in other fields (like education and humanities) that attract fewer foreigners, the total numbers have gone down. For quite a few (male) home students, the high opportunity costs of graduate education and the long-term perspective of an academic career apparently do not weigh up to the perceived attractions of careers outside academia that require no more university education than an undergraduate degree.

In recent years in The Netherlands, only 30% of successful PhD candidates find employment inside Dutch academia immediately following their graduation. Although this figure may well be too pessimistic because 43% of Dutch PhDs come from abroad (2011 data) and quite a few of them leave the country after graduation and may find university positions elsewhere, the impact on graduate student choice is crystal clear. When doctoral education is perceived as the golden route to academia and to academia alone, this state of affairs makes future students think twice before taking this risky road. As a result the pool of potential university teachers and researchers could shrink to undesirable proportions. To diminish these risks, Dutch universities enrich doctoral programs by broader skills training and career counselling, thereby enhancing post-graduate employability outside academia. A similar practice is recommended by a recent U.S. Commission on Pathways through Graduate School and into Careers (ETS & CGS, 2012). It reflects earlier U.K. policy proposals.

Universities that want to remain attractive career destinations should look carefully into labour market dynamics. I am often surprised by the lack of interest in what is going on in (international) job markets, or rather, the complacent attitude of quite a few universities. In comparison (international) corporations are doing much better by realizing the competitiveness of these markets and the need for offering attractive and transparent career paths, in particular if you would like to get the best and brightest interested in your organization.

TRADITIONAL MODELS OF JUNIOR FACULTY RECRUITMENT INADEQUATE

This brings me to my third topic: talent scouting and development of junior faculty. I remember the first time I used these labels in the company of university deans and rectors, some ten years ago. Are these not just new names for things we have been doing for ages already, they asked. Yes, of course, I said. But given the present scale of our institutions and the varieties in cultural background of our doctoral students and post-docs, we can no longer rely on our traditional informal approaches. We must deal with these issues much more structurally, professionally if you like.

The traditional conceptual model of university staffing combines the front door — house — exit sequence with supply-demand relations. Junior staff enters the university after graduate education (on the basis of some set of individual or group selection procedures), spends a shorter or longer period of time in house (depending on successful or failed promotions, and on available vacancies) and leaves to retire (in case of one of the "standard" academic careers) or to find employment elsewhere.

This basically is an elite model in that it presumes that aspiring academics will be prepared to wait in uncertainty and see after some time what the university has in store for them.

cartoon by Drew (http://www.toothpastefordinner.com)

At the same time, it is a model that reflects neither the dynamics of the labour market (the realities of competing employers and rivalling job or career options) nor changing conditions at the university (growing, shrinking, aging, rejuvenating).

ACTIVE SCOUTING AND COACHING OF JUNIOR FACULTY

In competitive and dynamic conditions (on both sides), such a model won't do. From the point of view of schools, talent growth shouldn't be passively observed, but rather be actively supported and developed. Academic careers, including their early stages, should be furthered individually and in terms of talent development, proven merit and opportunities for further growth, rather than solely being led by the need to find a replacement.

By talent-oriented career management, universities not only make sure that no talent will be wasted, but, equally important, they make it clear that they are offering attractive opportunities to the competent. In a way just like the traditional tenure track was meant to do, only with much more flexibility and tailor-made options. Typical talent guidance and support isn't only designed to retain. It is truly meant to motivate and offer optimal opportunities for career success to talented individuals.

One last aspect that deserves our attention in this context: are we sure that we offer career opportunities to aspiring junior faculty that are at the same time transparent and attractive? This is the case when career opportunities are attractive because they allow for individual creativity and advancement, and transparent because they are being made available and decided upon based on individual merit (the candidate's performance).

In this sense the German situation for a long time was rather unattractive for junior faculty, with long years of waiting before positions with a considerable degree of autonomy could possibly be gained, while the U.S. situation with its relatively large numbers of tenured faculty and tenure-track staff looked like paradise.

In recent years, however, both systems have been approaching each other by moving into opposite directions. In Germany in the rather empty space between tenured professors on the one hand and doctoral assistants and students on the other hand, new options have been designed. At the same time in the U.S., tenured and tenure-track staff has been reduced, while non-tenured staff and post-docs increased substantially. Though many people inside and outside higher education think of tenure-track appointments as the norm in the U.S., in reality tenure-track faculty are a dwindling minority on American campuses: while in 1975, tenure-track faculty accounted for 45.1% of the instructional staff, by 2009 they accounted for only 24.4% (data from AAUP).

I read these trends as adaptations to changed environments. German universities have adapted to increasing internationalization and growing cross-border mobility of doctoral students, post-docs and junior faculty. It just wasn't feasible anymore to stick to traditional national career patterns. U.S. universities, outside the very top segment, have had to adapt to changing budgetary realities. Limited growth or even decline and the need to be much more flexible have led to a growing part-time and non-tenured staff and a decline in tenured positions. In my view, both situations would benefit from more and structural talent-oriented career guidance. In a U.S.-type situation, it is the way to escape the negative impact of less attractive overall career perspective, while in a Germany-type situation it is the way to prepare and select senior researchers (*Nachwuchsgruppenleiter*) and associate professors (*Juniorprofessur*).

SENIOR FACULTY TOO APATHETIC

In his chapter on Comparative Reflections on Leadership in Higher Education (1994), Martin Trow included among the top six grave problems that face university presidents the problem of maintaining a flow of new scientists and scholars into departments and research labs, without institutional growth and with a large tenured and aging faculty.

Without a fair degree of mobility among senior faculty, renewal of the professoriate is a very slow process, in fact too slow for the university to respond to rapidly changing programs and projects and too slow to remain an attractive place for talented younger academics. Times are gone when universities were constantly expanding, adding programs and positions, and recruiting additional staff. These days change is more often realized by replacing existing groups and functions than by adding new ones. Under these conditions, a fair degree of mobility of senior faculty is very welcome.

Mobility is of course dependent on a multitude of factors and actors. A tenured professor at a nec plus ultra kind of institution has fewer reasons to consider a change than her younger colleague now teaching at a college and aspiring to engage himself in cutting-edge research. Similarly, a history professor has fewer attractive options outside the university than his colleague in the law department. In larger countries with Higher Education Institutions of different status, career mobility is more common than in smaller nations with a more or less uniform university system. And, at the end of the day, personal considerations of course play a key role, which by the way explains why the international mobility of senior faculty is much lower than that of juniors.

Should mobility in view of all these differences be left to individual decision-making? Usually this is the case. Up or out as a guideline in human resource management at universities is limited to non-tenured faculty. Career development of tenured faculty is seen and practised as just the individual responsibility of faculty members. The typical situation is one where most procedures and rituals are directed towards the moment of entry when someone is joining the tenured faculty. Career counselling as an ongoing activity throughout one's university employment is as far as I know still a rare phenomenon.

Senior staff mobility in terms of leaving to outside employment should not be seen as an isolated phenomenon. I like to see it as just one expression of career dynamics. And dynamics is what we need, for at least three good reasons.

QUI N'AVANCE PAS RECULE. TO STAND STILL IS TO MOVE BACK. WER RASTET, DER ROSTET.

Movement and change contribute to fitness for the job, including one's role in the organization and one's perception of where it is going. Movement across departmental or school borders, or even outside the institution should not be conceived as loss or betrayal but as a desirable broadening of one's expertise and a journey towards to new rewards. Only too often I've heard colleagues who finally dared to take such steps tell me or rather ask themselves, why didn't I do this earlier?

A second reason is the challenging complexity of university work and its increasing demands. In many research universities, teaching and learning have been rediscovered as a core responsibility for senior faculty, requiring new or refreshed competences and new tasks. Just think of phenomena like the international classroom, and the use or production of open educational resources.

My third argument is about university leadership roles. Sizable research universities need hundreds of leaders at group, department, school or institutional levels, in research as well as in teaching and learning, cooperation across disciplines and with external partners, in administrative roles and, last but not least, in human capital development. Career development cannot and should not be left to the personnel department or whatever more fancy labels these offices carry these days. Without the leadership and support of experienced academic peers, it just won't fly.

This kind of work on the quality and performance of senior faculty requires long-term strategies (few quick wins, but more healthy years ahead) and quite some enabling, motivating and facilitating labour. North American colleagues speak and write in this context about renewal of the professoriate in a variety of meanings, ranking from the rejuvenating powers of sabbaticals to replacement strategies. It is hard for me to judge how much of this is actually put in practice. In European settings it is a topic for discussion in specialist seminars and conferences, but I rarely meet enviable good practices. But where I see them they are extremely helpful. E.g. in Dutch research universities, senior faculty development has been a great help in campaigns meant to redesign teaching and optimize learning outcomes in undergraduate schools.

Are you satisfied with the dynamics of your senior faculty? It is a question that should be asked and answered more often. And be granted the status of a strategic question. It depends on the response to this question whether both the senior faculty and the institution itself will be aging in good health.

INDIVIDUAL VERSUS COLLECTIVE CAREER INTERESTS

Individual drive and motivation in the hearts and minds of faculty are some of the most important, if not the most important success factor in academia. In a way it is the secret of success. All of us instinctively prefer schools or research institutes with a culture of high performance and a practice of rewarding individual accomplishments.

Yet there is a downside to this. From my days as a university president, I clearly remember a conversation with one of our most visible economists. Have you, he asked, ever considered the opportunity cost of much of the work we do outside regular university programs and responsibilities? And if so, why are we allowed to be make available our time and expertise at such low prices?

His remarks made me think about the balance between individual faculty's career interests and university or departmental interests. I had often been talking about the research university as being more like a casbah than a company, thereby stressing the amount of creative freedom and entrepreneurial eagerness that senior faculty enjoyed and showed to — so I thought — the benefit of the university. But don't we risk going too far into this direction? Is there an acceptable equilibrium between private and individual interests of senior faculty and the good of the university?

It is clear that a relatively high degree of independence is one of the main attractions of a university career and one of the more important non-monetary rewards of a university career. It is also clear that many outside activities of senior faculty are valuable and visible connections with society, with serious and positive impact. In the context of contract evaluation and renewal, these aspects are usually recognized, on both sides of the table. Yet there is also substantial cost involved which most of the time is not accounted for. The absence of many high-ranking senior faculty from regular university program operations (be it in undergraduate teaching or in administrative roles) is a worrying illustration of this point.

Should universities be restraining this particular freedom? Or at least find better ways of balancing between private interest and collective good? I see at least three good reasons to indeed try to do so. In recent years budgetary pressures on universities have grown considerably. Above all in the public domain, this requires an extra prudent handling of issues of salaries and perks. Secondly, we are seeing an increasing need for academic integrity and independence. Too generous freedoms for individual faculty easily put these at risk. Researchers can divide their time between academia and the corporate world or other employers, they should not split their loyalties and academic norms. And, last but not least, universities actually need all the hands they have. This is true for all three priority areas: research, teaching and learning, and service and development. The present situation in quite a few countries where undergraduate education is left to temporary and part-time instructors and assistants, is both undesirable and risky in view of quality and reputation.

The procurement and maintenance of high-quality human resources are a key challenge for universities and their leadership. Yet the topic is often left to specialists to analyse and discuss in international forums. This paper has offered some assorted arguments to reconsider the traditional habitude of deans and presidents to speak about human resources in the presence of their colleagues by way of anecdotal evidence and success stories rather than analytically and strategically.

PART V

••••••••••••

Changing Nature
and Character
of Research Universities:
fast-developing countries

CHAPTER 17

The Search for Quality at Chinese Universities

Jie Zhang and Kai Yu

INTRODUCTION

Along with China's booming economy, the past three decades have seen tremendous progress in higher education in China. In 1982, only 1% of 18- to 22-year-olds had the opportunity to participate in higher education. The proportion in 2012 is now more than 26% (Yu, Stith, Liu & Chen, 2010), and China is likely to reach a 40% enrolment rate in higher education by 2020 (Ministry of Education, 2010). In the first decade of the new millennium, the income of all Chinese higher education institutions increased by almost 530%. The research universities enjoyed even faster growth. Shanghai Jiao Tong University's (SJTU) research income, for example, increased by 670% during the decade. The Chinese government has managed to further increase its education spending to 4.08% of gross domestic product (GDP) in 2012, which is 2,116.5 billion RMB (about US$345 billion), from a level of 3.66% in 2011. In this context, it has become a national endeavour to accelerate the process of building a number of world-class universities in China.

This paper argues that the calibre of a great university rests on the standing and competence of its faculty, and, therefore, the crucial factor in building a university of excellence is the creation of an outstanding faculty. The paper discusses the successful experience of Shanghai Jiao Tong University in assembling an internationally renowned faculty team. The paper concludes that Chinese universities have an opportunity to meet their urgent need for high-quality faculty, as the vast majority of Chinese who have studied abroad are interested in the idea of returning to China, either immediately after graduation or after gaining valuable work experience. This paper suggests a number of steps Chinese research universities and the leaders who oversee them can take if they wish to attract this talent back to China.

THE NEED FOR OUTSTANDING FACULTY

The calibre of a great university rests on the standing and competence of its faculty. The quality and commitment of the faculty determine the excellence of the university's academic programs, the quality of its student body, the reputation of its teaching and research, the resources it can attract from public and private sources, and its capacity to serve the wider society through public service (Rosovsky, 1991). Therefore, the crucial factor in building a university of excellence is the creation of an outstanding faculty. The increased investment in higher education in recent decades has reinvigorated the physical infrastructure of universities and colleges, meaning many Chinese higher-education institutions now enjoy first-rate facilities envied by their foreign counterparts. However, many continue to lack the "people" factor.

Recruiting staff of high quality is necessary for all universities and colleges, but for research universities it is imperative since they are competing, not only in their home market, where they may still benefit from domestic prestige, but also in the global market. There is perhaps no greater or more urgent challenge to the Chinese research university than to build and sustain a faculty of scholars who are creators and innovators of knowledge, teachers of distinction, who serve their institution and wider community in an effective and collegial manner, and who adhere to excellence in all their activities.

In 2006, Shanghai Jiao Tong University had around 3,000 teaching and research staff members, of whom only half held a PhD degree, and only 5.9% of the PhD holders gained their doctorate abroad. SJTU recognized the critical importance of faculty, and, in the strategic plan of 2007, the goal was set of assembling an outstanding and internationally renowned academic faculty that would match other world-class universities by 2020.

The history of most world-renowned universities reveals that they have generally evolved over the centuries of their own volition, and grown to prominence through incremental progress. SJTU could cultivate its own faculty, but, given the lack of local expertise in key research and teaching programs, particularly at graduate level, it would take too long to build up the required academic quality through natural progress. Therefore, the strategic decision was taken to rely extensively on recruiting from outside, in the first stage, and especially from abroad, in the search for an excellent faculty. This first-class faculty will then provide the mentoring that young scientists and researchers need and accelerate the cultivation of quality from within.

One major factor that can play a positive role in Chinese universities' search for excellent faculty is the large group of Chinese scientists and researchers working overseas. In the U.S., Chinese students represent the single largest source of foreign-born, doctorate-level scientists and engineers, and many have gone on to become innovative researchers and entrepreneurs. When it comes to brain drain, China is a reluctant champion. Many of the country's brightest have streamed out and few have returned; of the estimated 815,000 who left to study abroad between 1978 and 2004, only about a quarter came back (Cao, 2008). Chinese nationals comprise the largest number of foreign industrial hires in the U.S., and have historically had one of the highest stay rates. According to a report from the Oak Ridge Institute for Science and Education, more than nine of every ten students from China who gained a doctorate in the U.S. in 2002 were still in the country in 2007, the highest percentage of any foreign nation, compared with 33% for Japan and 41% for South Korea, for example (Finn, 1998).

However, after the deep recession that gripped Western economies in late 2007, there has been a prevalence of news reports of U.S. corporations restricting the hiring of foreign nationals and there have been deep cuts in funding for public universities. The bleak picture in much of the U.S. and the E.U. has been in stark contrast with China, which achieved an 8.7% growth in GDP in 2009, compared to the U.S.'s decline of 1.3%, providing a clear incentive for PhD graduates, as well as experienced scientists, to think twice about where to establish and develop their careers.

Now, with the country's economy booming and its strategy to reverse the tidal wave of scientific and research talent that has flowed out of China in the past two decades, more and more Chinese expatriates or *hai gui* (sea turtles), are starting to swim home. Motivated by patriotism, family ties, market forces, generous government schemes and the steadily growing and more secure Chinese economy, the long awaited homeward bound tide has finally turned far sooner and far more strongly than had been expected.

ASSEMBLING INTERNATIONALLY RENOWNED FACULTY

In recent years, considerable resources have been expended to upgrade university faculties by recruiting tens of thousands of scientists educated and employed in the West. The One-Thousand-Talent Plan offered scholars compensation equal to their salaries abroad, and as much as US$1.5 million in research funding (Xin, 2009). By the end of 2012, the Plan had recruited more than 2,000 academics, and SJTU alone has gained 76 full-time chair professors through this plan, one of the highest number of any universities in China. The premium salaries and generous research budgets provided by the university have helped to attract academics from abroad, but, to be successful, universities must also contribute to and complement them by offering professors an attractive remuneration package, a fulfilling career, a sense of purpose and a professional service.

An attractive remuneration package

Matching overseas salaries is the first challenge for Chinese universities. Relocation is a very significant commitment, especially for experienced professors who have family overseas. Although many of the recruited professors say that the salary was not the prime attraction, a salary level compatible with those offered in developed countries, at least in terms of purchasing power, will make the decision to relocate to China easier. The aim is to provide professors and their families with an attractive remuneration package so that the professors can focus on their teaching and research at universities without worries about degrading their quality of life.

There have been successful stories involving newly established universities in East Asia recruiting a large diaspora professor group. However, SJTU, like other traditional universities in China, differs in that it has an existing faculty, and it is not feasible to increase the pay of all existing faculty members to a level comparable to professors in developed countries. The university has therefore adopted a dual-track model, providing internationally competitive salaries to those hired academics who have an international reputation, and at the same time maintaining the pay structure for existing faculty members. To achieve this, SJTU has started fundraising campaigns to provide the additional money needed for international hires and to cater for the existing faculty.

Although salaries are important in recruiting and retaining faculty, the resources provided for research are perhaps even more vital. For those in laboratory-based disciplines, space, equipment and technical support are critical elements of the negotiation. Discretionary funds to support research assistants and graduate students can also prove decisive. Another key consideration for potential recruits is the possibility of future funding. With China's strong commitment to building a knowledge economy, it is expected that more funds will be injected into universities and research in the future.

A fulfilling career

Good salaries are not enough to attract and motivate high-performing academics; faculty members must also feel that they are part of a significant wider endeavour to ensure their full commitment towards the construction or renewal of the institution. A survey of intended returnees showed that about 60% of respondents listed expectations of a prestigious job back home as a "very important" or "somewhat important" reason for returning, while only 35% regarded greater economic rewards as decisive. Therefore, the attraction of more prestigious positions in China may be an equally influential factor. Along with national programs such as the One-Thousand-Talent Plan and Changjiang Scholars, SJTU has established programs endowed Chair Professors and Distinguished Professors to offer leading academics recognition for their achievements. The reputational or symbolic value associated with this provides added value for the returnee professors.

To attract and promote young scholars, the Special Research Fellow program has been established, which recruits young scholars who are assistant professors or have just completed post-doctoral training at the world's most prestigious universities. They are provided with generous start-up packages, encouraged to solve scientific problems in unconventional ways and helped to climb up the academic ladder. Many overseas Chinese PhD graduates express the desire to have a professional impact in their field, but this can be difficult to achieve in the competitive academic environment in developed countries. In contrast, many returnees who have gained a PhD or post-doctoral experience from prestigious overseas universities can expect a greater degree of autonomy in directing their research compared to their post-doctoral counterparts abroad, and some soon establish and lead their own research teams. Many of the young recruited scholars report that the opportunities to use their skills, the recognition of their research results, and the impact the results can make are more important than relatively good salaries.

A sense of purpose

Many recruits were already highly paid in overseas universities, and relocation to China means affecting family routines and a possible decline in living standards. Given the risks, distinguished scientists working abroad would have been unlikely to relocate to a new but unknown university if ethnic and emotional attachments to China had not been as important a factor to them as competitive salaries and career prospects.

Scholars with a strong emotional attachment to China were elated by the increased openness and economic progress of the country, and by improved conditions of universities. For them, this progress provided an opportunity to participate in a significant event and play a role in China's modernization, and to make an important contribution to their motherland. This sense of greater purpose, of advancing the discipline for the university and the country, and of shaping the development of China in the global context, has been a common sentiment among many overseas recruits.

A professional service

In order for the university to recruit new faculty members on the scale required to fill the large number of currently vacant positions, it will be essential to modernize and streamline the staffing and selection process. At SJTU a Green Passage system has been established to accelerate the staffing process and cater to the needs of professors who have been hired from overseas. This system helps to resolve issues — such as salary negotiations, welfare and living expenses — more quickly than if using traditional procedures. The profes-sional human resources (HR) team at SJTU efficiently help newcomers with navigating the bureaucratic hurdles of moving to China, with finding accom-modation and with integrating into the local community.

ACHIEVEMENTS OF RECRUITING AT SJTU

Efforts at SJTU to recruit international academics have been extremely suc-cessful. To date, the university has recruited over 300 professors from interna-tionally renowned institutions abroad, and in 2012 alone it received 269 appli-cations and interviewed 86 candidates. Furthermore, recognizing that building a strong academic team not only involves attracting experienced academics, but also achieving a balance between academics at the peak of their career and young scholars with promising academic futures, experienced professors are encouraged to initiate searches for promising young scholars in their disci-plines and to build up the faculty calibre. Since then, the backbone of the pro-fessoriate has successfully attracted a large number of talented young scholars.

Through the process of recruiting, and incumbent academics leaving, the overall faculty size has remained largely unchanged, but the calibre and struc-ture have improved greatly. The percentage of the faculty holding a PhD has increased by almost 30%, and the percentage holding a foreign PhD has more than tripled; now one in four PhD holders in SJTU gained their doctorates abroad. These qualifications are not only an indication of the calibre of the faculty, but they also represent a wellspring of academic capital used to form transnational research collaborations among networks of scholars.

Among the returnee professors are Ji Weidong, previously Professor of Law at Kobe University, Japan, an awardee of the Changjiang Scholar program; now Dean of the KoGuan School of Law at SJTU, Professor Ji is preparing the school towards achieving world-class status with a comprehensive plan of legal educa-tion reform; Liu Jianglai is a representative of young returned scholars, having completed his PhD in the University of Maryland-College Park and post-doc-toral training at Caltech; he is now in charge of the photomultiplier system in the PANDA-X dark matter search experiment, in the newly constructed 2,500m deep underground lab in Sichuan Province in southwest China.

Returnees bring with them an in-depth knowledge of world-class university culture and organizational practices, making them a valuable resource in aid-ing China's university development. As leading or promising academics in their respective fields, the returnee professors have increased the university's capacity to generate and apply new knowledge. Literature analysis has shown that returnee professors produce a greater number of important papers, which are cited more frequently, and are published more often in high-impact jour-nals than professors who remained in China for their whole research career.

The university's capacity for, and output of, research is significantly greater with the input of returnee professors. The volume of research grants received from National Natural Science Foundation of China (NSFC) increased 550% in the six years between 2006 and 2012. The university is also emphasizing the quality of its research; based on the Science Citation Index published by the Institute for Scientific Information (ISI), the number of citations increased 358%, representing a rapid improvement in the quality of scientific output. According to the latest figures from the Essential Science Indicators also by ISI, 15 disciplines at SJTU now rank in the world's top 1% in terms of the number of citations, and the positions of all disciplines are improving rapidly.

Table 1: SJTU Indicators in 2006 and 2011

Indicator	2006	2012	Growth
Faculty Number	2930	2760	– 5.8%
Faculty with PhD from overseas universities	5.9%	21.2%	259.3%
Funding from NSFC (in million RMB)	97.2	632.1	550.3%
Research Papers Published	2,169	3,519	62.2%
Research Paper Citations	2,742	12,555	357.9%
World's Top 1% Disciplines	5	15	200%

Figure 1: SJTU's Grants from the Natural Science Foundation of China, 2006-2012

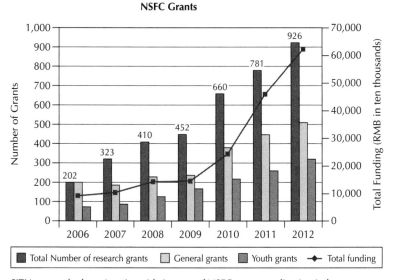

SJTU was ranked top 1 nationwide in term of NSFC grants application in last two consecutive years

CONCLUSION AND DISCUSSION

China already leads the world in the growth of scientific research and is now the second largest producer of scientific knowledge (Adams, 2010). In recent years, considerable resources have been expended to upgrade university quality in China, and it has become a national endeavour to accelerate the process of building a number of world-class universities. This paper argues that the calibre of a great university rests on the standing and competence of its faculty, and, therefore, the crucial factor in building a university of excellence is the creation of an outstanding faculty. This paper points out that Chinese universities have an opportunity to meet their urgent need for high-quality faculty, as the vast majority of Chinese who have studied abroad are interested in the idea of returning to China, either immediately after graduation, or after gaining valuable work experience. The experience of Shanghai Jiao Tong University suggest a number of steps Chinese research universities, and the leaders who oversee them, can take if they wish to attract this talent back to China.

Figure 2: Vision for faculty at SJTU in 2013 (figures in the left) and 2020 (figures in the right)

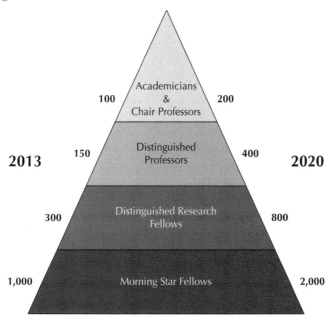

Despite the achievement of attracting high-quality faculty members, the university also realizes the challenges and difficulties associated with such recruitment. The "star" status associated with the returnee professors can have unintended negative impacts on the non-returnee faculty, such as decreased morale. Conflicts may arise between overseas returnees and faculty who are domestically trained, and between recent returnees and those who repatriated many years ago. How the university can help overseas returnee scholars efficiently increase their research network within Chinese academia remains another question.

Therefore, although the dual-track model currently adopted is required for attracting quality academics, the ultimate goal is that the two tracks should be merged into a modified tenure-track model. Salaries and compensation packages have been progressively increased for all faculty members, whilst also making them more flexible and performance-based. The Morning Star program was launched to help existing young faculty improve their performance, and so far the program has benefited 1,083 existing young academics in last four years, awarding 73 million RMB (about US$11.9 million). In addition, standards are being raised for academic faculty recruitment, retention and promotion, meaning the quality standards for domestic and international hires will eventually converge, as well as the pay. Pilot reforms have been started in selected departments to merge the two tracks, and the aim is to do this for all departments by 2020, when the university will have realized its goal of assembling an outstanding and internationally renowned academic faculty.

Globalization has accelerated the building of research universities, and also reduced the time that nations with rapidly growing economies are willing to wait for building such institutions. The case of SJTU illustrates how the quality of the faculty at a traditional university can be improved if the institution is astute in its perception of opportunities within a rapidly changing economic environment, is able to assimilate the required resources, and is pro-active and skillful in its approach to hiring internationally renowned professors, and thus enabling a university from an emerging economy to move rapidly into the league of world-class universities.

REFERENCES

Adams, J. (2010). "Get ready for China's domination of science". *New Scientist*, 2742.
Cao, C. (2008). "China's brain drain at the high end: why government policies have failed to attract first-rate academics to return". *Asian Population Studies*, 4(3), 331-345.
Finn, M. G. (1998). *Stay Rates of Foreign Doctorate Recipients from U.S. Universities*, 2007. Oak Ridge, TN: Oak Ridge Institute for Science and Education.
Ministry of Education. (2010). "China's New National Education Plan Aims to Build A Country with Rich Human Resources". http://www.moe.edu.cn/publicfiles/business/htmlfiles/moe/moe_2862/201010/109031.html

Rosovsky, H. (1991). *The university: An owner's manual*. New York, NY: W. W. Norton & Company.

Xin, H. (2009). "Help Wanted: 2000 Leading Lights To Inject a Spirit of Innovation". *Science*, 325 (5940), 534-535.

Yu, K., Stith, A., Liu, L. & Chen, H. (2010). *Tertiary Education at a Glance: China*. Shanghai/Boston, MA: Shanghai Jiao Tong University Press/Sense Publishers.

CHAPTER 18

Higher Education Model for Large Developing Economies

Raghunath K. Shevgaonkar*

INTRODUCTION

Education is the key to socio-economic development and character building. Higher education plays an important role in knowledge and wealth creation. Historically, one can find a good correlation between the spread and quality of higher education and the economic development of a nation. Scientific, social and economic developments in developed nations can be primarily attributed to the robust higher education systems those nations developed over a long period of time. Many European universities have a tradition longer than a few hundred years, whereas in the developing nations the modern education system evolved only in the last 100 years. In countries like India and China, although there were world-renowned universities in pre-Christ era, in the intermediate period the higher education system deteriorated due to many social, economic, geographical and political reasons, and today these large nations suffer from inadequate higher education systems. Although more than half the world's population lives in these countries, their knowledge and wealth contribution to the world are relatively small. With the industrial revolution, the economic gap between the western world and the Asian countries further increased. Countries like India and China continued to work with traditional practices without paying due attention to the modern approach to knowledge and wealth generation. The same thing happened in the middle Asian, African and South American countries. As a result, a large part of the world remained deprived of economic development. Large nations like India and China aspire to be major players in the modern world. However, this can become possible only with establishing a proper and robust higher education system.

211

PRESENT STATUS OF HIGHER EDUCATION
IN DEVELOPING COUNTRIES

According to the World Bank report published at the end of the last century, more than 80% of the world's population lives in developing countries as conventionally defined on the basis of per capita income. The developing world includes Africa, much of Asia, most of Latin America and large parts of the former Soviet Union. Although the developing nations exhibit wide economic, political, social and cultural diversity, the report discusses broad principles applicable to all the developing nations.

It is clear that in the 21st century wealth will not remain confined to factories and land, but will be distributed in the form of knowledge, skills and innovativeness of the people. The developed world has quickly reacted to the demands of the 21st century by redefining its educational priorities. However this could not happen for the developing countries. This is not because the challenges of the 21st century are not well understood by the developing countries, but they have many implementation issues due to their geographical, social and political conditions. One can therefore ask the following questions in the context of the developing countries: (i) what is the role of higher education in economic and social development? (ii) what are the major obstacles that Higher Education faces in developing nations? (iii) how can these obstacles be overcome?

These questions might appear trivial since the role of higher education in economic and social development is abundantly clear. However, in reality, during the last three to four decades the focus in developing countries has been mostly on primary and not tertiary education. (China, however, has provided more thrust for higher education in last decade.) Higher Education has remained under-funded by governments and consequently Higher Education institutions are politicized and poorly regulated. There is therefore a need to concentrate on Higher Education in developing nations. The report also points out that the modern Higher Education system has not remained limited to extending help in raising living standards and alleviating poverty, but has been forced to confront expansion, differentiation and a knowledge revolution. In recent times there has been a shift from class to mass in the Higher Education system in developing countries. More and more children are completing secondary education and are aspiring to get university degrees. Consequently the old institutions have grown in size to become mega-universities. Similarly a variety of new specialized institutions emerged in developing countries as compared to a small member of homogeneous universities that existed 50 years ago. The major impact of this quick expansion is the deterioration in the quality of Higher Education. Since major expansion is taking place in the private education sector, there is a need to explore what the private sector can and cannot deliver. For example, the private sector is mostly interested in professional schools and not in traditional university subjects. Government then should establish a mechanism for guaranteeing quality and for nurturing areas in which the private sector is unlikely to invest, like fundamental research, humanities and social sciences, liberal arts etc.

The internet transformed the outlook and the functioning of the world. More knowledge became accessible and those who got the skills to use it became powerful. The knowledge revolution therefore requires a new type of education. Higher Education should create intellectuals who are flexible and keep learning life long. In the present context Higher Education therefore becomes extremely important for the developing world. It is amply clear that although Higher Education alone cannot guarantee rapid economic growth, no sustained progress is possible without it.

The success of higher education lies in high-quality faculty, high-quality and committed students, and adequate resources. Developing nations primarily lack the first and the last of the three. By and large there are well prepared and committed pre-university student populations, but unfortunately there is an acute shortage of qualified faculty, and resources are meager. Faculty financial packages are the least attractive and therefore university faculty is the last option exercised by bright researchers. Due to the low paying capacity of the population in developing countries, revenue generation from tuition is negligibly small and Higher Education needs almost full financial support from the Government. Since the Government's priority in the developing countries is primary and secondary education, the developing countries spend far less on higher education than the developed countries on each student. It may however be pointed out that in developing countries individuals actually spend a higher proportion of their income than that in the developed world on higher education.

In addition to low financial resources, the developing countries suffer from poor governance.

Another important aspect of Higher Education in developing countries is insufficient scientific capacity. Academia in these countries also lacks strong linkages with industries. This pushes developing countries further behind the industrial nations in terms of their science and technology achievements, and widens global inequality. The key question for policy-makers in developing countries is what is the priority for science and technology education from a resource-allocation viewpoint? The answer widely varies from country to country. India and other Asian countries have provided proper thrust for science and technology education and have started playing a major role in development of software and manufacturing.

HIGHER EDUCATION IN INDIA – ISSUES & CHALLENGES

In India barring a few, most of the universities were established after independence from the British rule i.e., in the last 60 years (Note: At the time of independence there were only 30 universities in India). After independence (Colonial rule) in 1947, the visionary leadership of India put a thrust on technology education to make the Nation self-reliant and economically strong. A central regulatory body, the University Grants Commission (UGC), was established to define a higher education path for the country. A large number of state universities were established across the country to develop qualified manpower in all disciplines of science, engineering and technology, and humanities and social sciences (see Table I). The universities were primarily based on the British model with affiliated colleges that were physically isolated from the main university campuses. Although initially the universities were supposed to handle both undergraduates and postgraduates, slowly, the undergraduate teaching was shifted to the affiliated colleges and the university campuses predominantly became postgraduate. However, academic control, including the conduct of examinations, even for undergraduates, remained with the universities. The university functions got divided into two parts, postgraduate teaching and research, and the conduct of examination of the undergraduate students admitted in the affiliated colleges. Part of the university became an examination conducting board. Due to democratic processes involving the affiliated colleges, the functioning of university became sluggish and the quality of education deteriorated. Today a medium-size state university has 200-300 affiliated colleges with typical enrolment of 200,000 to 300,000 students. At large universities like Delhi, Mumbai, Pune, Kolkata, the number of affiliated colleges is as high as 500-600 and student enrolment more than half a million each. In the last 60 years the number of state-funded universities increased to about 300 and an equal number of privately funded universities have come into existence in last two decades.

Just after independence, as mentioned earlier, a few technological universities known as Indian Institutes of Technology (IIT) were established to meet the technological needs of the country by a special Act of parliament. These institutions were primarily based on the American Higher Education model and did not follow the affiliated college system. The institutions were single campus institutions with a good mix of undergraduate and postgraduate education and research.

To start with there were five IITs primarily located in different zones of the country i.e., Kharagpur (East), Bombay (West), Madras (South), Kanpur (North) and Delhi (North). Since that was the beginning of technical education in India, the Government of India encouraged mentorship from different industrialized nations for different IITs. Consequently, except IIT Kharagpur, all IITs received mentorship from the advanced nations — IIT Bombay was mentored by the USSR, IIT Madras was mentored by Germany, IIT Kanpur was mentored by the U.S. and IIT Delhi was mentored by the U.K. The mentorship not only provided financial and technical assistance, but imparted the

Table 1: Universities in India (2011)*

Institutes of National Importance	70
Central Universities	44
State Public Universities	302
Deemed to be Universities	132
Private Universities	146
Total Universities	694

*There were only 30 universities in India in 1950

educational ethos of the respective countries. This indeed resulted in some cultural differences between different IITs. However, over time all the IITs more or less converged to the American model of education. IITs provided a strong thrust on fundamentals and analytical skills, and produced graduates of international quality. IIT became a brand synonymous with quality in technical education. The number of IITs practically remained the same for almost 50 years. However, considering the need, the number tripled in the last decade. Today there are 16 IITs in India, including the original five.

In addition to IITs which were primarily technology institutions, a large number of central universities based on the American models were also established across the country. These universities are single campus universities covering all disciplines in science and humanities with a good mix of undergraduates and postgraduates. Jawaharlal Nehru University (JNU) at Delhi may be a good example of this.

To insure quality in higher education, the Government of India set up a National Assessment and Accreditation Council (NAAC) and a star rating criteria evolved over time. The star rating is based on overall performance in terms of NAAC score on a four-point scale, citation of research articles, patents filed etc. Although accreditation is not mandatory in India, good universities voluntarily obtain NAAC certification every five years. The institutions of national importance are exempted from the NAAC certification. Table II gives the number of universities for different star ratings.

While the modern university system was getting established in the country in the middle of the last century, the Government of India established a large number of research laboratories for area-specific fundamental and applied research under the banner of Council of Scientific and Industrial Research (CSIR). The mandate of these laboratories was to carry out research of national need without getting involved into teaching. As a result the research slowly moved from universities to these laboratories, research funds to the universities decreased and university research dwindled. Most of the state universities became teaching-centric examination bodies with less focus on research.

This model was in contrast to the western model where primary cutting-edge research is done in the university.

Table 2: Star Ranking of Indian Universities (214 Accredited Universities)

Star Rating	NAAC Score	Scopus Citations	Patents filed	Number of Universities
*****	>3.6	>6500	>500	24
****	3.2 – 3.6	3000 – 6500	>50	50
***	3.0 – 3.2	1000 – 3000	10 – 50	52
**	2.5 – 3.0	500 – 1000	1 – 9	44
*	2.0 – 2.5	100 – 500	–	44

The major disadvantage of this model was that the university students were deprived of exposure to cutting-edge research and their motivation to opt for research as a profession decreased. Due to improper exposure of the excitements in research, research became the last option for university graduates. This consequently resulted in a shortage of quality, research-oriented faculty in the universities.

In short, in the last 60 years, the Indian university system has undergone a massive expansion (See Table I). In addition to the state-funded universities, a large number of privately funded universities were also established in recent years. Today there are more than 650 universities in India, enrolling more than 10 million students, with about 1.5 million students in engineering and technology.

In spite of the massive expansion of the university system in India, the higher education gross enrolment ratio (GER) in India is just about 18%. When compared with other developing and developed countries, this GER is far below the satisfactory level (See Figure 1). For Asian countries this number is about 24% and in developed nations this number exceeds 70%. With the current number of higher education institutions, the GER in India will decrease in the next one to two decades because demographically India will become younger in the next few decades. It is therefore clear that even to catch up with Asian countries, the Higher Education system in India has to double within the next decade, and has to expand manifold within the next 30 years to become comparable to that of the developed nations.

India needs massive expansion and investment in research universities also (refer Figure 2 and Figure 3 for relative data). Today there is one research university for every 3 million population, whereas there is typically one university for every million population in the developed countries (see Table III). Research funding which is less than 0.5% of the GDP needs to be substantially enhanced as developed countries spend more than 2% of their GDP in research. Industrial investment in R&D also needs a transformational change.

Figure 3: Gross Enrolment Ratio for the Developed and Developing Nations [Ref. World Development Indicators 2012]

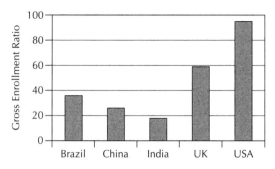

Figure 4: Number of Researchers

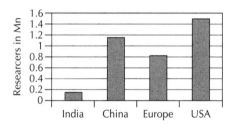

Figure 5: National R&D Investment

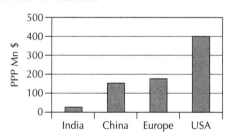

Table 3: Indian Universities and Population

Total Population in India	1.2 Billion
One University for	1.7 Million
Total PhD Awarding Universities	416
One Research University for	1 Million in Developed Countries
One Research University for	3 Million in India

HIGHER EDUCATION MODEL FOR INDIA

India's Education system has to undergo a massive transformation in the years to come, and the process has already begun. Education has been declared a high priority sector by the Indian Government and the funding has been enhanced manifold. However, mere enhancement of funds is not adequate to create a top-quality higher education system. Funds can create infrastructure and laboratories, but the creation of quality faculty is a long-drawn process. The major difficulty that India's Higher Education system faces today is an acute shortage of quality faculty. Today India produces about 10,000 to 15,000 Phds per year, including about 2,000 in Engineering and Technology. This output is just about 25-30% of the national need. Due to a shortage of quality faculty, undergraduate education also suffers and the employability of graduates diminishes. The Indian Education System is therefore in a most challenging situation. It needs rapid expansion without compromising the quality of education.

To fill the gap of quality faculty, India has done a commendable job in using technology for teaching. To start with, e-learning technology has been used in engineering education. On an initiative of the Ministry of Human Resource Development, under the National Project on Technology Enhanced Learning (NPTEL) the entire engineering curriculum in all disciplines has been developed in web and video lecture format. There are more than 600 courses that have classroom video content created by the best faculty available in the country (mostly from IITs). This content is made available to anyone and everyone across the country free of cost. A high bandwidth National Knowledge Network (NKN), which connects all the educational institutions, has been commissioned for dissemination of the e-content. In addition, efforts are made to reach masses outside the Institute premises through the mobile communication network. India has an excellent mobile network with 80% penetration; with low-cost mobile handsets and tablets, it is possible to take quality e-content to a large number of students. In India, therefore, e-learning (MOOC) has been playing an important role in handling the problem of the shortage of quality faculty. Indeed this may not be a permanent solution, but is an excellent interim choice.

Being the largest democracy in the world and a prospective major player in the global economy in the years to come, India's Higher Education system needs to deliver on three counts, namely skilled manpower, high-quality research and innovation. The three outcomes need conceptually different institutional set-ups. There may be some overlap between some or all of them, but a university or a Higher Education Institute needs to define its objectives clearly. Considering the scale at which the system has to work, it is difficult for an institute to perform equally well in all the outcomes. Even within an institute, it is difficult to find talent that has excellence in all three. Generally it is believed that research, innovation and teaching support each other. However, if the scale of operation is massive, as is the case in large, developing economies like India, institutions with three distinct priorities are a more effective model. The existing university system, with some modifications, will be more appropriate in the Indian context, instead of adopting the American university model. The model symbolically is shown in Figure 3. The model suggests three overlapping segments — teaching, research and innovation, and a university can choose relative proportions of them.

Teaching: The first segment that primarily focuses on teaching undergraduates can include all the affiliated colleges. An examination board can be created to efficiently conduct the examinations for the large student base. Teaching can be through the face-to-face mode or through a quality electronic mode. MOOCs may be used for imparting subject knowledge. Students can be empowered to define their course structure within some broad guidelines. Skills-based education can be made mandatory to make the graduate more employable. National agencies can assess the requirement of the specific skill sectors like administration, service sector, infrastructure development etc., and can dynamically upgrade the undergraduate curriculum. Although it is not mandatory, looking at the capability, a select class of students can be encouraged to interact with segments II and III. Faculty for this segment need not be PhDs since their primary responsibility would be quality teaching. However, they should have ample opportunities to overlap with the other two segments for enriching their knowledge. There should also be regular refresher programs for the teachers for updating subject knowledge. The performance of this segment should be assessed on the basis of the number of students graduated, their performance in competitive examinations and their placement.

Research: Research should remain primarily the responsibility of the state. Universities should focus on research and research-oriented teaching. Self-learning should become a regular practice instead of normal classroom teaching. E-content can be used for self-learning. Ample funds should be provided to the universities for doing research that is globally competitive. The faculty of this segment should address fundamental issues and grand challenges. The output of this segment should be measured in terms of funds attracted for research, and peer-reviewed journal and conference publications, articles, books etc. The faculty and students of this segment may interact with other two segments with a clear understanding that their primary responsibility is quality research. National agencies may define thrust areas of research from time to time, and the faculty of this segment should be able to align themselves with national priorities. In short, the faculty of this segment should be able to work with a free mind within broad research guidelines decided by the state.

Figure 6: Higher Education Model for Large Developing Countries

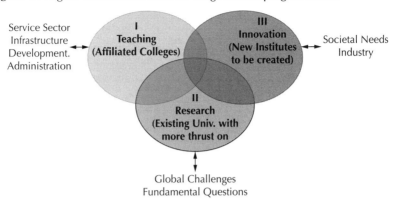

Service Sector
Infrastructure
Development.
Administration

I
Teaching
(Affiliated Colleges)

III
Innovation
(New Institutes
to be created)

Societal Needs
Industry

II
Research
(Existing Univ. with
more thrust on

Global Challenges
Fundamental Questions

Innovation: Innovation is the key word today. An innovation improves some aspect of human life. A good innovation enhances the benefit to cost ratio where the benefit could be in terms of comfort of life, monetary return, human safety etc., and the cost could be in terms of money or resources, physical effort, etc. Innovation requires out-of-the-box thinking, an ecosystem and different training needed for product development. Not every researcher in the university may have the temperament and passion to convert his/her ideas into a usable product. Innovation also needs a good feel for societal requirements. For innovation, new universities or institutions need to be set up with mostly postgraduate education. Since industry generally has a good feel for the market and community needs, its linkage with this segment is very crucial. Assessing societal needs, industry can project problems to academia and the academician can work with a specific focus on a problem. Academia should work on concept-proving and the prototyping of an innovative idea, and the ecosystem should take the idea to the user in the final product form. The innovation university therefore should have a technology-transfer unit and a science and technology park. The technology-transfer unit should help an innovator to incubate a company or to establish a link with a prospective industry. The unit should also conduct regular programs about how to create innovation. The unit also should help in patent filing and IP protection. The output of the faculty from this segment should be measured in terms of patents and their monetization potential. The faculty from this segment of universities should not be assessed on the basis of publishable research. Since generally a good product needs input from multiple disciplines, the system should facilitate multi- and inter-disciplinary research cutting across various branches of science, engineering and the social sciences, including the law. The curriculum should not be straitjacketed and should be decided by the faculty depending upon the broad topic in which an innovation is expected. This approach is the opposite of what a research university would normally follow where, first, all courses would be taught and then the research problem would be defined. The courses should be in small modules with a more practical orientation and open thinking. This segment may have linkages with the other two segments.

Innovation universities are practically nonexistent in India today. However realizing the importance of innovation in the 21st century, the Indian Government has established a National innovation council to promote innovative research. The University Grants Commission also has initiated schemes to establish innovation clusters in the existing universities with substantial funding over next five-year plan. The primary objective is to help develop innovative products that are India-centric. India-centric means a product which meets the needs of masses and which is inclusive, low-cost and sustainable. Since India is a multilingual, multi-caste, multi-religion system, innovation should cut across the boundaries of language, caste and religion. India therefore needs to develop its own educational framework since the model from the developed nations may not be suitable for Indian conditions.

It is therefore clear that a unique combination of teaching, research and innovation for university may not meet the needs of all societies. A variety of universities with different weightages given to the three segments, teaching, research and innovation, are needed in India. At present, since the thrust is on capacity-building, a large number of teaching-focused universities need to be created. However, as the country becomes more developed, the weightage for research must be enhanced. The education model proposed here is dynamic in nature and can be tuned to the requirements of individual nations. Considering the huge population, limited resources and complex society of India, there is a great potential for innovation. Also innovation created by and for India will be affordable to a majority of the global population that resides in developing nations.

SUMMARY

In this paper the challenges of higher education in the developing countries which account for more than 80% of the world's population have been investigated. Developing countries like India, China and some of the Latin American nations that aspire to be major players in the 21st century have provided thrust for higher education in the last two decades. However, there is still a long way to achieve the desired GER and the research capability. The Indian education system has been presented as a test case. A dynamic education model for large countries like India has been proposed. It is believed that the model will help in enhancing GER, research and innovation in the large developing countries, and will help in narrowing the gap between the developing and the developed world.

* The author is thankful to Dr. Ambuj Sagar, Professor of Humanities and Social Sciences at IIT Delhi for critical feedback on the manuscript of this paper.

REFERENCES:

Building Sustainable Higher Education, id21 Insights Education 7 (2008).

Careers360 March (2013). www.careers360.com.UNESCO report "Education at Glance" (2012).

UNESCO report "Trends in Tertiary Education: Sub-Saharan Africa" (2010).

UNESCO Institute of Statistics report "Global Investment in R & D" (2012).

UNESCO Institute of Statistics report "Human Resource in R & D" (2012). University Grants Commission reports, www.ugc.ac.in.

World Bank report on Higher Education in developing Countries — Peril and Promise (2000). World Development Indicators 2012.

CHAPTER

Challenges and Opportunities for Public Research Universities in Brazil

Carlos Henrique de Brito Cruz

F ederal and State-level support for higher education and research played a fundamental role for Brazil to develop a graduate schools system that awarded 13,912 doctoral level titles in 2012. The number of scientific articles authored by scientists working in Brazilian higher education institutions and published in international journals grew from 2,000 in 1980 to 38,000 in 2012 (TR Web of Science data, 2013).

In the Brazilian higher education system, research-intensive universities exist because higher education and research are supported by public funding provided through two complementary streams, plus a smaller fraction sourced from business. One is the institutional funding to universities that covers salaries for faculty and staff, plus the basic operation costs of the institutions. By law, public universities cannot charge any tuition for both undergraduate and graduate courses. The second funding stream is the competitive peer-review processes, operated by (public) research funding agencies at the national and state level. Business funding for university research contributes a small fraction of the total research funding in most Brazilian universities, with a few notable exceptions.

Of the 190 universities in Brazil in 2011 (INEP, 2011), 102 were public. Among the private universities, on average, only 24% of the faculty has a PhD degree, and practically none of them qualifies as being research intensive. Among the public universities, on average, 54% of the faculty has a PhD degree, and for only 14 (11 federal and 3 state universities) of those more than 75% of the faculty has that title.

Besides having faculty qualified to lead research, it is expected that research-intensive universities offer a broad range of graduate courses, which are instrumental in defining the connection between education and research that underlies these institutions. Applying this additional criterion, the estimated number of 14 research-intensive universities mentioned above reduces to the 10 universities shown in Table 1.

Having 21% of the faculty among the public universities in Brazil, these 10 universities responded, in 2012, for 55% of the doctoral titles awarded in Brazil, for 68% of the number of scientific articles published by authors from Brazil in Web of Science journals, and for 88% of the citations received in the scientific literature.

Presently, one of the most important challenges for these universities is that of obtaining higher impact. By "impact" we mean two main dimensions: (1) intellectual impact, measured for example in the number of citations received in the international literature; and (2) societal impact, measured for example in terms of assisting the competitiveness of business and the effectiveness of public policy. This does not mean they do not already have a strong impact in the development of Brazil. They do, e.g. in terms of qualified personnel they graduate and get positions in business or in other universities in Brazil. Most of them also have intense ties with business, and their scientific articles receive a good fraction of the citations to Brazilian-authored articles. The point is that there is room to grow, and the taxpayer and their representatives expect that. In the following we describe some of the initiatives that were put in place to this end, focused mainly in (1) developing university-industry research collaborations; (2) developing international research collaborations; and (3) developing long-term, high-impact research.

Of course, the list shown in Table 1 is only indicative and it is dynamic. Younger universities (the case of the Federal University of ABC comes to mind) are climbing the ladder quickly and will soon have the breadth of fields and graduate doctoral programs to be considered research-intensive. A small number of private universities, such as the Pontifical University of Rio de Janeiro and the Pontifical University of São Paulo might also be included.

DEVELOPING UNIVERSITY-INDUSTRY/GOVERNMENT RESEARCH CONNECTIONS

In addition to a steady flow of graduates to industry, research-intensive universities in Brazil have been working to intensify their research connections to business through two main mechanisms: (1) joint university-industry research projects; and (2) start-up company generation, mostly led by former students.

Table 1: Size of faculty, percentage with a Doctoral degree, number of Doctoral thesis approved in 2012, and number of Web of Science documents for Brazil and for the ten universities in Brazil qualified as research-intensive universities.

Region/University	Faculty	%DR	DR Thesis approved	Web of Science Documents
Brazil	129.716	54%	13.912	34.393
Sum for the ten universities below	27.854		7.597	23.549
University of São Paulo	5.860	99%	2.439	7.712
State University of Campinas	1.739	99%	853	2.534
Federal University of São Paulo	1.216	95%	308	1.561
University of the State of São Paulo	3.625	95%	852	2.716
Federal University of Minas Gerais	3.027	83%	626	1.903
Federal University of Rio Grande do Sul	2.570	82%	767	2.068
Federal University of Rio de Janeiro	3.791	81%	773	2.310
Federal University of São Carlos	1.226	79%	220	820
University of Brasília	2.513	77%	365	843
Federal University of Santa Catarina	2.287	77%	394	1.082

Sources:
Faculty and percentage with Dr degree: for federal universities, INEP's Statistical Summary, 2011; for state universities the respective Statistical Yearbooks, 2012
Number of Dr Thesis approved: CAPES database, 2012
Number of Web of Science Documents: Thomson Reuters InCites, 2012

Most, if not all, of the universities listed in Table 1 have offices directed at developing opportunities for joint research. They look for partnerships with industry and, to a lesser but still relevant extent, with government. For the universities listed for which there is data available on the value of the research contracts with industry, the percentage of the total research expenditures falls between 5% and 8%, which is comparable to the average value for universities in the U.S. (NSB, 2012).

The number of opportunities for joint university-industry research has been growing, and research funding agencies like the National Funder of Studies and Projects (FINEP) and the São Paulo Research Foundation (FAPESP) offer special programs to match funds to those of companies looking to contract research at universities.

FAPESP operates a program through which the foundation enters in an agreement with partner companies to jointly announce calls for proposals to select the projects to be co-funded. The portfolio of companies using this program has been growing and includes Microsoft, Agilent, Braskem, Oxiteno, SABESP, VALE, Natura, Petrobrás, Embraer, Padtec, Biolab, Cristalia, Whirlpool, Boeing, GSK, BP, BG and PSA (Peugeot-Citröen). The calls invite proposals that might be for two-year research projects up to 10-year research plans for a joint Engineering Research Center (ERC) hosted in a university.

In some cases the partner is a governmental organization, a Secretary or Ministry. To mention an example, the researchers of the FAPESP-BIOTA program, who lead several research grants to study the biodiversity in the State of São Paulo, developed a longstanding interaction with the State of São Paulo Secretary for the Environment and assisted them in creating more than 20 pieces of legislation for environmental conservation (Joly *et al.*, 2010). In Bioenergy, researchers from the FAPESP BIOEN Research Program are working with UNESCO in a SCOPE assessment of the impacts of large scale bioenergy production.

Start-up creation is also a target for the research-intensive universities in Brazil. The State University of Campinas describes on its website a list of more than 200 start-ups originating in the last 20 years, generating thousands of jobs and opportunities for young students. Again, FINEP and FAPESP offer programs to fund small business R&D that are similar to the SBIR program in the U.S.

DEVELOPING INTERNATIONAL RESEARCH COLLABORATIONS

Increasing international research collaboration can help to increase the intellectual impact of the research. Most of the universities listed in Table 1 have been developing programs for international collaboration. The University of São Paulo (USP) is one of the most effective in this endeavour, and, besides having a good number of active exchange agreements, has recently organized a joint graduate course with Ohio State University and Rutgers University, in topics related to plant sciences.

In 2012 the Ministry for Science and Technology of Brazil announced an ample program to send students from Brazilian universities for stays up to 12 months in universities abroad. The program, named Science without Borders, offers opportunities for students in fields of study considered strategic by the Brazilian government and invites collaboration with industry. The announced target is to send 100,000 students in four years. Most of these are undergraduate students who will attend classes that will contribute to their courses. A smaller fraction is composed of graduate students who will either do a full PhD abroad or spend 12 months working in research related to the thesis they are doing in Brazil. As of August, 2013, 35,138 students had been supported. Of these, 26,682 were undergraduates, 3,718 were doctoral students enrolled in Brazil who went for a 12-months stay, 746 were doctoral students enrolled in a full doctorate abroad, and 1,989 were post-doctoral fellows (CNPq, 2013). The sheer magnitude of the program will bring important results for the education of the students involved and also for the establishment of international networks in research.

In the state of São Paulo FAPESP has been developing an important strategy for creating opportunities for research collaboration for researchers in the state. FAPESP maintains cooperation agreements with research funding agencies, higher educational and research institutions and business enterprises. The international cooperation covers a broad range of countries and agencies (FAPESP, n.d.-a), including the U.K. Research Councils, the Agence Nationale de Recherche in France, the Deutsche Forschungsgemeinschaft (DFG) in Germany, the National Science Foundation and the Department of Energy in the U.S., the Danish Council for Strategic Research (Dk), the Fundação para Ciência e Tecnologia (Portugal), the Academy of Finland, the Consejo Nacional de Ciéncia e Tecnologia (Argentina) and other funding agencies.

To foster the preparation of joint proposals, FAPESP has agreements with universities in most of these countries, through which seed funds are offered for teams of researchers to work together and prepare full proposals to be jointly submitted.

In addition to this, FAPESP has been organizing a number of scientific events (FAPESP Week Symposia) in key hubs like Washington DC, Toronto, Boston, Tokyo, Madrid and London. In each of the FAPESP Week Symposia, researchers from São Paulo, Brazil, and invited colleagues from the region present their recent results and discuss the ongoing collaborations, creating opportunities for the funding agencies to interact directly with the collaborating researchers and assess the progress of the collaborations. FAPESP's strategy and instruments for international collaborations are described online (FAPESP, n.d.-a) The number of joint research projects supported by FAPESP grew 20-fold, from eight in 2005 to 150 in 2012.

The strategy for international collaboration also includes bringing foreign scientists to São Paulo. FAPESP's program of post-doctoral fellowships is open to foreigners willing to come to Brazil. In the Natural Sciences the percentage of foreign post-docs supported by the foundation grew from 15% in 2007 to 34% in 2012. In the Life Sciences the change was from 4% to 11%. In 2012 FAPESP awarded more than 920 post-doctoral fellowships. All proposals are selected through peer-reviewing and applications can be submitted in English.

Additionally, the Young Investigator program selects scientists with a few years of post-doctoral experience, demonstrating outstanding research leadership capabilities (FAPESP, n.d.-b). Funding includes a fellowship, plus a research grant. In 2012, 88 young investigator awards were granted for researchers to start their careers in São Paulo, in the Natural Sciences and Engineering.

For outstanding, experienced researchers who have a permanent position outside Brazil, FAPESP offers the São Paulo Excellence Chairs (SPEC). The candidate must commit to spend not less than 12 weeks per year for five years, leading a research project hosted in a university in the State of São Paulo. The 12 weeks do not need to be continuous. The grant covers funds for equipment, consumables, trips, fellowships for students and post-docs, as well as expenses to travel to Brazil. The host institution in São Paulo will pay a salary for the weeks spent there leading the research.

In order to foster international research experience by the recipients of its fellowships, FAPESP offers for the 3,000 undergraduate, the 6,500 graduate students and the 2,000 post-doctoral fellows who have FAPESP fellowships in universities in São Paulo an additional fellowship for a stay of up to one year to work in a research laboratory of their choice abroad.

Finally, to enhance the visibility of the research environment in São Paulo and to facilitate interactions with prospective candidates, FAPESP created the São Paulo Schools of Advanced Science. Each School runs from one to three weeks and is led by a researcher in São Paulo, who invites colleagues from Brazil and from abroad to be lecturers. Around 100 doctoral students can attend, at least half of those coming from other countries, all fully supported by FAPESP funding. Started in 2010, the program has supported the organization of 38 Schools so far (ESPCA, 2013).

DEVELOPING LONG-TERM, HIGH-IMPACT RESEARCH

FAPESP created the Research, Innovation and Diffusion Centers (RIDC) Program in 1998 with the objective to offer outstanding research groups in São Paulo the opportunity to pursue a long-term research plan, breaking away from the two- or four-year cycle of grant duration. The expectation was that with a long-term contract the group would be able to pursue higher-risk research objectives. Following international experience, FAPESP requested, in return for the longer term and higher than average value of the funding, that each centre have a core of world-class research, and use it to exploit two additional objectives. One is to create opportunities for innovation through university-industry and/or university-government interactions to assess and/ or assist in the creation of public policies; the other is to use the advanced research experience to assist science education, impacting the public awareness about science and the quality of science education in basic schools. By adding these two objectives to the core research mission of each centre, FAPESP seeks to maximize the social benefits created by the research done.

A first round of the program supported 11 centres from 2001 to 2013. The centres were selected in a competitive call for proposals which had a 10% success rate, using international peer-review. The results were excellent in all three fronts: high-impact research, technology-transfer and innovation, and public awareness and science education.

In May 2011 FAPESP announced the call for proposals for the second round of the program. 90 pre-proposals were received and 150 reviewers contributed to the Phase 1 selection process preparing 207 reviews. Of the 90 initial pre-proposals, 44 were selected and invited to submit full proposals for Phase 2 of the selection process. The invited full proposals were submitted by 6 February 2012.

In May 2013, FAPESP announced the 17 new Research, Innovation and Dissemination Centers (RIDCs) selected for funding for a period of up to 11 years, subject to continuation reviews on years 2, 4 and 7.

Funding for the 17 RIDCs will come from FAPESP and the host institutions (funding faculty salaries, technicians, support personnel and infrastructure). It is estimated that for the 11-year duration of the program, the total funding for the 17 centres will be above US$680 million, with US$370 million coming from FAPESP and US$310 million in salaries from the host institutions. Additional funding will be obtained by each centre from industry and government organizations.

The 17 RIDCs bring together 499 scientists from the State of São Paulo and 68 scientists from other countries. The research topics covered by the centres include the following: food and nutrition; glasses and glass-ceramics; functional materials; neuroscience and neurotechnology; inflammatory diseases; biodiversity and drug discovery; toxins, immune-response and cell signalling; neuromathematics; mathematical sciences applied to industry; obesity and associated diseases; cellular therapy; metropolitan studies; human genome and stem-cells; computational engineering; redox processes in biomedicine; violence; and optics, photonics and atomic and molecular physics.

The 17 centres started in 2013 are:

- Food Research Center — FoRC, University of São Paulo;
- Center for Research, Teaching, and Innovation in Glass — CEPIV, Federal University of São Carlos;
- Center for Research and Development of Functional Materials — CDFM; Unversity of the State of São Paulo;
- Brazilian Research Institute for Neuroscience and Neurotechnology — BRAINN; University of Campinas;
- Center for Research on Inflammatory Diseases — CRID, University of São Paulo;
- Center for Research and Innovation in Biodiversity and Drug Discovery — CIBFar, University of São Paulo;
- Center for Research on Toxins, Immune-Response and Cell Signaling — CeTICS, Butantan Institute

- Research, Innovation and Dissemination Center for Neuromathematics — NEUROMAT, University of São Paulo;
- Center for Research in Mathematical Sciences Applied to Industry — CeMEAI; University of São Paulo;
- Obesity and Comorbidities Research Center — OCRC, University of Campinas;
- Center for Research in Cell Therapy — CTC; University of São Paulo;
- Center for Metropolitan Studies — CEM; Brazilian Center for Analysis and Planning (CEBRAP) and University of São Paulo;
- Human Genome and Stem-Cell Research Center — HUG-CELL, University of São Paulo;
- Center for Computational Science and Engineering — CECC, University of Campinas;
- Center for Research on Redox Processes in Biomedicine — REDOXOME; University of São Paulo;
- Center for the Study of Violence — NEV, University of São Paulo;
- Optics and Photonics Research Center — CEPOF, University of São Paulo.

CONCLUSION

Public support for research-intensive universities has been decisive in Brazil. In addition to federal funds, some other states appropriate substantial funding for higher education and research.

In the state of São Paulo, which responds for 33% of Brazil's GDP, three public universities have their budget appropriations set at 9.57% of the state VAT revenues, through a Governor's Decree from 1989. Additionally, the Constitution of the state guarantees for the São Paulo Research Foundation 1% of all state fiscal revenues. Federally funded universities do not have the same kind of autonomy, but have seen climbing budgets in recent years.

Universities and funding agencies have been fostering university-industry/ government interactions, the internationalization of higher education and academic research, and the search for high-impact research. Several programs exist in Brazil for sending students and researchers for short stays abroad and for bringing foreign scientists to Brazil. There are substantial challenges, such as the language barrier. Even so, the number of international joint research projects has grown intensely in the last seven years, and the same has happened to the number of young foreign post-doctoral fellows coming to Brazil, especially to the state of São Paulo where there is an aggressive program of fellowships.

Public research universities face growing demands from society to display more direct relevance in social and economic development. This happens especially in relation to university-business relations, but also with respect to the social impacts of higher education and academic research. Universities are more and more pressed to focus on research that either helps business competitiveness or heals the sick or makes poor people richer. While trying to answer these calls, it remains essential for research-intensive universities to remember that their commitment to that research that makes mankind wiser and to its connections to education is what makes them singular to society.

REFERENCES

CNPq (2013). "Science without Borders Control Panel".
   http://www.cienciasemfronteiras.gov.br/web/csf/painel-de-controle
ESPCA (2013). São Paulo School of Advanced Science.
   http://www.bv.fapesp.br/en/98/sao-paulo-school-of-advanced-science-espca
FAPESP (n.d.-a). Sao Paulo Research Foundation. http://www.fapesp.br/en/6812
FAPESP (n.d.-b). Sao Paulo Research Foundation. http://www.fapesp.br/en/4479
INEP (2011). "Sinopse Estatística da Educação Superior 2011".
   http://portal.inep.gov.br/superior-censosuperior-sinopse
Joly, C. A. *et al.* (2010). "Biodiversity Conservation Research, Training, and Policy in São Paulo", *Science* vol. 328, p. 1358.
   www.sciencemag.org/cgi/content/full/328/5984/1358/DC1
NSB (2012). "Science and Engineering Indicators 2012", Appendix Table 05-10.
TR Web of Science data (2013). Thomson Reuters: Web of Science.
   http://thomsonreuters.com/web-of-science/

CHAPTER 20

Challenges in Establishing
a Top Research University

*Nam P. Suh**

INTRODUCTION

The historical development of research universities and their roles in society has been articulated in many articles and documents. Since their inception, distinguished research universities have generated leaders in virtually every field and created scientific and technological advances that have affected the welfare and well-being of humanity. Top research universities have also contributed to creating national wealth through the generation of knowledge, technology innovation, job creation and establishing new business enterprises and public policies. To reap similar benefits, many countries have invested in higher education, but the results have been mixed. For instance, it has been difficult to match the likes of MIT, Harvard, Columbia and Cambridge.

The purpose of this paper is to describe the challenges associated with elevating a university to a world-class university and to present qualitative observations on both the role of government and the influence of the calibre of institutional culture in strengthening and establishing top research universities.

DIFFERENCES IN SUPPORTING HIGHER EDUCATION
AND RESEARCH UNIVERSITIES AMONG OECD NATIONS

Typical goals of modern research universities are to generate educated human resources, create basic knowledge, innovate and improve technologies, and promote public service in order to contribute to health, prosperity and welfare in their nations and the world. To achieve these goals, different models and approaches have been advanced and tried. In many nations, there have been continuing debates on proper and equitable ways of supporting research universities.

In some countries, such as the United States, Korea, Japan and Turkey, two research university systems co-exist: public universities supported by taxpayers and private universities that must secure their own financial support from non-governmental sources. In contrast, many European nations mainly have public universities that are supported by their central or local governments, although some private universities do exist.

Many arguments have been advanced in support of each one of the two models: public universities supported wholly by government versus private universities. When universities receive governmental support, the bureaucracy of government tends to exert control either directly or indirectly, since government operates according to regulations and rules to comply with governing laws. Even private universities that do not receive much public support can be under tight government regulations.

The higher educational system of the United States is an exception in that its two university systems, public and private, function well, serving the public interest without the kind of government control that exists in many other countries, because the Federal government does not fund universities. Many American private universities have long histories of excellence with complete independence, receiving no direct financial support from government. Furthermore, the U.S. research support system for universities is diverse, effective and highly competitive, thanks to the vision articulated by Vannevar Bush in *Science, the Endless Frontier*.

Historically, different countries have a variety of different educational and support systems, some with strong government support. The OECD nations make significant investment in education. On average, OECD nations spend about 4~5% of GDP on education. However, the actual expenditure can be much larger. For instance, in Korea, families spend an extra 2.8% of GDP for education. On average, Korean families spend an estimated 8% of their household budgets on tutoring and after-hours programs for each child. This high cost of education for families is one of the basic causes for Korea's low fertility rate of 1.2 — a potential social and national problem. The investment made in education by Korean families is among the highest in the world. Indeed, the sensitivity of this issue emerged as a major political issue in the 2012 presidential election in Korea. To get votes by capitalizing on the high cost of education, many politicians demanded that the tuition of all universities be reduced by 50%. This simple-minded approach to higher education is emblematic of the political approach to complex problems faced by many nations and their universities.

The large investments made in education in Korea and other Asian nations have contributed to their rapid economic development. For example, Korea's GDP per capita (in terms of purchasing power parity — PPP) is on par with those of many nations of the European Union. Korea has become a leading nation in many industrial sectors, including shipbuilding, cell phones, consumer electronics, automobiles and steelmaking. This rapid economic development and industrialization have been attributed to its high educational level and its large investment in education.

STRATEGY OF KAIST TO BECOME ONE OF THE BEST RESEARCH UNIVERSITIES IN THE WORLD

The goal we established was to catapult KAIST to the rank of the world's best research universities, à la MIT. Both KAIST and MIT are great universities with similar aspirations and goals, and equally excellent human resources, but there are major differences in governance, financing, history and culture. MIT is the highest-ranked research university in the world per the QS ranking of 2012. It is a private university with rich tradition and a large endowment. It was founded in 1861, 110 years before KAIST was established in 1971. Both institutions are research-intensive, with similar research funding per faculty and an almost equal number of undergraduate and graduate students.

We adopted the following strategic approach: "Solve the most important problems of humanity in the 21st century."

We identified energy, environment, water and sustainability (EEWS) as some of the most important problems that must be solved in the 21st century. Specifically, we chose the reduction of CO_2 as a major goal. As results of this focused effort, we were able to initiate the R&D effort for the On-Line Electric Vehicle (OLEV) project in 2009. Also at the same time, we created the Mobile Harbor (MH) project. We developed both of these complex systems in two years. OLEV is now commercial.

These two projects are typical examples of the research done at one end of the research spectrum, i.e. technology innovation. The other end of the research spectrum is basic research. This philosophy of emphasizing the two ends of the research spectrum at KAIST is a result of the observation that the research done in the middle of the research spectrum has limited impact.

To achieve the goal of becoming one of the leading research universities, we also decided to increase the faculty size from 400 to 700 in order to reduce the ratio of the number of graduate students per faculty member. Departments were encouraged to hire as many faculty members as they can recruit, provided that they satisfy the highest standard of quality established for faculty. Although government did not fund many of these additional faculty hires, we were able to manage the additional cost. We proved that research universities must fund their operations largely with research funding.

This strategic goal also required the construction of modern physical facilities for research, education, dormitories, sports, health care, international activities and housing for international faculty. During the period of 2007-2013, we built 14 new buildings. These buildings were financed from a variety of sources, i.e., gifts, government funding and other funds.

One of the most important undertakings at KAIST was the I-4 education, a new format of learning and teaching. Under this new educational format, there were no formal lectures in the classroom. Instead, students would listen to the lectures available on the Internet and come to class to solve problems with their fellow students in a pre-assigned group of six students with the help of TAs and professors. Students learn through discussion with other students while solving assigned problems. I-4 is over-subscribed because of its increasing preference among students.

OBSERVATIONS FROM VARIOUS RANKING OF RESEARCH UNIVERSITIES

In recent years, many universities have begun to pay more attention to rankings of universities by organizations such as the QS World University Rankings and Times Higher Education (THE). Although the specific details of the ranking process are subject to questions and debates, the general trend and the overall comparative picture provided by the rankings may be informative.

The following observations may be made based on the QS World University ranking and other relevant information:

a. According to the 2012 QS ranking, six private universities in the United States, headed by MIT, are among the top 10 research universities in the world. Four universities of the United Kingdom are also in the top 10. Among the top 20 universities, 13 are U.S private universities. Of the top 700 universities, 130 are in the United States. A distinguishing characteristic of the U.S. universities, including public universities, is that they are mostly free from government control. Although universities have to comply with government regulations when they receive research funding, government control of private universities is relatively minimal. State governments support all public universities except the military academies. A university dependent on funding from a state government may be subject to more control by the state. However, in comparison to the government regulations exercised in other nations, public universities in the United States are relatively free to make most of their own decisions. Also, the U.S. has provided more support for university research than many other nations through such agencies as NSF, NIH, DARPA and ARPA-E. In addition, American universities benefit from the American culture of charitable donations.

b. Young universities in Asia, founded since 1962 (less than 50 years old), are rapidly rising up in ranking.

c. There are 19 Asian universities (excluding seven in Australia and one in New Zealand) and 21 European universities (excluding 18 U.K. universities) in the top 100. What is remarkable is the fact that excluding the United Kingdom, only two of the European universities — ETH (13th) and EPFL (29th) of Switzerland — were ranked in the top 30.

d. If we exclude the U.K. universities, there is only one European university in the top 20 — ETH of Switzerland — and only two European universities in the top 30.
    Many of the prestigious European universities are public universities. ETH and EPFL are supported by the Swiss federal government and have more autonomy than other Swiss universities, which are supported by regional governments, the cantons. The cantons regulate their universities tightly, making it difficult for the universities to innovate and transform themselves. The funding for ETH and EPFL seems to be unique. They receive a lump-sum budget from the ETH board.

e. Most prominent universities in Sweden, Denmark, Norway and Germany are public institutions funded by the central or local governments. In France, there are two kinds of higher educational systems, universities and grandes écoles. Universities are usually public. Grandes écoles, mainly devoted to engineering and business administration, can be public or private. Most prestigious ones are public. One-fourth of research in France is conducted at and through CNRS. Many of these universities seem to be bound by the budgets they get from government and, as a consequence, are beholden to government in pursuing their institutional goals.

f. Korea and Japan have both public and private universities. In the ranking of Korean universities conducted by the Korean *JoongAng Daily*, KAIST was No. 1 for five years in a row. Some of the best universities used to be public or national universities, but that is gradually changing. Many private universities have been moving up in the rankings.

g. In Korea, the Ministry of Education, Science and Technology (MEST) controls all national universities tightly and even exerts control over private universities. KAIST has made some independent decisions, which have strained the KAIST relationship with MEST. All administrative staff members of the national universities are civil servants belonging to MEST. Private universities are also subject to control by MEST.

h. Most universities in Europe and the U.S. charge tuition. ETH Zurich charges 1,160 CHF for two semesters, plus 128 CHF for other fees. At KTH in Sweden, undergraduates pay as much as 145,000 SEK (about $21,300) per year. The tuition at the Technical University of Berlin is US$1,000 per year for E.U. students and as much as US$15,000 per year for international students. The cost of education at private American universities can be substantial, as much as $50,000 a year for tuition alone. At the state universities the tuition is less, around $3,000 per year.

ROLE OF GOVERNMENT IN THE DEVELOPMENT OF TOP RESEARCH UNIVERSITIES

Universities should not be treated as a "regulated business"

Most governments are under pressure from taxpayers and politicians to be impartial and fair in distribution of financial resources to universities, which often translates into uniform and equal funding. As a result, in many countries with many national universities, the available financial resources are equally divided among all national universities, taking away the incentive to be more competitive. The faculty and administrators get used to the comfortable life that comes with the tranquil environment when there is no need to strive to be the best.

When governments administer universities as "regulated business" like the postal service or public transportation, great universities cannot exist. A solution to this problem is to allocate most of the educational and research funds of the nation in special agencies (e.g., foundations, research projects agencies, etc.), after providing minimum support to its national and public universities to cover the basic cost of operations. These agencies should create competitive grant systems.

Governmental regulation of universities

In countries still in development phase, a limited control of universities by government may be necessary to maintain a minimum standard for higher education. However, for OECD nations, governmental regulation may hinder the emergence of outstanding research universities. Government should provide sufficient room for competition, while guaranteeing a minimal level of support for public research universities.

There are many ways governments regulate universities. One common method is requiring government approval of decisions made by the university administration. The approval power often covers personnel appointments, budgets, purchasing, regulations, the number of faculty members, the number of students who can be accepted, tuition charges, etc. Another method of control is the creation of rules and regulations. Under this system, even sub-standard universities will survive regardless of their quality and great universities cannot emerge. This tendency towards the mean is the current situation in many countries.

Lump-sum support of the base budget of universities

It appears that the Swiss model of lump-sum support of ETH and EPFL by the federal government of Switzerland is the ideal model for public research universities. However, Switzerland is an exception.

At KAIST, the basic budget provided by the government pays for the minimal expenses of a tuition-free institution. Such support has been essential for KAIST's development and achievement of its current status. However, now that KAIST has to make another quantum leap to be among top 20 of the world's best universities, KAIST needs much greater financial resources and institutional freedom. The government should simply guarantee a minimum lump-sum support to KAIST to cover the basic operational cost. KAIST should raise the rest of its budget from other sources.

Maximum Freedom to Achieve the Primary Goals of the University through Competitiveness and Self-Determination

A research university must establish its goals and missions clearly. The goals are typically related to the primary mission of the university: education, research and public service. Then it must establish explicit strategies, policies and tactics to achieve the stated goals. In this process, the university should not be encumbered by extraneous factors that are not related to its primary missions.

The Board of Trustees and the Retention of the Power of Approval

One of the prerequisites for a strong research university is an independent board of trustees, free from political influences. A good example for a public university is the University of California system. Under the California constitution, its Regents, who have "full powers of organization and governance" subject only to very specific areas of legislative control, govern the university. The governing article states "the university shall be entirely independent of all political and sectarian influence and kept free therefrom in the appointment of its Regents and in the administration of its affairs." At the University of California, there are 26 Regents, 18 of whom are appointed by the governor of the state for 12-year terms to insulate the board from political influence.

A leading research university should have a large number of board members selected from those who have valuable administrative experience (e.g., former presidents of universities, corporate CEOs), major donors (because donors help fund the university), alumni, leaders in science and technology, and international leaders. The board members should be appointed for at least five years to provide continuity and independence for the board. Many private universities in the United States have boards of trustees with more than 50 members, led by a small executive committee consisting of about 10 members.

CONSTRUCTIVE AND ETHICAL CULTURE: PREREQUISITES OF RESEARCH UNIVERSITIES

A distinguishing characteristic of a top research university is the culture of the university, which takes many years to establish. It is embedded in the beliefs, ethics, aspirations, fears, attitudes and expectations of faculty, students and staff. Culture is transmitted through people — professors, staff and students — over many generations. For young institutions, it is important to start establishing the right kind of culture from the beginning, because it is difficult to transform a well-established culture.

There are many common attributes of a constructive university culture: a high standard of ethics and honesty, respect for colleagues and for their achievements, sharing of the value system that enables scholars to make their intellectual contributions, and open discussion with colleagues to elevate the overall level of understanding. Such a culture does not tolerate unethical behaviour such as the fabrication of data, plagiarism, fabrication of misleading stories to attack a target, sexual harassment or other unjust actions. In many universities, most people possess the qualities that are worthy of a great university. However, a small group of people who do not share these basic qualities can poison the culture of the university. A great university must also maintain a culture that promotes, rewards and respects diverse views. A great university is one where those who have made outstanding scholarly and professional contributions are respected. Without these qualities, a great university cannot survive the test of time. If the faculty is led by those who have not made significant scholarly or professional contributions, but are engrossed in campus politics, the culture of the university will become politicized and eventually deteriorate.

Scholars should compete primarily with history, striving to emulate and surpass the intellectual giants who have affected the history of their fields and, in some cases, the history of humankind. A culture that allows creative and unorthodox scholarship, free from coercion of any kind, must permeate throughout the university for serious inquiries to proceed. Such a culture is a prerequisite of a great university.

Perhaps more than in any other institutions, academic culture tends to prize aspects of the status quo. It resists any change that affects the professors themselves. This alone can be good in some situations but also harmful, depending on the issues involved and whether one is the proponent of a change or the subject of the proposed change. One must expect major resistance when proposing a change. Once again, this aspect of the university culture is neither good nor harmful, but how people react to and deal with proposed changes is an important element of the culture. The desirable culture is one in which changes are rationally discussed and debated.

The changes proposed at universities should be considered in the larger context of the institutional needs. However, this practice is not always the case. When the author proposed that the Department of Mechanical Engineering at MIT broaden the discipline of mechanical engineering from a physics-based discipline into a discipline that is based on other scientific fields and design in addition to physics, some senior faculty members strongly objected. As a testament to the strength of the MIT culture, the board of trustees (called the MIT Corporation), the upper administration and the department faculty handled the difficult transition constructively. The author's experience at the U.S. National Science Foundation was similar, although the transition there involved the large community of the United States. In recent years, KAIST has gone through more significant transitions — a much stronger tenure policy, a department-centric system, increasing faculty size by 50% without departmental quota, a new research structure, instruction in English, etc. All these transformations at MIT, NSF and KAIST yielded positive results, although they were difficult changes.

RECIPE FOR DEVELOPING A GREAT RESEARCH UNIVERSITY

A great research university is created — not born — through many decades of effort and hard work by many who toiled for long hours. To become such a university, there are a few pre-requisites that one should consider.

Requisite 1: Goals

The mission and goals of a research university should be clearly stated and articulated. As discussed earlier, at KAIST, the goal was to "become one of the top research universities in the world" by solving some of the most important problems of humanity in the 21st century. We identified these problems to be "energy, environment, water, and sustainability (EEWS)" and four years later we added healthcare, education and defence (HED) to the original list.

Requisite 2: Strong faculty

KAIST hired 350 new faculty members without getting full government support. By hiring outstanding faculty, the overhead they brought in generated enough revenue to pay the research expenses and salaries. The lesson is that research universities must generate revenues based on outstanding research. Tuition paid by students cannot and should not pay the research expense.

Requisite 3: Strong Governance and Organizational System

a. Department-centric system
In a complex research university, the power to make important decisions should be delegated to those who best understand the issue. This philosophy requires a department-centric system, in which a department head is in charge and makes important decisions on personnel, finance, space and academic programs in consultation with the faculty. Sometimes the decisions made by the department head may not necessarily be based on the majority opinion of the faculty, since the department head may have information that is not generally available to others. In this system, the department head should be the boss.

b. Asymmetric decision-making process
To enable the department head to exercise his/her decision-making power, the upper administration should not force the department head to reverse a decision in the negative (e.g., not to hire a particular candidate). However, the upper administration must review the department head's affirmative decisions, since their implementation may have campus-wide ramifications.

c. Faculty Hiring
At most universities, the central administration assigns a fixed number of faculty positions to each department mostly based on past history. However, such a system has shortcomings. The department may perpetuate itself by filling vacancies that were created by retirements with professors who have similar traditional backgrounds to the professors just retired. Under such a personnel policy, the departments may not hire to staff newly emerging fields. Furthermore, the field-specific hiring in a given department may overlook the best-qualified person who happens to be in another field. Therefore, an alternate way is to open up the hiring process so as to hire the best-qualified professor who can open up new frontiers of knowledge.

d. Tenure policy for faculty
Top research universities must have a fair and strong tenure policy. Tenure policy is needed to protect both the professor and the university. A strong tenure system is also required to attract the most qualified faculty to the university.
At KAIST, a stringent tenure system was introduced in 2006. Some of the professors were denied their tenure under the new policy,

which was a new practice in Korea, because previously most professors had received tenure once they were hired. Because about a half of the professors at KAIST did not have tenure, this new tenure policy — a process that allows a maximum of eight years to acquire tenure — has created a great deal of tension on campus, as well as opposition by the faculty "union". However, this process is now firmly in place at KAIST.

e. An ideal ratio of graduate student/faculty
Often there is a debate within universities about the right size of the graduate and undergraduate student bodies. The answer depends on institutional goals. At a research university, an ideal ratio of undergraduates to graduate students seems to be about four to six. The optimum number of graduate students per faculty member in science and engineering seems to be about six so as to allow the professor to be engaged in research with the student.

f. Admissions policies to offer opportunities to those with limited chances
One of the major tasks of a research university is to admit the most qualified undergraduate and graduate students among those who apply for admission. The research universities also have an obligation to admit the "unpolished rough diamond". At KAIST, we accepted up to 150 freshmen from rural and deprived regions based on the recommendations of the principals of their high schools (only one recommendation per high school), oral examinations and interviews. About 80% of the students admitted through this process performed as well as those from the highly selective science high schools, but the last 20% could have done better if KAIST had offered remedial courses before enrolling them to the regular freshman class, a lesson learned.
For a research university to be competitive, it must also attract the brightest and most capable students globally. Research universities in English-speaking countries have a clear advantage in attracting foreign students. With the ease of migration, the countries that can attract the brainpower will have competitive advantages in many fields of human endeavour, especially in science and technology.

g. Elections for presidents, deans and department heads by the faculty
Many universities elect their presidents, vice presidents, deans and department heads by vote of the faculty. This practice has many shortcomings. It leads to inbreeding of hiring only their own graduates, splits the faculty and creates a continuing battleground for next election. It is unproductive. It works against the idea that universities must serve the public by bringing the best scholars and professors

regardless of their background. The board of trustees should select the president through a search process and the president should appoint all vice presidents and deans.

h. Merit-based compensation system
To attract the most qualified professors and do justice to those who contribute the most to a university, the compensation system must be merit-based, recognizing the difference in supply and demand of professors in different fields. When market forces are ignored, universities either underpay or overpay their faculty members, practices that are ultimately unfair from the viewpoint of those who actually pay the cost of maintaining a university.

i. Generation of gifts for new buildings and faculty chairs
Universities are not profit-making organizations. Universities need benefactors who are willing to support special activities with their private wealth as a way of repaying what society did to nurture their own success.

Requisite 4: Academic and Research Programs

a. Interdisciplinary collaboration across departments
Many research universities emphasize interdisciplinary and trans-disciplinary research. One way of achieving these goals is to conduct large-systems interdisciplinary research projects that involve the design of complex systems, which necessitates collaboration among colleagues with diverse backgrounds.

The OLEV and MH projects at KAIST required the expertise of many professors and researchers from many disciplines. They also needed participating companies to defray costs that were in several tens of millions of dollars over two years. What these projects have demonstrated is that research universities can conceive major technological innovations that are large and complex, and successfully execute them in a relatively short time. These projects demonstrate that theory-based design of large complex systems and implementation by building actual systems can be done at leading research universities.

b. Creation of interdisciplinary education and research for better education
It is reasonable to assume that education will undergo a significant transformation because of technology. There is no need for so many professors to teach the same subjects every term. In theory, the English-speaking countries need only one professor of, for instance, physics to teach freshman physics. Students can listen to the lectures stored on the Internet. Then education can be tailor-made for each student — mass customization of education. At KAIST, we have

initiated the I-4 Educational Program to change the educational system to a learner-centric system from a teacher-centric system. Currently, the number of applications of students to enrol in I-4 exceeds its capacity.

Requisite 5: Cultural issues related to creativity and ethics

The culture of a university is the most distinguishing difference between the top research universities and others. Among the many elements of a university culture, two important ones are related to creativity and ethics.

Perhaps the most convincing argument that the university culture matters in nurturing creativity is the observation that the same individual can become more or less creative when the person goes to another university. It may be attributed to the fact that in top-tier universities there are more incidences or occasions that stimulate and inspire creative thinking because of its institutional dynamics, quality of human interaction, respect for creative achievements of their colleagues and history of successful creative activities.

As noted before, ethics at top research universities may be equally or more important than creativity. The absence of ethics in a university can be corrosive over a period of time, permeating the entire university and affecting the core of a university system. At a university, there should be no room for plagiarism, plotting to hurt others, bias, prejudice and slander. Everyone should be treated equally irrespective of religion, national origin, school background, family and regional ties, race, etc. Furthermore, there should be genuine respect for those who have made major scholarly contributions.

Requisite 6: Relationship with Government

A strong government is needed. All universities must respect government policies, since they are concerned about the overall welfare of a nation. Governments deal with much larger issues than a university does and must satisfy many different constituents. That is the reason people in democratic countries have delegated so much power to their governments, since in such a government the people ultimately hold the power.

Universities also have their own responsibilities and obligations, which must be respected by politicians and governments. Universities are legal entities created to fulfil special needs of society and serve the long-term welfare of a nation and humanity. In many cases, universities need government support and government needs strong universities to achieve national goals. Under normal circumstances, there should be a symbiotic relationship between universities and government.

In some countries, government tends to dictate its terms to universities, because government is more powerful and authoritative than universities. Governments control financial resources and can dole out special favours to interest groups, if they choose to. In some countries, government controls the board of trustees by appointing many civil servants as the trustees and by limiting the number of non-government trustees. They even remove those who have made major financial and intellectual contributions from the board so as to control the board of trustees.

CASE STUDY TO TEST THE THEORETICAL FRAMEWORK FOR A LEADING RESEARCH UNIVERSITY

The development of KAIST since 2006 is a prototype of a case study for development of a major research university. Its world ranking has gone up from 196th to 63rd, and to 24th in engineering and IT. In several fields of engineering, it is in top 20, which is a remarkable change. However, to confirm the theoretical framework discussed in this paper for a top research university, it will be interesting to conduct more case studies.

CONCLUSIONS

a. Leading research universities have made major contributions to the development of human resources, generation of the knowledge, major technological innovations and economic growth of their countries.

b. While the importance for strong research universities is clear, the actual establishment of high-quality research universities has been difficult in many countries for a variety of reasons. The best universities feature outstanding faculty, the staff and highly competitive students who can generate and implement creative ideas to solve important problems of humanity. Equally important are the financial resources to attract talent and create state-of-the-art facilities that enable innovative research.

c. Concurrent with the need to satisfy the requirements for a leading research university, there are two important issues that have not been articulated as much as the others in the past. The first is regulation of universities, either directly or indirectly, by government. Many universities under tight government control have not reached the top ranks, and often they are not competitive in attracting the most knowledgeable and forward-thinking faculty and staff.

The second issue is the culture of a research university. Leading research universities create a culture that directly respects and rewards accomplished scholars and professors, dedicated staff and outstanding students for their intellectual and scholarly contributions. They also create an environment where unethical behaviour is not tolerated.

d. Leaders of the best universities must articulate a shared vision and clear goals, and create collaborative teams to develop detailed strategies for success. They also must identify multiple financial sources, and, in the case of public universities, gain governmental and societal backing. Leaders must then bring out the very best qualities in the community members that comprise their universities, encouraging dedication, teamwork and innovation.

* *The author wishes to thank Kristian Jaewon Lundberg for his assistance.*

CHAPTER 21

The Asian Tiger University Effect

John Niland*

INTRODUCTION

A common wisdom is that we are now entering the Asian Century, having travelled the American century in the 1900s and the British century in the 1800s. This reflects the array of impressive economic indicators emerging in the East. As the *Australia in the Asian Century* white paper (Australian Government, 2012) notes, in the past 20 years alone China and India have "almost tripled their share of the global economy", and the Asian Development Bank estimates that by mid-century "an additional 3 billion Asians could enjoy living standards similar to those in Europe today, and the region could account for over half of global output". (ADB, 2011). Such profound change prompts many questions, not the least being the implications for the world's research universities.

The quest for world-class universities in Asia has been a topic of interest for some time (Niland, 1998), with a growing literature of policy analysis (Tan, 2008) and comprehensive case studies (Altbach & Salmi, 2011) emerging in recent years. While the story with China and India will continue to dominate, equally interesting questions lie with a subset of other countries often referred to as the Asian Tiger Economies: Hong Kong, Taiwan, Singapore and Korea. Their stunning economic growth over the past several decades has already lifted living standards to developed-country levels for many of their citizens. They have also laid strong foundations for developing first-rate university systems, with some comprehensive universities, such as Hong Kong University and the National University of Singapore, already well-established in the top band of world-class universities. But this is just the start, for a wave of new, more agile universities may well be on the way.

One marker is the rankings of newer universities — those under 50 years old — by QS and THE. Impressively, the QS top seven in the under-50s group also make it to the top 100 of the main ranking table. And five of that seven are from three of the four tiger economies: Chinese University of Hong Kong (CUHK), Hong Kong University of Science and Technology (HKUST), Nanyang Technological University (NTU), Korea University of Science and Technology (KAIST) and Pohang University of Science and Technology (POSTECH). Taiwan seems to be the exception in the nexus between tiger economy and tiger university: National Yang Ming University, at rank 37, is the only Taiwanese university to appear in the young list, while Taiwan National University, at 134, is the only Taiwanese university to rank in the top 200 of the main list. (O'Leary, 2012). A similar profile appears in the Times Higher Education World University young list (THE, 2013) where POSTECH is one, HKUST is two, KAIST is five, CUHK is 12, NTU is 16 and National Yang Ming is 30.

Against this background emerges the idea of the Asian Tiger University. No model is invariable and none of the three rapidly rising star universities taken as reference points for this paper carry all elements discussed below. But a mix of core features can be identified. The typical tiger university is newly established, usually purpose designed to fast track to eminent international standing as a research-intensive university. It is extremely well funded, at least in comparative terms, and serves both as a magnet for international recruitment of faculty and students, and as a beachhead for change in sibling (even national flagship) universities which have followed more traditional (and leisurely) paths of development. It is more often specialist than comprehensive, generally with an emphasis on science and technology. It is well embedded in nation-building strategies, and it is expected to reciprocate with its own deep determination to rise to the top in the minimum time. Thus, "the young aristocrat" or "young gun" or "princeling" universities (as they are sometimes called) in the tiger economies are being cast both as contributors to social enhancement and aerobic economic advancement, and as beneficiaries of that dynamic. Like a country's flag carrier airline of an earlier era, they are expected to build the national reputation (and do so probably with a better cost: benefit fit!)

This paper aims to address three main issues.

- To understand the environment or general context within which the Asian tiger university effect or dynamic is emerging: why Asia, why now?
- To examine the key core strategies being implemented by several Asian tiger universities, notably Singapore Management University (SMU, established 2000), Hong Kong University of Science and Technology

(HKUST, established 1991) and South Korea's Pohang University of Science and Technology (POSTECH, established in 1986).
* To assess the <u>overall impact</u> of the tiger university effect on the various stakeholders, both at home and abroad.

THE GENERAL CONTEXT

"Singapore universities today … exist in a complex societal and economic ecosystem and interact with many parties — research institutes, business, government agencies and the wider community." (Tan, 2008: 138). Beyond this, relevant ecosystem elements in the tiger economies include issues of demographics, geography, IT capacity, IP security, judicial integrity and the rule of law, governance norms, cultural commitment to education, personal and corporate attitudes to philanthropy, and much more. Salmi (2011: 342) speaks of "the weight of the tertiary education ecosystem in influencing the performance of research universities in seeking to achieve world-class status", making reference, *inter alia*, to quality assurance, the regulatory framework, vision, leadership and reform capacity, and resources and incentives.

For the purposes of this discussion, the focus is on five of the ecosystem elements that seem particularly critical to the tiger universities referenced here: economic momentum; aspirational society; higher education environment; lively public policy climate (for the advancement of universities onto the world stage); and global portals.

National Economic Momentum

To state the obvious, it is no accident that higher education has fared better in developed economies, and best under growth scenarios: "For much of the nation's history, American universities recognized that their existence and success were intertwined with the economic fortunes of the nation. Economic growth, in turn, has been inexorably tied to the increase of new knowledge and an educated population." (Schramm, 2008: 19). A similar story is evident in Europe, where the Prussian government was supporting the Humboldt model "because it promised to assist in national development and help Prussia — and later Germany — to achieve international power and influence". (Altbach, 2011: 15).

The higher education systems in Asia are the latest, and most intense, variant on this particular compact between government and gown: national pride is clearly part of the mix; well-founded goals for economic growth are more ambitious; and the compact is set to a much tighter time frame than has been evident in other eras — yet another reflection of the raw competitiveness that comes with globalization. A sense of urgency prevails, and this helps shape the strategies in higher education systems generally, and for the tiger universities in particular. The comparison is made even more stark by Schramm's assessment that "the United States has watched its universities slip further from economic relevance … as other countries have been more ambitious about establishing the vital link between university research, student education and economic growth". (Schramm, 2008: 25). And in this "race to the top", more than "bragging rights are involved … for a world-class university system is a powerful engine for economic development, and research is the fuel powering that engine". (Normile, 2012: 1162).

National economic momentum, together with the drive of the educationally aspirational society, is key in understanding the "why Asia, why now" aspect of the tiger university dynamic.

Aspirational Society

Education is widely seen as central to societal aspiration in Asian cultures. One particularly strong example is South Korea, where words like "thirst", "mania" and even "abnormal" have been used to describe "education's hold on South Korea's collective psyche and its shaping of society." (Morgan, 2010: 1). As Duderstadt et al. (2008: 282) note, Korea's "Confucian culture has long placed a high premium on Education", leading to an extremely high proportion (80%) of high-school graduates going on to college. But there are two sides to this coin. The style of its mass higher education system has also been fingered for reinforcing Korea's tendency towards monoculture, and denying universities a strong research dimension. The advent of the tiger university strategy, in particular the emergence of KAIST and POSTECH, together with enhanced government funding, has bolstered Korea's research effort. New and less hidebound, these two rising stars have also led the way in meeting government priorities for a balanced set of admission criteria to better reflect a more nuanced sense of merit. One lesson seen time and again, in Singapore and Hong Kong as well as in Korea, is that the tiger university creates a beachhead for reform elsewhere in the country's higher education system.

In Asia, success in the education domain is particularly prized (in contrast, say, to Australia where academics often complain about the national obsession with international sporting success!), and students seem more driven to keep company with the best. Against this background, governments (and private sponsors) have more scope to differentiate, and to implement funding strategies that in many western countries would face serious opposition on equity grounds. Another effect of the high valence on education is mega-philanthropy, examined shortly.

The media in Singapore, Korea and Hong Kong widely report rises in the rankings of their universities, and the tiger universities are becoming prominent locally for their international standing. This, in turn, boosts their capacity to compete with the flagship universities for top students, and to some extent mutes the flow of the most talented local high school graduates to brand name universities in the U.S. and the U.K. From an early stage, POSTECH attracted the top 1% of high school graduates, and by the ten-year mark several of SMU's schools were level pegging (at least) with NUS and NTU in the student quality stakes. In 2013, undergraduates at the SMU Law School (established in 2006) won the Singapore division of the prestigious Jessup International Mooting Competition, and placed second in the world finals. Oddly, though, HKUST spent its initial decade with a stronger reputation abroad than at home, and its undergraduate admission profile was nothing special, but by the 20-year point that had changed dramatically.

Educational Environment

The tiger university is not established, nor could it develop, in a vacuum. Important elements of the prevailing ecosystem include: a network of established universities which in one dimension are supportive and in another are competitive; a mature administrative framework for oversight of the university sector, including external quality monitoring and assurance; public policy provisions that accept, preferably promote, differential funding and in other ways foster the new university (in much the same manner as tariff protection does in the infant industry proposition of international trade theory).

In Hong Kong the university sector is overseen and shaped by the University Grants Committee (UGC), an intermediary between the Government and the universities. It distributes a total of US$585 million annually to the eight universities for research, of which about 20% is through a competitive grants system. International scholars sit on an array of discipline panels that channel funding support to projects based on merit, (as opposed to formulaic block grants for each university based on student numbers). Over the past ten years the UGC has leveraged its funding authority to shape the system in ways important to the development of top-line research universities. One outcome might be seen in Hong Kong's unparalleled success in the various rankings exercises: three of its universities now place in the top 50 of the QS rankings. Put another way, over 50% of Hong Kong's students attend a university in the top 75 of the various recognized ranking regimes. This is one important element of the higher education ecosystem that stimulates HKUST (and CUHK for that matter) to rise as strongly as it has.

Singapore displays a similar quality profile. Two of its four universities currently rank in the top 100 of the main ranking regimes, and over 70% of enrolled students are at NUS or NTU. As to Korea, a much higher proportion of students go on to post secondary education, there are many more universities and those ranked highly are generally smaller, with the result that the same quality profile for the sector is not so evident.

Lively Public Policy Climate

The language of public-policy pronouncements in the tiger economies is alive with references to higher education hubs, world-class recognition, eminent international alliances and so forth. It is tempting to sometimes see this as an exercise in hubris, but the record in Korea, Hong Kong and Singapore speaks for itself. In each country, the advancement of higher education is a front foot public policy issue, and this creates an ideal environment for the tiger university dynamic.

In Hong Kong, the move in 2012 by all eight universities in the UGC system from a three- to a four-year undergraduate degree standard came as part of perhaps the most intense government-initiated reform to a university sector anywhere in the world in the past 25 years. The liveliness of the public policy climate in Hong Kong is also reflected in the government's pursuit of merger between the HKUST and CUHK. Ultimately abandoned in 2004 because of a bruising public debate and fierce opposition from HKUST (reflecting its tiger culture), we see that not all national strategies to advance higher education arrangements follow the planned path. The idea behind the merger proposal was to create twin peaks of excellence, with the merged entity joining HKU at the top table of world universities (Niland, 2004). It can be argued that the serious threat of merger spurred HKUST (and to some extent CUHK) to even stronger performance. As O'Leary notes, by 2012 HKUST was the top-ranked Hong Kong university in the QS regime, and the leading university in Asia by this measure (although this order was reversed in the 2013 THEWUR listings, highlighting the relative volatility and variability of these exercises).

In Singapore, higher education is a headland public policy issue, and government, through its Ministry of Education (and to some extent its Economic Development Board), actively shapes the sector in ways that would probably be resisted in Europe, Australasia and North America where university culture is more laissez faire.

Global Portals

Some university systems, as well as their component institutions, are more globally engaged than others. The tiger university dynamic is best fostered where the broader national system drives international engagement. Government involvement is critical, and can range from visa regimes designed to facilitate international student enrolment and faculty recruitment, to strategic funding, such as for major research projects that meet standards set through international peer reviews. Each of the reference countries illustrates in their own way how to build windows on the world — the global portals.

In Hong Kong, a third of the University Grants Committee's members are from overseas. They are mostly serving or former university heads and in the past 10 years have been drawn largely from the U.K. and the U.S., but also from Australia, the Netherlands, Singapore and China. Major reviews of the system, conducted every ten years or so, are led by overseas experts, as are particular enquiries into specific problem issues. The 13 panels of the Research Assessment Exercise (RAE) are all led by overseas academics of international standing. The Hong Kong government further enhances its global portal by funding 135 new doctoral fellowships each year to attract "the best and brightest students in the world to pursue their PhD studies in Hong Kong institutions", assigned on a competitive basis. For Hong Kong, another important portal is the higher education strategy of China. One example is the Shenzhen Campus Project in the Pearl River Delta, sponsored by municipal authorities, which has drawn a significant cross-border presence from six of the eight universities in Hong Kong.

With Singapore, the global culture in higher education is advanced through many initiatives. Prominent is the region's most active and well-funded program to bring into the country elite overseas universities for deep collaboration with local universities: medical schools at NUS by Duke University and at NTU by Imperial College, the Yale-NUS Liberal Arts College, the MIT cornerstone stake in the new fourth university, Singapore University of Technology and Design (SUTD), and the mentoring of SMU by the Wharton School in its start-up phase. Also of note is the standalone branch campus of INSEAD. Another indicator of the strength of Singapore's global window is CREATE (Campus for Research Excellence and Technological Enterprise) which leverages Singapore's strengths as a doorway to Asia for elite universities and corporate research labs wishing to set up their own bases nearer the action. The support funding is impressive, said to be about US$400 million over 5 years, and has attracted some nine entities from an array of elite universities including Cambridge, MIT, UC Berkeley, ETH, Teknion-Israel, as well as Shanghai Jiao Tong and Peking Universities. All will partner with Singapore universities in various ways, including hosting their PhD students.

The Korean University system has been less global in outlook than Singapore and Hong Kong, but this is changing. There is a stronger effort to adopt English as a mode of instruction at its leading universities, with POSTECH becoming a bilingual campus in 2010 and English the mode of instruction for most undergraduate and all postgraduate courses. The government is sponsoring the Songdo Global University Campus (SGUC). Located in the Incheon Free Economic Zone (IFEZ), it operates as "a university complex, where foreign universities are located together" and offer their own degrees. A special independent administration manages campus facilities (Jung, 2011).

Each of the three countries builds its own style of global portal. The details vary, but the central purpose is constant: to create a global-rich cultural setting to further foster international alliances at the discipline and individual-researcher level, and to promote cross border faculty collaboration, not to mention enhancing the international recruitment of faculty as the sector continues to expand. This all builds a virtuous, self-reinforcing circle which is a necessary (though not sufficient) condition to deliver on the tiger university ideal.

THE CORE STRATEGIES

The first prerequisite for the development of a tiger university is an overall ecosystem that will be supportive of this ideal. The second prerequisite is a set of specific strategies adopted by the tiger university to carry forward its rapid rise to international prominence. The list of potential strategies is long, and their effectiveness will vary from country to country. Those that seem to be core, judging from the journey travelled by HKUST, POSTECH and SMU, relate to: differentiating themselves from other institutions in their national system; tapping into patrons with deep pockets; engaging the strategic hand of government; adopting modern management systems for both academic and administrative domains; attracting eminent international partners and leveraging from this the recruitment of first-rate faculty; consciously crafting a university culture which prizes research and global engagement; and purpose-designed governance, both at the institutional level and for the academic community. Enviable campus facilities also figure prominently.

The *Sui Generis* factor — be Different

Inevitably, the tiger university promotes itself as breaking the mould in ways that matter: degree structures; teaching modes; special, even unique, areas of disciplinary concentration; geographical location; eminent partnering institutions; influential sponsors; a special institutional spirit, energy and drive ... the list goes on. The tiger university needs to present itself to stakeholders as something really new, a breath of fresh air, but still with its feet on the ground. For prospective students and their parents, this may come across as better career paths in a rapidly changing world; for prospective faculty, the magnet may be the opportunity to work in an exciting environment with top-notch infrastructure and premium funding to support the type of research that supercharges the CV: "flocking to Asia for a shot at greatness", as Normile (2012:1) describes the phenomenon. The danger, always, is that the start-up will be seen as an upstart. Thus the whole *sui generis* package needs to make plausible the declared goal of reaching world standing in 20 to 30 years, not the traditional 100 years plus. Credibility is critical.

For POSTECH, lines of differentiation started with its patronage from POSCO (Pohang Iron and Steel Company), leading to an extremely well-funded specialization in science and technology. Early on, POSTECH launched a lively marketing campaign to prospective students across the country, highlighting: their unprecedented level of resourcing; full fee waivers; free on-campus accommodation and other forms of student support; their academic excellence; and their positive differences. As Rhee (2011: 107) notes, "historically, such promotional activities simply were not practised by universities, least of all by elite universities". As with SMU and its energetic marketing program, POSTECH broke tradition to better compete, and in ways which were soon taken up by the legacy institutions themselves.

For SMU, the niche narrative was built around its introduction into Singapore of the North American four-year undergraduate degree arrangement, rather than following the three-year British model prevailing at NUS and NTU. SMU also adopted faculty structures and promotion review processes common at American universities. It was described as a private university (albeit mostly built with public funds) which enabled the Government to see it as Singapore's first "autonomous" university with a "corporate style" governing body. Within several years, NUS and NTU had been translated into autonomous universities. Equally important, SMU was Singapore's first specialized university, as distinct from the much larger conurbations at NUS and NTU. All these unique design features were consciously built into the model developed by the Government, or they flowed from it. (Tan, 2008: 132). For HKUST it was the tag line "be different — do not duplicate" which guided much that unfolded.

From this orientation the tiger universities in Singapore, Hong Kong and Korea became beachheads for change across the sector, a key impact which is considered in the final section.

Patrons with Deep Pockets

A feature common to young universities on the rising star path is a massive funds infusion in the start-up stage. This can arise from several sources: for SMU it was a particular premium funding formula implemented by government; for HKUST the initial boost came from a high-ranking community institution, the Hong Kong Jockey Club; and for POSTECH it was corporate benefaction from POSCO. This is not dissimilar from the U.S. for what are now many of its world-class universities, but there the benefaction was private from the beginning, with names such as Carnegie, Rockefeller, Mellon, Cornell, Stanford, Hopkins and Duke obvious examples. One hypothesis is that such state, corporate or community benefaction, as distinct from private benefaction, more strongly sets the new university into a type of nation-building obligation, and this is certainly reflected in the tiger university dynamic.

In Hong Kong, the Jockey Club is a wealthy non-profit entity, with a deep commitment to supporting higher education. This is well reflected in its foundation pledge in 1987 of US$192 million, or two thirds of the start-up costs for HKUST. As the HKUGC observes, "the success of HKUST today (simply would) not have been possible without HKJC's generosity." POSTECH's endowment is largely donated POSCO stock valued at about US$2 billion today, give or take market fluctuations. One downside is that the dominance of its leading Patron to some extent "makes it more difficult to reach out to other potential sponsors and donors" (Rhee, 2011: 123). And, as with SMU (and HKUST to some extent), the model of small classes limits the pool of alumni to be tapped. Most challenged on this front is POSTECH which in the period 1990-2012 had produced just 15,097 graduates: 2,455 Phds, 6,733 MSc and 5,909 BSc.

SMU's endowment and surplus, at the ten-year mark since its founding, was about US$700 million, built up through donations and the Government providing three-to-one matching of private donations in the period 2000 to 2004, and thereafter one-to-one matching, which is standard in Singapore (and to some extent, in Hong Kong). Completing the picture, the Government allows 2.5 times of tax deduction per dollar donated. One donor is reported to have calculated that these policies "effectively mean that every $1 contributed could potentially become $8 for the endowment". (Appell, 2013).

The sheer scale of the start-up funding, not to mention the patron's profile, creates a halo effect, which gives the new university some greater credibility in articulating its grand plans for world-class status in a short time. In this, the physical face of the new university is also important, and patrons have played a major role here at all three tiger universities. For SMU, a cornerstone element in its government funding was a new, purpose-built campus, adjacent to the financial district. POSCO provided a remarkable facility for POSTECH, and the various patrons for HKUST ensured an iconic campus development at Clearwater Bay. All of this gives comfort to potential faculty and students who might otherwise demur about involvement with what in reality is an unproven entity. A striving new university needs a good "story" to attract top students and faculty, and there is perhaps no better start than storied funding. By contrast, many of the world's blue ribbon universities have a large and often quite wealthy alumni cohort, who fill the patron role, with Stanford currently the outstanding case.

Strategic Hand of Government

In Asia, the targeted development of a particular university into the company of the best of Europe and North America means that government quite openly exercises its hand in more actively shaping research focus, areas for teaching emphasis and the needs of human capital planning. For the tiger university, this figures as part of their contribution toward nation building. Certainly research universities in the West are now familiar with the "piper's tune" rule, as Newby noted in quoting the British cabinet minister on the point that universities could indeed hope for a return to traditional autonomy, but they should then also expect medieval levels of public funding! (Newby, 2008: 61). But the role of public policy and the contingent funding that comes with it, is more intense in Asia, and perhaps more accepted, though not without some concerns being expressed from time to time. It is in this context, for example, that a Yale-NUS leadership group recently emphasized that "the administration will not be instituting any speech restrictions (and that) faculty members and students must judge for themselves the best manner to express their ideas, determining the balance of sensitivity and provocation." (Davie, 2013b).

In Singapore, a key strategy has been preserving post-secondary sector boundaries and offering differentiated funding, reflected in the clear distinction made between the four public institutions on the university side of the institutional divide, and the five public polytechnics on the other. Unlike Australia and the U.K., Singapore has firmly resisted upgrading "adjacent" institutions into the university sector, which in terms of outcome has been to the benefit of both universities and polytechnics. By setting SMU into the university sector (rather than upgrading a polytechnic to it) the government clearly signalled an expectation of higher scholarship, particularly in world-class research. It is too early for SMU to be considered in the institution-wide ranking exercises such a ARWU, QS or THEWUR, but one indicator of early success is the various discipline-specific ranking regimes based on referred articles in top-line academic journals. Thus, after just 12 years, SMU ranks 3rd in Asia and 52nd globally in the UTD list for Business; 3rd in Asia and 66th globally in the Tilburg University rankings in Economics; for Accountancy in the BYU regime it ranks 4th in Asia and 44th globally (on a par with the London School of Economics). By 2012 the Lee Kong Chian Business School had become the youngest ever to gain both AACSB and EQUIS accreditation.

Another critical requirement from the Singapore Government was the adoption of the North American four-year undergraduate degree standard. Also important, SMU has been shaped as a niche university, as has Singapore University of Technology and Design (SUTD), the newest rising star, where MIT plays a similar guiding role to that of Wharton for SMU (see para 42).

In Hong Kong, a number of polytechnics were brought into the university sector in the 1990s, but by 2009 the UGC had drawn the line on research standards expected, and, despite an intense campaign for elevation, determined that the Hong Kong Institute of Education, which for historical reasons was part of the UGC regulatory framework, nonetheless should not take on the university title. In another sweep of the government hand, the overall higher education budget is effectively top sliced for the Research Grants Council (RGCHK) to operate a competitive bidding process. This has facilitated funding that is differentiated by excellence, an essential building block for the tiger university as it moves past start-up stage. Thus, by 2009 HKUST's application success rate was 47%, ahead of 36% for the other two (and somewhat older) research universities. As Postiglione notes (2011: 65), the amount awarded per HKUST faculty member was almost double that for any other university (although some allowance should be made for variable discipline mix).

Modern Management Systems: Academic and Administrative

A feature common to SMU, HKUST and POSTECH is their departure from management styles common in legacy institutions. All three eschewed elected deans and opted for appointment by a high-level search committee, internationally focussed, with a core of members coming from the school in question. With HKUST this provided useful precedent for HKU when, in 2003, it departed from 100 years of tradition in favour of international searches for deans over internal elections. This helped reshape the budgeting system, with greater devolution of responsibility (with accountability) to the dean and others at the school level.

POSTECH, reflecting its origin with strong private sector patronage, imported POSCO's "management techniques and systems, albeit selectively", thus avoiding "bureaucratic red tape and decision-making procrastination", argued to be evident in many of its older colleague institutions. Beyond this, the university plan carried performance indicators, published on the website, detailing metrics, timelines and deadlines. This represented a "massive departure" from management practices in Korean university circles in the 1980s. (Rhee, 2011: 108).

Academic management systems at SMU initially drew heavily on Wharton's experience and input (the first president was a senior professor on leave from Wharton), applying the Wharton governance handbook from day one to facilitate a fast-track start-up. More recently, INSEAD thinking (reflecting the background of the fourth president) has been influential, as for example with the introduction in 2013-14 of responsibility centre accounting, and a business process improvement unit (incorporating the Six Sigma Methodologies), which together drive both cost efficiency and transparency, as well as developing management skills to deliver better productivity, efficiency and innovation. Beyond this, annual performance reviews for senior academic managers were introduced early on, and then extended to the academic ranks, where annual remuneration adjustment varies under a bell curve, and follows specific merit reviews (rather than the more traditional method of the U.K. and Australian systems of essentially automatic increases, uniform across the faculty). Two further design features served to boost research performance. First, and in another departure from the style of NTU and NUS, SMU remuneration incorporates the "ninths" system of North America, which reinforces the role of individual performance in adjusting total remuneration. Second, differentiated appointment and promotion modes operate. In the teaching and practice tracks, faculty face lighter research requirements but heavier teaching loads, and vice versa in the tenure track. The challenge has been to give legitimacy and standing for practice or teaching faculty in an environment where research is so prized.

The North American tenure clock of seven or eight years has been adopted by HKUST, POSTECH and SMU, and draws on significant input from leading overseas academics in the referee process. Inevitably, some fail to gain tenure, and in an Asian context this can be quite problematic, even traumatic. Also, the more limited array of alternate job opportunities, particularly in Singapore, presents a further difficulty for those who fail to secure tenure or contract renewal.

Eminent Partners, Top Faculty

One effect of globalization is that virtually all research universities build international alliances, for purposes ranging from student exchange to faculty research collaboration. For the tiger universities the imperative is towards a deeper and more complex collaboration than the norm. As with the eminent patron, the eminent partner institution can accelerate credibility, particularly important in the start-up phase when external perceptions of the new university are formative. This strategy served SMU well, as the association with Wharton and then Carnegie Mellon University helped encourage senior research faculty from overseas to take up permanent and visiting appointments, and to join research project teams. In Singapore the CREATE initiative bolstered this effect. Partner immersion to help initial planning and institutional development is also evident with the role of MIT at SUTD. The level of funding from Singapore to attract and sustain these eminent partner relationships is not published, but is doubtless significant.

While the start-up phase for the tiger universities in Hong Kong and Korea also has seen partnerships with top-tier offshore universities, both HKUST and POSTECH have concentrated more on industry alliances. HKUST early on established the Research and Development Corporation (RDC), a wholly owned subsidiary dedicated to commercializing faculty research and innovation, and pushing the university into the global world. At POSTECH the relationship with POSCO led to the early establishment of a world-class particle accelerator, whose effect was to draw in eminent scholars to collaborate with POSTECH researchers. Their jointly authored papers gave a small and young university a remarkable opportunity to feature in top-line journals, adding both to POSTECH's recognition factor, and enhancing standing in international league tables, which in turn contributed to a virtuous circle for offshore faculty recruitment. This is a classic tiger university dynamic, where "academics from around the world are taking jobs in Hong Kong and Singapore …

lured by generous budgets and a welcome sign for foreigners". (Normile, 2012: 1162).

At HKUST, an important element in the recruitment dynamic was the founding president Woo Chia-wei who, as "the first person of Chinese descent to head a major university in the United States", leveraged this distinction into recruiting excellent faculty, "a key factor in its rapidly won success". (Postiglione, 2011:77). The parallel at POSTECH is where a high-profile foundation president who, with the encouragement of POSCO, exercised greater authority than normal for Korean private universities in recruitment, implementing a two-step process. First, tap the high end of the Korean scientist and engineer pool in the U.S., and then fund them to energize the recruitment of rising star faculty from the U.S. and Korea: "Every year since then, the backbone professoriate has successfully attracted a large number of talented young scholars". (Rhee, 2011: 108).

Consciously Crafted University Culture

Each of the three tiger universities referenced here has made conscious efforts from the very beginning to embed into the academic culture a deep commitment to research and the need for strategies to build international recognition. While these values are common in promotional material and vision statements of most universities, the hard reality is that it takes a deep commitment to deliver on the ideal. The drive (even hunger) for recognition needs to go beyond building any individual's CV, to the core spirit of the whole university. In some respects this runs counter to the norm in academic communities where store is placed on self-determination and individual autonomy, which is one dimension of academic freedom. So, much depends on the founding leadership's capacity to not only inspire with the vision, but in quite pragmatic ways to structure systems and implement standards that reinforce the desired institution-wide culture; it does not happen automatically or organically.

Recruitment of the founding cohort of research committed professors is critical, and one strategy has been to bring in eminent scholars on extended visiting appointments to demonstrate the priority being given to research excellence, and to help recruit and mentor the first cohort of younger scholars. The tenure and promotion system discussed earlier is equally important, and again there is a clear indication that each of SMU, HKUST and POSTECH, from the outset, adopted strong research standards in promotion and tenure matters. In many respects the first ten years are the most formative, and research culture is particularly difficult to retrofit.

As with faculty, a university's culture both influences and is influenced by the student body. SMU, for example, looks for prospective students with more than high grades. In 2013 a range of faculty-led panels is interviewing all 7,000 short-listed applicants to fill its entry positions, which in 2012 numbered 1,900 places (www.smu.edu.sg). The filter is to find students with high grades who will prosper in the four-year undergraduate environment. Employers are said to speak of the SMU difference: students that are "a distinct breed, outspoken, confident and willing to tackle the unfamiliar" (Davie, 2013b).

The physical quality of campus at all three tiger universities also has helped shape culture, by encouraging students and faculty alike to feel they are in a special place. This in turn dovetails with and enhances academic aspiration. Universities, it seems, can proudly operate in diminished physical conditions (as with the artist's garret!) once they have made their world reputation, but certainly not before that these days.

Fit for Purpose Governance Framework

Governance in a university setting can be taken to mean that system of checks, balances and oversights which give legitimacy to decision-making. Two broad levels operate: institutional governance relates to the university's governing body, and the roles and responsibilities it reserves to itself and board committees; and academic governance, which assigns roles and responsibilities for running the institution to the President, and on throughout the academic hierarchy. At both levels the tiger university often displays arrangements quite different from the general pattern in the legacy universities (although, of course, there is variation in detail). This reflects both the Asian context and the core objective of fast tracking the new university to a world standing.

At the institutional level, the governing body of the aspirant start-up university tends to be smaller and can be found to operate more along "corporate" rather than "representational" (some might even say "collegial") lines. At POSTECH and SMU, for example, no trustees are elected and none are drawn from the ranks of students or faculty (at least at this stage), as is common in legacy universities.

In the start-up phase the governing board of the tiger university tends to reserve greater decision-making to itself (but can be expected to step back over time). Similarly, the president is more inclined to a centralized approach with academic administrative roles. This way, it might be argued, the board and a president can sharpen the strategic focus and shorten timelines in the growth path. This contrasts with the standard culture in large established research universities where over many years the faculty have driven a lower centre of gravity for decision-making on academic matters such as recruitment and promotion, and sometimes in what are posited to be related issues, such as budgeting and strategic direction.

There is a delicate balance between centralism to set and embed the culture and the planned growth path on the one hand, and on the other hand staged devolution to meet best practice and the expectations of academic communities, particularly where recruitment of top, overseas scholars is key to the strategic plan. This highlights a critical issue in the launch and early development of the tiger university: how to shift the governance centre of gravity, and to what timeframe? At SMU, for example, an academic subcommittee of the Board of Trustees had prime carriage of the faculty appointment process in its first decade, but now, in the second decade, this role has been delegated to the President in consultation with a committee of eminent professors (internal and external). Important aspects of budget responsibility are also being devolved from the relevant Board level committee. By the third decade, with the research culture well and truly set, both academic and institutional governance should have matured. The critical issue is that a plan for transition over these three trimesters of gestation, so to speak, needs to be well understood, for there will be challenges, with competing interests at play, between those who want to preserve their level of authority through time and those who want a faster track for devolution. Timing is of the essence.

THE OVERALL IMPACT

The pace of Asian university development in the past several decades is without precedent, and the trajectory of the tiger sub-species is even more spectacular. What are the implications: will the tiger university in time be seen simply as a precocious and passing phase in the 1,000-plus year history of university evolution, perhaps ultimately swamped by the digital revolution, or by re-energized legacy institutions? Or do we now have an alternate model for the research university of the future? Will the tiger university bring fundamental changes to the higher education system in which it nests? Will governments pull back strategic support as goals are met, or will the success of the tiger university keep the model rolling forward? Has a tiger university "bubble" been brought on by the rise of ranking regimes?

We are only at the beginning of the phenomenon examined here, so it is really a case of "watch this space". However, five themes or propositions do emerge from what we have seen so far from the cases of SMU in Singapore, HKUST in Hong Kong and POSTECH in South Korea.

The first proposition is that the key elements driving the dynamic of the tiger university are not stand alone, but rather form an interlocking web. Hefty early phase funding has an obvious practical value, but it also serves to quickly establish credibility for the new university's rather grand vision, which then helps recruit top overseas research-oriented faculty who might otherwise hesitate to join a start-up. Sparkling, purpose-built campuses burnish the nascent halo. This in turn lays down important elements of the culture that is being consciously developed. At the same time, donors are more inclined to feel they are putting good money after good money. And, with the enhanced resourcing base, the academic community is more inclined to accept governance with a centre of gravity that is higher than in many legacy institutions, thus facilitating focus and strategy development. Each of these elements can be examined separately, but in reality they are interlocking and reinforce one another in a virtuous circle.

The second proposition goes to the powerful role model for the tiger university offered by key elements of research universities in the U.S. Elite American universities show a keen interest in giving guidance, in return for elegant funding arrangements and a door to Asia for their own global footprint. Ironically, this is at a time when many leading universities in the U.S. are seen to be under significant pressures post the GFC, and even from a higher education bubble. (Thiel, 2010).

The third proposition is to do with the symbiotic nature of the relationship between the tiger university and the overall higher education system in which it lives. Interestingly, it both "draws strength from the other research universities … and … becomes a catalyst for those universities' reforms." (Postiglione, 2011: 92). Reform pressure grows out of advancement strategies common, if not unique, to the tiger universities: tenure regimes; management systems; marketing and promotion styles; governance practices; recruitment strategies; remuneration adjustment linked to performance reviews; new modes of learning; nodes of research concentration … and much more. Building such beachheads for change undoubtedly is part of government strategy for enhancing practices and lifting standards across the higher education sector in each country. In time, one of the most significant roles of the tiger university will be seen in its impact as an agent of change for other universities. But in time the tiger university will also need to reinvent itself.

The fourth proposition is that the tiger university is a direct consequence of globalization and the emergence of university ranking regimes. Without these two (necessary but not sufficient) forces, the young aspirational university would be more anonymous, and would find it difficult, if not impossible, to shake up the established order.

The fifth proposition is that, notwithstanding its stunning success, the tiger university model is not without potential downside effects. Some observers may worry that the core and critical role of government in the early phases of development will in time become a barrier to full autonomy and the vibrancy of academic debate, as well as curiosity-driven research, at least as these hallmarks of higher education are understood in the West. Another concern arises in the minds of those who see significant benefit in students from the science and technological quadrant, or those in the business, economics, law and accountancy quadrant, co-mingling on campus and in classrooms with others from across the discipline spectrum. Some would question the certainty of the Asian miracle running for another decade or two, let alone a whole century;

will the loss of serious economic momentum shift funding priorities away from the tiger university? Another worry may be the loss of energy and focus as a young and rising star reaches middle age. And, of course, the "coming avalanche", as Barber *et al.* (2013) describe the higher education revolution ahead may not play out well for the tiger university, as amalgamations and other rationalization measures emerge.

So, on balance, where does this leave the idea of an Asian Tiger University Effect? While there are many factors to play out, it seems safe (or at least as safe as any broad conclusion on the future form and substance of the world's research universities) to see the rapidly rising stars in Asia as an interesting new development, and one of several forces playing on the traditional paradigm of higher education.

* I am grateful for feedback on an earlier draft from Antonio Borges, Glyn Davis, Bruce Dowton, Arnoud De Meyer, Simon Marginson, Gavin Moody, Gerard Postiglione, Mark Wainwright and Ross Williams, none of whom bear any responsibility for errors of fact or judgement that may persist.

REFERENCES

ADB (Asian Development Bank) (2011). *Asia 2050: realizing the Asian century*, ADB, Manila, www.adb.org

Altbach, P.G. & Salmi, J. (eds), (2011). The Road to Academic Excellence: The Making of World-Class Research Universities, World Bank, Washington DC.

Altbach, P.G. (2004). "The Costs and Benefits of World-Class Universities", *Academe* (January-February).
http://www.aaup.org/AAUP/CMS_Templates/AcademeTemplates/AcademeArticle.aspx?NRMODE=P/

Appell, D. (2013). "Singapore's Approach to Endowments are Rare in Region", *Pensions and Investments*, 18 February.
http://www.pionline.com/article/20130218/PRINTSUB/302189992

Australian Government (2012). *Australia in the Asian Century*, Canberra. asiancentury.dpmc.gov.au/white-paper

Barber, M., Donnelly, K. & Saad, R. (2013). *An Avalanche is Coming: Higher Education and the Revolution Ahead*, Institute for Public Policy Research, London.

Davies, M. (2012). "Can Universities Survive the Digital Revolution?" *Quadrant Online:*
http://www.quadrant.org.au/magazine/issue/2012/12/can-universities-survive-the-digital-revolution

Davie, S. (2013a). "No Topic Off Limits, Yale-NUS Report Says", *The Straits Times*, 7 April.
http://www.straitstimes.com/breaking-news/singapore/story/no-topic-limits-yale-nus-report-says-20130405

Davie, S. (2013b). "7000 candidates ... and SMU will interview them all", OSU, 11 April
http://www.overseassingaporean.sg/articles/d/7000-candidates...-and-smu-will-interview-them-all

Duderstadt, J. *et al.* (2008). "The Globalization of Higher Education" in L. E. Weber and J. J. Duderstadt (eds) *The Globalization of Higher Education*, Economica, London.

Jung, H. (2011). "South Korea: Global Campus for Foreign Universities", *World University News*, 21 January.
http://www.universityworldnews.com/article.php?story=20110122084850765

Marginson, S. (2013). "Global Perspectives on Education and Poverty", AERA Annual Meeting, San Francisco, 1 May.

Marginson, S. (2013). "The Rise of Higher Education and Research in East Asia and Singapore", Moscow, 17 April.

Morgan, J. (2010). "Appetite for Education".
www.timeshighereducation.co.uk/414509.article

Newby, H. (2008). "The Challenge to European Universities in the Emerging Global Marketplace" in J. E. Weber & J. J. Duderstadt (eds), *The Globalization of Higher Education*, Economica, London.

Niland, J. R. (1998). "The Challenge of Building World Class Universities in the Asian Region", public lecture at National University of Singapore, 25 June in L.E. Weber & J.J. Duderstadt (eds), *The Globalization of Higher Education*, Economica, London, 2008 and http://onlineopinion.com.au/view.asp?article=997.

Niland, J. R. (2004). *Integration Matters*, Report of UGC Working Party, UGC Hong Kong.

Normile, D. (2012). "Flocking to Asia for a Shot at Greatness", *Science*, Vol. 337, pp. 162-166.

O'Leary, J. (2012). "The Rise of Asia's Young Universities", QS *Top Universities*, 29 May.
http://www.topuniversities.com/where-to-study/region/asia/rise-asias-young-universities

Postiglione, G. A. (2011). "The Rise of Research Universities: the Hong Kong University of Science and Technology" in P. G. Altbach & J. Salmi (eds), *The Road to Academic Excellence: The Making of World-Class Research Universities*, World Bank, Washington DC.

Rhee, B. S. (2011). "A World-Class Research University on the Periphery: The Pohang University of Science and Technology, the Republic of Korea", in P. G. Altbach & J. Salmi (eds), *The Road to Academic Excellence: The Making of World-Class Research Universities*, World Bank, Washington DC.

Salmi, J. (2011). "The Road to Academic Excellence Lessons of Experience", in P. G. Altbach & J. Salmi (eds), *The Road to Academic Excellence: The Making of World-Class Research Universities*, World Bank, Washington DC.

Schramm, C. (2008). "Reinvigorating Universities in an Entrepreneurial Age" in L. E. Weber & J. J. Duderstadt (eds), *The Globalization of Higher Education*, Economica, London.

Suh, N. P. (2008). "Globalization of Research Universities in Korea", in L. E. Weber & J. J. Duderstadt (eds), *The Globalization of Higher Education*, Economica, London.

Tan, T. T. K. (2008). "Building Singapore's University Education System in a Globalized Word: Issues, Policies and Challenges", in L. E. Weber & J. J. Duderstadt (eds), *The Globalization of Higher Education*, Economica, London.

THE, (2013). Times Higher Education World University Rankings. http://www.timeshighereducation.co.uk/world-university-rankings/2012/one-hundred-under-fifty

Thiel, P. (2010). http://www.thielfoundation.org/index.php?option=com_content&id=14:the-thiel-fellowship-20-under-20&catid=1&Itemid=16

LIST OF ACRONYMNS

ADB – Asian Development Bank

ARWU – Academic Rankings of World Universities (Shanghai Rankings)

BYU – Brigham Young University

CMU – Carnegie Mellon University

CREATE – Campus for Research Excellence and Technological Enterprises

CUHK – Chinese University of Technology

ETH - Eidgenössische Technische Hochschule

HKU – Hong Kong University

HKUST – Hong Kong University of Science and Technology

IFEZ – Incheon Free Economic Zone

INSEAD – Institut Européen d'Administration des Affaires

KAIST – Korean University of Science and Technology

MIT – Massachusetts Institute of Technology

NTU – Nanyang Technological University

NUS – National University of Singapore

POSCO – Pohang Iron and Steel Company

POSTECH – Pohang University of Science and Technology

QSWUR – Quacquarelli Symonds World University Rankings

RDC – Research Development Corporation

SGUC – Sangdo Global University Campus

SMU – Singapore Management University

SUTD – Singapore University of Technology and Design

THEWUR – Times Higher Education World University Rankings

UGC – University Grants Committee (of Hong Kong)

UTD – University of Texas - Dallas

PART VI

••••••••••••

Summary and Conclusion

CHAPTER 22

Summary and Conclusion

James J. Duderstadt and Luc E. Weber

I n June 2013, the leaders of many of the world's leading universities gathered in Glion-above-Montreux to participate in the IX Glion Colloquium to consider the challenges and responsibilities facing their institutions in an era of rapid change. Today, most nations recognize the critical importance of education, research and innovation to their economic prosperity, social well-being and security. They also understand the importance of research universities as key resources in providing these assets. Yet today, these important institutions are being challenged by the powerful forces of demographic change, globalization, environmental risks, hypercompetitive markets, failing governments and disruptive technologies such as information and communications technology, biotechnology and nanotechnology.

The Colloquium was organized into five topical sessions:

- the changing purpose, role and relationship of research universities
- the changing nature of discovery, learning and innovation
- the cost, price, and value of higher education
- the changing nature and character of research universities: developed countries
- the changing nature and character of research universities: developing countries

To provide a framework for the discussion in each session, participants prepared papers that were distributed in advance of the meeting. Although the format of each session allowed the presentation of brief summaries of these papers, most of the session consisted of open discussion of the issues raised both by the topic and the papers.

This summary chapter has been written to pull together several of the key points made by the participants and arising during the discussion phase of the

sessions. These summaries have been provided in an order that conforms to
the sessions of the Colloquium.

SESSION 1: THE CHANGING PURPOSE, ROLE AND RELATIONSHIPS OF RESEARCH UNIVERSITIES

Chairs: Howard Newby and James Duderstadt
James Duderstadt: Research Universities and the Future of America: A Study by the
National Academies of the United States
Heather Munroe-Blum: The Strategic Repositioning of Research Universities to
Fulfill their Global Priorities
Hunter Rawlings: How to Answer the Utilitarian Assault on Higher Education
Chorh-Chuan Tan: The Changing Nature and Character of Research Universities:
New Paradigms

The crucial importance of the research university as a key asset in achieving economic prosperity and security is widely understood, as evidenced by the
efforts that nations around the globe are making to create and sustain institutions of world-class quality. Yet, while America's research universities remain
the strongest in the world, the nation's commitment to sustaining the research
partnership among governments, industry and universities has weakened in
recent years, putting this leadership at risk. In response to this concern, in
2010 the United States Congress asked the National Academies (of Science,
Engineering and Medicine) to conduct a major study of the future of the
nation's research universities and provide recommendations to address the
challenges facing these institutions.

The National Academies effort raised several key concerns: The policies
and practices of the United States government no longer placed a priority on
university research and graduate education. In the face of economic challenges and the priorities of aging populations, the nation's states no longer are
either capable or willing to support their public research universities at world-
class levels. American business and industry have largely abandoned basic and
applied research and today are largely ceding this responsibility to research
universities, but with only minimal corporate support. Finally, American
research universities themselves have failed to achieve the cost efficiency and
productivity enhancement in teaching and research required in an increasingly competitive world. The study provided a series of recommendations to
strengthen the partnership among universities, federal and state governments,
philanthropy and the business community in order to revitalize university
research and speed its translation into innovative products and services.
In addition, it recommended actions to streamline and improve the productivity of research operations within universities, and ensure that America's

pipeline of future talent in science, engineering and other research areas remains creative and vital, leveraging the abilities of all of its citizens and attracting the best students and scholars from around the world. This study has ignited a decade-long effort to elevate the priority of American's research universities.

Although Congress requested this study within the framework of contributions to the nation's economic strength and security, this ran the risk of intensifying the pressure on American universities from both government and the public to adopt a purely utilitarian mission, both in the education of their students and in the research they conduct. In fact, many of the most important missions such as educational breadth, basic scholarship and even disciplines such as the social sciences have come under attack by powerful political forces, undermining public trust and confidence.

Research universities in other Western nations are facing similar challenges. Even as they attempt to address urgent global challenges such as world poverty, health and education, they are hindered by the instability of government funding and the erosion of public understanding and support. This growing lack of public trust is a serious challenge, although perhaps it is also because our institutions have become more important to the needs of society. Clearly it suggests that research universities must re-configure their relationships with the government, the private sector and civil society in order to build on their strengths and reaffirm their contributions domestically and internationally.

Here the contrast with the experience of universities in rapidly developing Asian economies is profound. Not only are institutions in knowledge-intensive economies such as Singapore given high priority and strong funding, but they are strongly encouraged to pursue strategies for achieving global leadership through new paradigms that leverage more effectively and explicitly on the synergies between research and education, and between research and the translation of basic research findings into new thinking, products, services, concepts, policies and practices, since these represent very important dimensions of the overall value proposition of research universities and enable them to possibly leapfrog more established institutions. The National University of Singapore provides an excellent example with its innovative development of global educational programs through partnerships that provide both a portal and a bridge to several of the world's leading universities; its fascinating partnership with Yale to build a liberal arts college in Singapore: and its CREATE initiative to build international research "collaboratories" in key areas such as human, energy, environmental and urban systems.

SESSION 2: THE CHANGING NATURE OF DISCOVERY, LEARNING, AND INNOVATION

Chair: Heather Munroe-Blum
Lezek Borysiewicz: Research Funding: Trends and Challenges
Arnold van Zyl: The Role of Universities in Regional Development
James Duderstadt: The Impact of Technology on Discovery and Learning in Research Universities
Patrick Aebischer: Can the IT Revolution Lead to a Rebirth of World-Class European Universities?

The session began with a presentation on the changing nature of research sponsorship in the United Kingdom, a pattern that was also becoming apparent in much of Europe and North America. Sponsors were shifting from providing peer-reviewed research grants to university investigators to grand challenge initiatives with large grants made to interdisciplinary research centres addressing more pragmatic objectives associated with social or economic goals. While this approach addresses the broader character of transdisciplinary research, it also makes even more competitive — and perhaps more routine — traditional research grants and projects. The development of the European Research Area will stimulate still further evolution, particularly with its emphasis on innovation and technology transfer and large-scale research facilities. Hence there will be a growing challenge to funding agencies to keep sufficient funds available for individuals (not large collaborations) where much of the originality in research occurs, while focusing their attention on the amount of funding they are willing to provide rather than dictating the research that will be done with these funds (with a similar caution to industry). For universities, the challenges will include developing academic structures to enable discipline-based units to deliver multi-disciplinary research, combining grand-challenge approaches with investigator-led research, and improving the efficiency of translation of research results into societal benefit.

The third mission of the research university, to transfer knowledge through various forms of community engagement, was an important topic of discussion for this session. In the broadest generic sense, the third mission encompasses the interrelationship between a university and its non-academic partners. Universities need to put the issue of individual human rights and concerns for the environment at the centre of their inquiries. They need to actively engage and enter into alliances with a number of stakeholders. Yet the nature of this engagement must reflect the strong difference in the needs of developed and developing nations. For example, today much of the focus of university engagement in Europe and America addresses economic needs for technology transfer and innovation, although this sometimes raises concern about shifting their centre of gravity away from teaching and fundamental research and may result in the degradation of the university to an extended, externalized research facility for industry (e.g., is Stanford still a university?) In sharp contrast, in Africa there is a need for more immersive engagement of students and faculty in working/caring in a resource-limited environment. In a sense, universities must use their own environments to create optimal modalities for achieving (and demonstrating) their relevance and impact.

Perhaps the most significant changes in learning and discovery (teaching and research) today are being driven by rapidly evolving information and communications technologies. Hence much of the discussion of this session involved new approaches to education, such as massively open online courses (MOOCs), cognitive tutor systems, or Carnegie Mellon's Open Learning Initiative. This is also happening to research (e.g., MOO"R"?) through crowdsourcing, simulation-based research, big data and data mining. In fact, there were several references to frequent claims that today higher education is on the precipice of an era of extraordinary change as such disruptive technologies challenge the traditional paradigms of learning and discovery. To be sure, one of the major reasons for the continued surprises we get from the emergence of new applications — the Internet, social networking, big data, machine learning — arises from the unexpected directions taken by these technologies that evolve at an exponential pace. We have learned time and time again that it makes little sense to simply extrapolate the present into the future to predict or even understand the next "tech turn". These are not only highly disruptive technologies, but they are highly unpredictable. Ten years ago nobody would have imagined Google, Facebook, Twitter, etc., and today nobody really can predict what will be a dominant technology even five years ahead, much less ten!

Because of their recent appearance and rapid growth, MOOCs received a great deal of attention during the discussions. To be sure, through the use of online access, social networking and data analytics, this learning paradigm is capable of providing educational access to extremely larger populations, particularly important in underserved areas. It also establishes visibility and attracts talent (and perhaps eventually even revenues) to those institutions that are leaders in this movement. Yet it was also acknowledged that such online courses were very different from a campus-based education. It was clear that it is a time for experimentation, including rigorous measurement of educational results, before we allow the technology tsunami to sweep over us!

The same might be concluded for the new paradigms for research and scholarship driven by new technologies. Certainly the language of research is changing to embrace concepts such as clouds, data mining and disciplinary convergence. If one subscribes to the view that there is a paradigm shift from hypothesis-driven to data-correlation-driven discovery, then the culture of scientific and engineering discovery and innovation is changing as a result of access to data, computational technology and social networks. But while these approaches augment the traditional scientific method of observation, conjecture, experiment and theory, they certainly do not replace it.

SESSION 3: THE COST, PRICE, AND VALUE OF HIGHER EDUCATION

Chair: Nam Pyo Suh
Luc Weber: Who Is Responsible for Providing and Paying for Higher Education?
Howard Newby: How and Where Are Dominant Funding Models Steering Higher Education and Research?
Ronald Daniels: Fault Lines in the Compact: Higher Education and the Public Interest in the United States
Linda Katehi: The Challenge of Transition in Public Higher Education

This session dealt primarily with the financial aspects of higher education. A wide spectrum of issues was discussed in the session. The facts that higher education provides value to both individuals and broader society and can be supported either by the public purse or individual fees, raises issues of economic policy, social policy and, of course, politics. The complexity of these considerations was illustrated by the degree to which minimizing the fees charged to students can actually have a negative impact on equity since it tends to preferentially subsidize higher-income students at the expense of those of modest means. Because of the impact of an educated population on society, a strong case could be made that higher education (including both teaching and research) was a public responsibility, although student fees can also be justified because of the economic impact of education on the earning capacity of graduates.

While this initial discussion was of a general nature, many other issues were country specific. The most discussed was the decreasing government support for higher education at public universities, which led to the discussion of impact of higher tuition, particularly in nations like the United Kingdom where tuition has recently replaced government funding. Another frequently discussed issue was the importance of research funding, which comes mostly from governmental sources. The impact of decreasing investments in higher education by the public sector on the quality of higher education drew much attention, with the University of California as perhaps the most extreme example, since this world-leading institution has lost almost two-thirds of its state support over the past decade. Other issues discussed were the complex relationship between universities and government, the need to embrace ICT to reduce costs and to improve the quality of learning, and the importance of developing effective relationships with industry.

There was a consensus among the presenters that many universities are indeed struggling with inadequate funding for quality education and research. Since many universities depend on government funding for research, this may lead to governmental interference of the research agenda. This trend is greater in countries that have a monolithic structure for funding research. In the U.S., several funding agencies pursue diverse research agendas, which enable its universities to have a wider flexibility in pursuing their research goals. Industrial support of academic research is important, especially in engineering, but the actual level of research funds provided by industry is relatively small.

There was a general sense that the relationship between universities and governments needed to be renegotiated and better aligned with well-established public goals that were sustained by strong public trust and confidence. Yet, notwithstanding the many challenges identified by all participants, the overall tone of the discussions was positive. All the participants appeared to be confident that they could improve their own research universities, even though the current uncertainty at those universities caused by the worldwide economic downturn poses challenges and demands imaginative solutions.

SESSION 4: THE CHANGING NATURE AND CHARACTER OF RESEARCH UNIVERSITIES IN DEVELOPED COUNTRIES

Chair: John Niland
Alain Beretz: Can the French System Support Competitive Research Universities?
Antonio Loprieno: Contemporary Challenges for the Swiss and Continental European System
Eva Akesson: A Research University for both Academic Excellence and Responsibility for a Sustainable Future: Does the Swedish Model Work?
Sijbolt Norda: Human Capital, the Oft Forgotten Key Challenge for Universities

This session began with a discussion of experiences from four different European nations: France, Switzerland, Sweden and the Netherlands. France was particularly interesting, since it faced the challenge of creating world-class research universities from a dual system of universities providing mass education and "Grandes Ecoles" providing rigorous technical training for the economic and political elite. The nation has embarked on a series of excellence initiatives to create perhaps five to ten major research universities that are globally competitive and capable of attracting the best researchers and students. This requires a competitive strategy to increase funding, faculty and student mobility, competition and institutional autonomy.

Swiss institutions continued to be well-funded and globally competitive, but they are undergoing a major structural and cultural transformation to better align themselves not only with the Bologna model but also with leading research universities around the world. Here the shift is from the Bildung/Ausbildung organization of the traditional European "universitas", with disciplinary concentration occurring at both the college and graduate level, to a broader undergraduate education to prepare students for an intensely focused disciplinary training at the graduate level. Beyond this, the predominant model of the Swiss university has distanced itself from the traditional administratively decentralized, professorially driven and state-controlled institution to reach a higher level of stakeholder diversity, corporate identity and executive efficiency.

Focus on research, personalized instruction, global understanding of the role of the university in society: these seem to be the main features — and the main challenges — of the contemporary Swiss academic landscape. In many respects, this evolution dovetails quite well with the demographic expectations of our knowledge society.

Sweden is also characterized by generous government support of universities and strong research reputations. Yet its practice of government selection of research priorities narrows the academic activities of its universities. Institutions are characterized by high insularity and little mobility on the part of faculty and students. And, perhaps most seriously, the imposition of high tuition and visa restrictions for international students has decimated their enrolment and threatens to cripple the ability of Swedish universities to adequately participate in an increasingly global scholarly community.

Although the Netherlands also continues to sustain universities with a global presence, there are major concerns about the approaching turnover of faculty in Dutch institutions. Serious attention is being given to making academic careers more attractive to young people while encouraging senior faculty to achieve a better balance between the career interests of individual faculty members and university collective interests. Academic leadership will be key in both efforts.

SESSION 5: THE CHANGING NATURE AND CHARACTER OF RESEARCH UNIVERSITIES IN RAPIDLY DEVELOPING COUNTRIES

Chair: Leszek Borysiewicz
Jie Zhang: The Search for Quality at Chinese Universities
R. K. Shevgaonkar: Higher Education Models for Large, Developing Economies
Carlos Henrique de Brito Cruz: Challenges and Opportunities for Public Research Universities in Brazil
Nam P. Suh: Challenges in Establishing a Top Research University
John R. Niland: The Asian Tiger University Effect

A particularly impressive presentation was made concerning China's remarkable achievement in increasing higher education participation of 18- to 22-year-olds from 1% in 1982, to 26% in 2012, with a goal of achieving 40% in 2020. In parallel with this massive effort to increase access to higher education is China's concerted effort to elevate several Chinese universities to truly global leadership in research and graduate education. To achieve a faculty capable of such quality, Shanghai Jiao Tong University has implemented a dual-track model, providing internationally competitive salaries to new faculty with international reputations. However, salary and compensation packages have been progressively increased for all faculty members, while making them more flexible and performance-based.

India faces a comparable challenge in scale, with an estimated need for higher education that is three times the current capacity of existing universities, and a population that is becoming even younger. While the Internet has provided the country with the economic boost from the off-shoring of jobs from America and Europe to India's strong science and engineering graduates of its elite IIT and IIM systems, the nation is still losing the top 10% of its graduates through brain drain. India's key focus areas are involving extensive use of online education for massification, e.g., now providing its entire engineering curriculum in all disciplines through web and video lecture format; adequately funding research at global standards; and developing a strongly entrepreneurial culture to provide innovative solutions to local problems. Since India is at the interface between developed and developing nations, its strategies are relevant to 70% of the population of the world

Yet a third example was provided by Korea's efforts to transform KAIST (the Korean Advanced Institute of Science and Technology) into a world-class institution of the quality of MIT. This has required not only a major investment of resources, but, as well, a significant change in institutional culture that allows, promotes, rewards and respects diverse views. KAIST has dramatically raised the standards for faculty achievement, selecting research topics well-aligned with areas of strength that would attract global attention and working closely with key industrial partners such as Samsung, Hyundai and Daewoo. It has been fortunate in being able to tap the talent pool of outstanding applicants, accepting less than 1% of those who applied to KAIST after a rigorous secondary education.

The final discussion of this session concerned the efforts of other "Asian Tigers" (Singapore, Hong Kong and Taiwan) to build outstanding research universities. The stunning economic growth of these societies over the past several decades has already lifted living standards to developed country levels for many of their citizens. They have also laid strong foundations for developing first-rate university systems, with several of their universities, such as Hong Kong University and the National University of Singapore, already well-established in the top group of world-class universities. But this is just the start for a wave of new, more agile universities that may well be on the way. The pace of Asian university development in the past several decades is without precedent, and the trajectory of the Asian tiger sub-species is even more spectacular. These initiatives have certainly benefited from strong investments and government commitment. They have also leveraged their relationship with leading universities in America and Europe, while focusing on areas where they could rapidly move into leadership positions. These efforts have also benefited from strongly aspirational societies (e.g., a Confucian philosophy that greatly values education) and a government approach that was not only collaborative but also highly strategic.

SESSION 6: A GENERAL DISCUSSION

The Colloquium concluded with a general session both to evaluate the format and substance of the papers and discussions and to identify possible topics and formats for future efforts. The 2013 IX Glion Colloquium was somewhat more homogeneous than earlier colloquia in that almost all participants were either current or former university leaders rather than a mix of participants from higher education, business, government and foundations. The participants believed that this facilitated a somewhat more engaged and focused discussion, both in the formal sessions and during the various associated events (luncheons, dinners, travel events, informal discussions). They also agreed that those papers and presentations that were analytic considerations of particular topics rather than descriptive of particular institutions were the most informative (although using particular institutions to illustrate a more general issue was felt to be highly effective).

The participants believed that the truly global character of the event was one of its strong points. Of particular value were the discussions that revealed the sharp contrasts between developed and developing nations, different regions (Asia vs. Europe vs. America vs. Africa), and different types of institutions.

Composé par Economica, 49, rue Héricart, 75015 PARIS
Imprimé en France. - JOUVE, 1, rue du Docteur Sauvé, 53100 MAYENNE
N° 2129249P - Dépôt légal : novembre 2013